The LAKE COUNTIES

The LAKE COUNTIES

CUMBERLAND WESTMORLAND

ARTHUR MEE

BRACKEN BOOKS
LONDON

The Lake Counties

Previously published by Hodder & Stoughton, London, in 1937

This edition published in 1994 by Bracken Books, an imprint of Studio Editions Ltd, Princess House, 50 Eastcastle Street, London W1N 7AP, England

ISBN 1 85891 208 3
Printed and bound in Guernsey by The Guernsey Press Co Ltd

TRIBUTE

To John Wilson for his valuable services in connection with this book

for the pictures to Sidney Tranter, Art Editor, And to the following photographers:

Messrs. Abraham, H. Bell, Brian Clayton, Fred Crossley, J. Dixon-Scott, Herbert Felton, H. J. Smith, E. W. Tattersall, W. F. Taylor, Country Life; and to the Stationery Office, the L.M.S. Railway, the Royal Commission on Historical Monuments, and the West Cumberland Development Council

The Lake Country

IT is an astonishing piece of England, the greatest surprise and delight that awaits the English traveller who has not been this way. It has deep solitudes, majestic heights, and the solemn beauty of still water, a grouping of natural beauty uncommon in this country and here seen at its best.

It has not the vastness of Switzerland, and yet it is a veritable mountain land. In Switzerland or in Tyrol we may at any time be in a valley 5000 feet above the sea before we begin to ascend a mountain of 8000 feet and so have but 3000 to climb. That is actually what we may climb in Lakeland. Nearly all the Lakeland dales are but a few hundred feet above the sea, a fact which must not be forgotten in comparing our own mountains with the Alps. Scafell with its 3210 feet, is more than 3000 feet above Wastdale, lying at its base, and the bed of Wastwater is below sea level.

The Lake mountains of England spring suddenly and loftily from low green valleys, and so abound in swift changes from soft and quiet beauty to rugged grandeur. They are a medley of hills closely compressed, as if Nature had tried to place as much of her handiwork as possible on a small show-ground.

If we imagine Lakeland as a circle about 90 miles round we may form some conception of one of the most remarkable natural kingdoms Nature made in carving out the earth. Rivers and glaciers, rain and frost, wind and every kind of weather have made Lakeland what it is. Sometimes the rocks are covered by material borne on glaciers, now thinly spread, now thickly laid, and so it is that we have strange contrasts of vast masses of barren rock and hillsides clothed with living beauty.

One who knows this country well has said that for colour the Lakeland mountains are unsurpassed in Europe, and indeed this world of grandeur passes from the russet brown of winter into the deep green of the bracken in summer, and it is the crimson heather that tells us that another year is passing to its close. Primrose and daffodil, foxglove and bluebell, all come to Lakeland in due season.

Into this circle of 90 square miles Naturė has packed 180 mountains that rise at least 2000 feet. Over 60 of them are 2500 feet and eight of them about 3000 feet. With these 180 mountains there are 64 lakes, every fourth a big one.

The 15 chief lakes are Windermere, the biggest in England, over ten miles long and nearly a mile broad; Ullswater over seven miles long, with three and a half square miles; Bassenthwaite, four miles long, and Derwentwater, nearly three miles long, but both equal in their area, about two square miles; Ennerdale Water and Wastwater, each a little over a square mile; Thirlmere, which has been enlarged, and Hawes Water, which is being enlarged, to supply Manchester with water; Crummock Water, which is just under a square mile; Lowes Water which stretches for over a mile and lies 430 feet above sea level; and Grasmere, Buttermere, Rydal Water, Elter Water, and Brother's Water which are much smaller in size but are as beautiful as their bigger neighbours.

Making way for us through this wondrous country are 20 mountain passes, cleaving a road through the hills or between their tops, and what is so delightful in these days is that half these passes allow no wheeled vehicle to mount them, but wait for him who walks, tempting him up their steep, winding, lonely, and often rocky ways. Here at least the pedestrian is king.

Lakeland belongs to three counties, for it makes its way into the industrial world of Lancashire, so unlike itself; part of it lies in Cumberland, with its sea-coast and its Scottish border; but it is Westmorland that is incomparable, a cameo of natural beauty unmatched as a whole in these islands. No part of it is out of sight of its impressive hills, and much of it is ridged by some of the loftiest of our mountains.

It reaches the sea only through the narrow estuary of the River Kent, and it has only one considerable town—Kendal, with 15,000 people. It lives chiefly on its pastures, with a little scattered mining and quarrying, and a welcome survival of ancient crafts; for the rest it depends on its charms as one of the most fascinating places of England, drawing to it sooner or later all lovers of beauty. In Spring or Summer its few main roads are thronged by those who can find time only to "glance and nod and bustle by," but all the year round it is haunted by ramblers who have succumbed to its spells, and who, knowing the passes and peaks where wheels never run, have there enriched their hearts with its memories.

More intimately than any other county Westmorland remains the haunt of the poet who, above all the rest, looks Nature in the face and feels himself her child. Wordsworth was born in Cumberland and schooled in Lancashire, but it was here he made his home. Here in a little cottage at Grasmere which anyone can see he wrote nearly all the poems that rank him as supremely great. Here he lies at rest, and his spirit is the magnet that draws men to this place. What he wrote of the young Shepherd Lord of the grim Clifford race, tamed into gentleness in the seclusion of these majestic wilds, was true of Wordsworth himself:

Love had he found in huts where poor men lie;
His daily teachers had been woods and rills,
The Silence that is in the starry sky,
The Sleep that is among the lonely hills.

It is the spirit of this matchless piece of England where we may wander lonely as a cloud, and where Mother Nature shapes her children as she will. Nowhere else could Wordsworth have thought of Nature making a little Lady:

She shall be sportive as the fawn
That wild with glee across the lawn
Or up the mountain springs;
And hers shall be the breathing balm,
And hers the silence and the calm
Of mute insensate things.

The floating clouds their state shall lend
To her; for her the willow bend;
Nor shall she fail to see
Even in the motions of the Storm
Grace that shall mould the Maiden's form
By silent sympathy.

The stars of midnight shall be dear
To her; and she shall lean her ear
In many a secret place
Where rivulets dance their wayward round,
And beauty born of murmuring sound
Shall pass into her face.

Another memory of the poet is recalled between Grasmere and Ullswater.

Close by the lonely Grisedale Tarn is a big stone, hard to find, with an inscription saying that here Wordsworth parted from his brother John, who was going on what proved to be his last voyage, his ship being wrecked in 1805 and nearly all on board drowned. It must have been for him one of the saddest places in all Lakeland.

It is true, of course, that Lake scenery was known before Wordsworth's day. Thomas Gray passed this way in the year before Wordsworth was born, but to him the mountains rose "very rude and awful with their broken tops." They were a turbulent chaos of mountain behind mountain, rolled in confusion. There was no intimacy with the mountains here; they were to Gray a hundred nameless hills, except Skiddaw and Helvellyn and a few crags towering close by the wayside. Yet the truth is that there are fifty mountains in Westmorland alone which have distinct personalities and are known in all their moods by thousands of travellers. Doubtless they would have come to be the playground of England if Thomas Gray instead of William Wordsworth had introduced them to us, but never would they have been the same. Wordsworth has bathed them in a poetic radiance that will never fade, and has made them a place of pilgrimage for all who feel a kinship with Nature and are sensitive to her delights.

Only Windermere is open enough to give a fairly wide and distinct view of Lakeland, and those who would know it as it is must walk. Let us take one walk over the hills where the eye can range across mountain and vale, far as well as near. If we come to Windermere and walk up the Troutbeck Valley we can work our way gradually up the hillside to a dip in the range near Garburn pass, and then strike up the first peak, with the curious name of Yoke. We are on a rather narrow mountain ridge with a switchback top, and the next rise is Ill Bell. The next peak is Froswick and the next Thornthwaite Crag, beyond which the range spreads out broad and flat, and the rise is gradual. We are on a grassy peaty sheepwalk a mile wide, with peaks and precipices at the eastern edge. Here the Romans were before us; here on this grassy plateau 2663 feet above the sea they made one of their roads right along the ridge of this range. Today it is called High Street, and the Roman road can still be traced for fifteen miles. To this lofty plateau the shepherds of Lakeland bring the lost sheep that have strayed from distant mountains and joined their flocks, and here they are sorted and returned to their owners.

As we stand at this fine point on the edge at Thornthwaite Crag we are five long mountain miles from everywhere and we have a view westward over Lakeland. The view extends from Morecambe Bay northward to the sudden rise of the mountains.

First comes the Lancashire group in the district quite clearly, the clear-cut summit of Coniston Old Man, the waving line of the Carrs, and the massive strength of Wetherlam looking down on the depression of Wrynose Pass, which separates the Coniston cluster of peaks from the great central mountain knot of the district. There in succession we see the well-named line of Crinkle Crags, the fine peak of Bowfell, and, farther off, Scafell and Scafell Pike, with a deep chasm between them, and to the right the steep upthrust of Great Gable. All these fine hills are peaks springing from a widely sprawling common base. More to the right and nearer rise those singularly illusory twin-peaks the Langdale Pikes, which from here take their true proportions. No mountains of Lakeland are so much photographed. They have a look of two lions side by side, one hidden except his head. Their outline captures the eye.

It is only by such walks as these that the true character of these mountains can be judged. We see the great Helvellyn falling down sheer on its eastern side into deep glens, with narrow ledges striking off several hundred feet below the summit and linking up the mountain with outlying ridges or peaks. The narrow ridge of Striding Edge runs out with a foot-track along its rather giddy top, which in a few hundred yards joins the wider ridge of Grisedale Valley. A strong wind on these lofty slopes will whirl a man off his feet like a drifting leaf, but on a fine day we may take a narrow ledge called Swirrel Edge, and between these two Edges are the finest ascents of Helvellyn. Deep down between Striding and Swirrel Edges lies the little pear-shaped lake Red Tarn, looking as if we could throw a stone into it. This is the place where the traveller died who was watched over by his faithful dog, as Sir Walter Scott and Wordsworth both describe in poems. Seen at any season, either in clear sunshine or when clouds are scudding across the face of the dark precipices, or when snow is draping them in gleaming drifts hundreds of feet deep along the mountain walls, it is profoundly impressive.

Over Helvellyn in the distance are two neighbouring mountains, standing by themselves, which mark the northern limits of Lakeland, Skiddaw and Saddleback, two Cumberland heights best reached from Keswick. Skiddaw, though bold to look at, is not worth the climb, but Saddleback is a noble mass. It has a glorious two-mile walk along its summit, overlooking Thirlmere and Derwentwater, with the lovely vale of Borrowdale at Derwentwater Head backed by the haunting peaks of the Scafell range, giant of all these famous peaks where for three miles nothing falls below 2500 feet.

We have walked up the High Street to see one view, but, magnificent as it is, it is not finer than the view from half a dozen other mountain heights that command the different lakes: from Coniston Old Man, in Lancashire, with its vista of Coniston Water; from Red Pike, in the west, with its lovely vistas of Buttermere, Crummock Water, Ennerdale Lake, and Lowes Water; or from Great Gable, an outlying mass of the central mountain knot, overlooking Wastwater, and set right in the midst of the grandest and loneliest of the master mountains of this wondrous land—Great End, Scafell, and Scafell Pike, the precipiced Pillar mountain, and all the deep valley clefts that climb upward to this wild topmost region of storm and cloud that is the cap of England.

Forty acres of Scafell Pike, all land over 3000 feet, belongs to the National Trust as the Peace Memorial to the men of the Lake District who fell in the war. Another Peace Memorial is a few miles away, some 3000 acres including the summits of Great Gable, Kirk Fell, Green Gable, and Great End, and extending down to the height of 1500 feet. This magnificent area was given to the National Trust by the Fell and Rock Climbing Club as a memorial to its members.

Just below the summit of Great Gable, 2949 feet high, and one of the great tests of the rock climber, is a tablet, with the name of the club, and a relief map of nearly three thousand acres of mountain heads around, and below it this tribute and story:

> In glorious and happy memory of those whose names are inscribed below, members of this club who died for their country in the European War, 1914–1918, these fells were acquired by their fellow members and by them vested in the National Trust, for the use and enjoyment of the people of our land for all time.

The club has 450 members, and the names of 20 who were members are inscribed in honour, high among the mountain peaks they loved.

Westmorland shares the shores of Windermere with Lancashire. Ullswater (the other lake vieing with Windermere and Derwentwater) has its Patterdale end in Westmorland but the county shares the other end with Cumberland, the boundary passing down the middle. Hawes Water in Mardale is the only great lake that is entirely in Westmorland. But the county has an abundance of smaller lakes and tarns, high and low, many of them linked most impressively on the recessed shoulders of fine mountains.

First among the smaller lakes are Grasmere and Rydal Water, gems in the valley of the Rothay, but only to be seen in perfection from the Loughrigg Terrace Walk and Red Bank above the southern side, and not from the main road. The tarns have to be seen, of course, with the mountains which they grace. In Little Langdale are four low-lying tarns beloved by Wordsworth, and all domestic in their setting. At the head of Little Langdale the mountains begin and they are half within Cumberland, for the boundary runs from summit to summit. Boldly and sternly they rise from their rocky heights.

Tarn after tarn we pass as we climb, and from the slope of Fairfield to Red Screes, overlooking the top of the Kirkstone Pass, is one of the most exhilarating walks, up and down over four summits, to be found in the world. The range that is all in Westmorland is the Ill Bell and High Street range, with the Kirkstone Pass and Ullswater on one side and Kentmere and Mardale on the other. The slopes round the head of High Street are pitted with tarns delightfully placed.

But the Cumbrian Group, as the geographer calls the mountains of Lakeland, are not the only mountains in those two Lakeland Counties. The Pennine Range, the backbone of England, forms their eastern boundary, with Wild Boar Fell 2323 feet high on the south, Cross Fell, 2892 feet high, towering above the valley of the Tees where that river forms the boundary between the two counties; and the rugged group of crags which carry the Range into the Cheviots. For mile after mile stretches this great limestone range, its steep slope facing Lakeland, the great parting of the waters which flow with greater speed westward than down the long valleys of the eastern counties.

None of the rivers of these two counties can be called navigable, and this is particularly true of the Eden. This river is 60 miles long, receiving the waters of the river Eamont where it leaves Westmorland after flowing from Lake Ullswater, and the river Irthing, which gathers countless streams from the Pennines in the north-west of Cumberland. Another river fed by these Pennine heights, and also by the Cheviots, is the Line, which joins the Esk, the river which for some miles divides England from Scotland.

Through the heart of Cumberland flows the river Derwent with a length of 40 miles. It rises in Sprinkling Tarn near Scafell, flows through Derwentwater and Bassenthwaite Lake, and, having received the river Cocker at the busy town of Cockermouth, reaches the sea at Workington. Wordsworth's river Duddon, 15 miles of beauty, forms thc boundary between Cumberland and Lancashire, actually rising at the Three Shire Stones where Westmorland meets these two counties. Two other Lakeland rivers which are more important to other counties are the Tyne, fed by many tributaries in the Pennines, and the Lune, which leaves Westmorland for Lancashire at Kirkby Lonsdale.

There are innumerable streams which sing their way down every valley, frequently leaping precipices and splitting up into sparkling bands of light which make the waterfalls of the Lake Country as attractive as any in the world. The praise of the Falls of Lodore has been sung by Southey (perhaps too much), and other exquisite falls are those of Sour Milk Gill from Easedale Tarn, Mill Beck from Stickle Tarn, Langdale, and Stock Gill Force near Ambleside.

At times these falls and rivulets are in full measure, at others they are mere trickles, for the Lake Country, though it is the rainiest part of England, is not always drenched with rain. It is true, of course, that its mountains condense the moist air flowing in from the Atlantic, but a drought in England is also a drought here. The fact is that when rain does fall in the Lakes it falls heavily, and heaviest in a few square yards at Seathwaite in Borrowdale, which has an astounding average rainfall of 150 inches.

It is a wrong impression that has gone abroad that the Lakes have an undesirable climate. If that were so men would hardly have sought them as dwelling-places down the ages. The people of the Stone Age and the Bronze Age have left evidences of their sojourn all over them. It was in Solway Moss, indeed, that the famous stone axe with the wooden handle was found. There are many barrows, and many of the Stone Circles which speak of the religion of civilised races before the Romans came. There is a Circle near Keswick, and near Little Salkeld is the famous group of stones known as Long Meg and her Daughters. Two British routes cross Westmorland, one coming in from York over the Pass of Stainmore, the other following the valley of the Lune out of Lancashire and going over the Pennines into Northumberland.

But it was the Romans who built great roads in these two counties, as we have seen, the most thrilling being High Street, on the high ridge facing Helvellyn, which for many miles can still be traced. If Cumberland has not the unique remoteness of Westmorland, if it has wide stretches of industrial region that can hardly be called haunts of peace, it has something that must stir the sense of wonder in every traveller who comes to it, in some ways the most remarkable monument in England, the Roman Wall of Hadrian. We ride by it from East to West of England and for miles we are spellbound by this majestic spectacle. On both sides of us are the vast solitudes of these great northern spaces, and we are walking where the Romans walked, where they built this mighty wall, their forts and camps, with more than half their stations in Cumberland, and with fascinating relics of their occupation just across the border. And this great ride along the road from which the Romans dominated the district for 400 years brings us to a famous place which dominates it still with its historic appeal, Carlisle and its wonderful Cathedral.

It has masonry from the wall built into it. Nowhere in

Cumberland indeed are we very far from something Roman, and often we find stones carved by Romans, Norsemen, and Normans everywhere about us. Bridekirk has a Roman altar, and keeping it company is one of the most interesting fonts in England, with fine carving of strange animals and sacred scenes believed to have been wrought by Richard of Durham 800 years ago. Dearham has also a Roman altar, a fascinating Norman font carved with strange creatures, and three little pieces of carving from Saxon England. Gosforth has not only the cross known to all antiquarians and carved a thousand years ago, but a rich store of ancient carved stones by Saxon and Norman craftsmen. Great Salkeld has another rare collection including a Roman altar and a grand Norman doorway. Irton has a fine cross a thousand years old. Scaleby has a broken Roman altar in its simple church, and Newton Arlosh has timber in its lectern and its pulpit older than Christianity itself, for it was made of bog oak from the marshes. Bewcastle has the gaunt grey ruins of a castle built almost entirely of masonry from the Roman Wall which runs near by, and it has one of the most famous crosses in the land set up as a Victory Column 12 or 13 centuries ago. Burgh-by-Sands has a grand church with stones and carvings that were old even when they brought the body of Edward the First to lie in state there after his death on the marshes while on his way to crush the rebellion of Robert Bruce. Ravenglass, once the foremost port of north-west Britain, has Roman walls about 12 feet high, perhaps once part of a Roman House, and Over Denton has a church remarkable for having a chancel arch which was once a Roman gateway. Here it happened that the Saxons building their church found a gateway suited to their needs among the Roman ruins; it happened also at Corbridge over the Northumberland border, where the Saxons carried the arch of the gate of the Roman town across the fields and set it up in their tower.

All travellers through Lakeland know its few old towns. Westmorland's most historic town is Appleby, known to the Romans, Saxons, and Normans. It has a sycamore under which John Wesley preached, and a school at which two of George Washington's brothers learned their lessons. Kendal, the grey old town of Westmorland in the lovely valley of the river Kent, has a rich storied past and much treasure in its safe keeping. Here began the extraordinary love story of George Romney, and here is treasured the prayer book of a Kendal girl who became the lucky widow of Henry the Eighth, Catherine Parr. It now makes blankets and carpets, and entertains tourists as one of its chief industries, but once it made the famous Kendal Green cloth which brought it into Shakespeare. Penrith, where Wordsworth's mother sleeps, is the ancient capital of Cumbria and has a castle, a church full of interest, and charming oldworld peeps. The new capital of Cumberland is, of course, Carlisle, the city of border ballads and border history with its castle of grim memories, a museum full of Roman sculpture, and a cathedral which, though half of it has been burned down and its Norman arches are all agley, has carving unsurpassed in England in its choir, and one of the grandest east windows anywhere. Cockermouth has two famous old houses, in one of which Wordsworth and his sister Dorothy were born, the other being the prison-house of Mary Queen of Scots. Keswick is known to holiday-makers in great multitudes, and has drawn pilgrims for generations by its association with Wordsworth, Shelley, Coleridge, Southey, Ruskin, and De Quincey.

The group of great houses in Lakeland is one of the best in any small county. There is Levens Hall, with all the grace Elizabethan builders and craftsmen could give it, and one of the loveliest gardens in England; Naworth Castle, built round its 14th-century fortress, with Saxon foundations in its tower, long the home of the earls of Carlisle; Sizergh Castle, home of the Stricklands for seven centuries, built round its old pele tower and flanked by Elizabethan wings: the picturesque Greystoke Castle; and Lowther, often called the Pride of Westmorland.

Of ruins there are those of Calder Abbey, with its ivied walls sheltering in a hollow under the fells; Lanercost Priory so lovely in the valley; Shap Tower in its great solitude, and

Kendal Castle on the hill; Cockermouth Castle, Dacre Castle, and a little host of others. The picturesque pele towers built for defence against the raiders from Scotland are everywhere about the Northern Border.

So richly endowed by Nature it is difficult to see what this wonderful country lacks except the crowds that would destroy it. To many of us Lakeland is perhaps some magic lake like Windermere, Ullswater, or Derwentwater, or perhaps the lovely little Rydal Water. To others it may be one of the towns or some particular small place—or perhaps a valley such as Borrowdale, with its smooth fells and rocky crags, its wooded slopes and rich pasture, the music of running water, and the rare magic of the lake. To myriads it will be Grasmere, the epitome of all that is best in Lakeland, made enchanting by Nature and enriched with the spirit of Nature's master poet. But in truth there is no part of England where so much of it all is beautiful and so little spoilt.

We ride about for hours enraptured by the little farms, the stone walls creeping up the hills, the grandeur of the peaks, the solemn stillness of the lakes, the glory of the trees and the mystery of the rocky heights, with rich pastures here and there, and everywhere a winding road and now and then a cottage.

Village after village we remember—Crosthwaite like a fairyland in spring; Firbank a tiny hamlet among the grandeur of the Pennines and Kirkby Stephen looking up to some of the finest scenery in the land; Kirkby Lonsdale beloved by Ruskin with its old medieval bridge, and Temple Sowerby with the loveliness of the Eden Valley about it; Troutbeck snuggling in the Kirkstone Pass; Askham with the cottages on the green, and Matterdale still with the host of nodding heads which filled the poet's heart with such deep pleasure and set it dancing with the daffodils.

Westmorland has 790 square miles with 65,000 people, and Cumberland is twice the size and has four times the number of people. Westmorland is more completely beautiful, but Cumberland has a character of its own. It touches the borders of

Durham and Northumberland and shares both their ancient story and their modern distress. It has a coast-line of about 70 miles and looks across the Solway Firth to Scotland and the Irish Sea to Ireland. It has the highest point of England, Scafell Pike, so that we may climb to its peak and look out on the four kingdoms, and it has part of lovely Ullswater, seven miles long and in places 200 feet deep. It was the scenery of Cumberland that captivated John Ruskin in his youth and gave him the deep love of nature that thrilled him in old age. He chose to die among the Lakes in which his love of beauty was born. Three other fine lakes has Cumberland—Bassenthwaite, Derwentwater, and Thirlmere. Except for Windermere, it has all the biggest lakes, and it has as its boundary the famous River Duddon which Wordsworth loved, sharing it with Lancashire. Wordsworth was cradled in Cumberland, and by this famous river he sat dreaming of the mystery of Life.

But it is as a whole that we must judge Lakeland, and as a whole it must be declared unparalleled for beauty in these islands. It has a past older than history and its share in the historic period when our island was part of the Roman Empire. It has its association with poets and scholars: Coleridge, Wordsworth, and the generous-hearted Southey, Dr Arnold of Rugby and his poet son, Mrs Hemans and Harriet Martineau, all loved this piece of England and made it their home. Here also was born John Dalton. Here began the love stories of Romney and Scott.

Lakeland has its roll of honour, its lakes and mountains, a remarkable variety of scenes and strangely varied hamlets and towns; it has the Roman Wall rooted in so historic a past; it has a height on which we may stand on a fine day and look out of England into Ireland, Scotland, and Wales; it has miles of coast washed by the sea, and miles of border with the Scottish heather beyond it.

So richly blessed by Nature, Lakeland has not unworthily paid Nature back by giving to mankind the master poet of the hills, the dales, the little daisy, and the running stream.

CUMBERLAND

Fragments of Splendour

ABBEY TOWN. The pathetic fragments of its lost splendour are scattered far and wide; long before we reach it we see them, odd-looking stones in houses, bits of carving built into barns. They are all over this countryside, dominated for centuries past by the great and wealthy abbey of Holme Cultram.

The old church left standing in Abbey Town is but a part of the nave of the abbey church, and strange is the feeling it gives of a splendid thing brought low. Its walls are the noble 13th-century arches of the nave, blocked up and pierced again with windows that would better suit a puritan chapel; at the east it ends abruptly with a wall and goes on as ruined foundations outside; and it only stands at all because the people begged the destroying Thomas Cromwell to leave it as a great aid and defence against the Scots.

Within a century of the dissolution of the monasteries Abbey Town had proved itself unworthy of the great church left in its care. They let the tower fall and built it up again; then somebody set the whole place burning, and it became a ruin.

The 18th century saved what could be saved, the 19th restored it, and the great Tudor porch is now a little museum of old things rescued. The museum itself has one of the finest pieces of Norman architecture in Cumberland, the magnificent west doorway, with its five moulded arches and its eight pillars with carved capitals. It is 16 feet high and stands in a wall 8 feet thick.

The porch was built by Robert Chambers, an abbot who did much for his abbey not long before it was dissolved. In it are the remains of his tomb carved with a variety of figures and with the chained bear that he used as a pun on his name. He is carved in his robes, with praying monks on either side.

Near by is a stone to the kinsman of a 13th-century abbot; another to his wife; and another to a 14th-century abbot. Finely cut with a cross is the tombstone of Robert Bruce's father, the lord of Annandale; and carved with a staff under a canopy is that of Abbot Rydekar, who died in 1434. Dating from the years after the monks had gone are two other tombstones, one to a lady murdered by a pistol shot in her own house and the other to a 17th-century man who "Gave almes freely to the poore."

One of the bells was here with the monks, and in addition to many old pieces of carving are a few patterned tiles of 600 years ago, and two old chests. Outside in the wall is a richly decorated niche for a statue.

There is a modern inscription to the man who was the last abbot and then the first rector, and another to Joseph Mann, who on his farm here did a great service to farmers when in 1826 he invented a crude reaping-machine, one of the primitive forerunners of the first reaper invented by Cyrus McCormick a year or two later.

One of the windows has a beautiful figure of St Mary, in memory of Sister Martha Mark, who was more than worthy of her name. She was nursing in the Boer War, and again through the Great War.

Downfall

AIKTON. We can stand here in a quiet country lane and look across the Solway Firth, but it is not the sight of Scotland that thrills us: it is the great grass-grown mounds by a wayside farm in the hamlet of Downfall.

Downfall it has been since its Hall was burned down by the Scots, and the grass-grown mounds are all that is left of that great place. They bring to us an echo of the tragedy of Thomas Becket, for here lived Joan de Morville, whose father was one of Becket's murderers, and in the shelter of the church porch is a richly carved stone believed to have been on the coffin of her father, Hugh de Morville.

The little church among the elms at the top of a lane has something from its Norman days, for, though its chancel arch has lost its pillars, the scalloped capitals are as the Normans left them, and the crudely carved bowl of the font is probably theirs. The nave arcade is 14th century, and the little piscina with the flower-shaped drain would be the work of the same masons.

The black-and-white roof has four stout rough-hewn beams where they have been for centuries, and in the turret hangs a bell which was ringing before the Reformation, though we found it cracked, and ringing, alas, no more.

The Smiling Lady

AINSTABLE. Four roads run away through fields and woods, leaving at the crossways some white farm dwellings and the church on the hill where John Vesty preached for 57 years. After two miles the road stops by an 18th-century farmhouse known as the Nunnery, tucked away in a glen where the Croglin and Eden meet.

Eight centuries ago a convent was founded in this green refuge. One of its walls can still be seen; from the well sunk in the foundations of the house the nuns perhaps drew their water. Near the farms, on the roadside, rises a mysterious, solitary square pillar about ten feet high bearing a panel set in newer masonry with the astonishing date 1088.

We leave its riddle unexplained, and come back to the church, first built about the same time as the convent. What it was like when faithful John Vesty came in 1680 we can only guess from fragments the rebuilders saved, such as the Norman pillar piscina; John Denton's gravestone cut with a crested helmet, sword, and four shields, in the 14th century; a headless sandstone figure 36 inches high, holding a shield; an old gravestone with a cross; and a bird with spread wings—perhaps St John's eagle.

By the altar lies a beautiful red-sandstone lady in a long gown and winged headdress, who has been smiling at a secret thought for 500 years. She was the wife of John Aglionby, who lies armour-clad on the other side of the altar, his bearded head resting on a helmet. He is wearing gauntlets and his dagger hangs from his belt. There are marble inscriptions to the Aglionbys of the 18th and 19th centuries.

In the old church John Leake was baptised in 1729. He became a famous doctor, founded a hospital for women in Westminster, and was buried in the Abbey.

The Napoleon of Watling Street

ALLHALLOWS. Lying where the hills of Lakeland die away into Solway Plain, it has two churches old and new. The new one has a good window showing the Ascension; the old one goes back to Norman times and was seldom used when we called.

It stands locked and alone, treasuring the memory of a good man sleeping within its walls, and no one who fetches the key from the vicarage will regret it, for the monument of George Moore is worthy of the man. In white marble his head and shoulders are carved, portraying his fine face and very human personality, and of him this is written:

He served his generation according to
the will of God, and fell on sleep.

George Moore was born at Allhallows soon after Trafalgar, and from working as a boy at Wigton he went to conquer London with half-a-crown in his pocket. He may be said to have done so, for he was soon employed by a firm of lace sellers, and from that time fortune continued to smile upon him. As a traveller on the road he was so successful that they called him the Napoleon of Watling Street.

Enormously rich, he was equally generous. He helped to found schools and hospitals, homes and missions; he tried the experiment of running a Reformatory for thieves at Brixton; he did a great deal for his own county; and his humility was such that he chose to pay the fine of £500 rather than hold the high office of Sheriff of London to which he was elected.

In his prosperity his thoughts turned back to this place, and he came to live at the great house Whitehall close to the old church. Death came to him tragically in 1876. He had started his march to prosperity on the roads, and the roads, in that age of rural tranquillity, were to bring him to his doom, for the Napoleon of Watling Street was travelling to speak at a meeting in Carlisle when he was knocked down by a runaway horse. He died at the inn where, half a century earlier, he had slept as an unknown boy going to London; and he lies in the little mortuary chapel of this church, with the monuments of his two wives close to his own.

Charting the Trackless Deep

ALLONBY. It has the sea and fine sands to enjoy, a long line of Scottish hills to look at across the water, a certain quaintness of plain old houses, and one thing to see in the very plainest of early Victorian churches. It is a marble monument carved with the head of Joseph Huddart, who was born here in 1741 and lived to win a place for himself in the story of navigation.

As a boy he went to the vicar's school and built model ships; as a man he built a real one and sailed in it far and wide. For two things he is remembered: his charting and surveying of the coasts and ports he visited in the East, and his invention, after seeing a mishap caused by a broken cable, of a new way of making cables so that the strain fell equally on the different strands of yarn. Going into business with his idea he grew rich and died in London, being buried at St Martin-in-the-Fields; but it is right that he should have a memorial in this church by the sea, for he did much, as the inscription tells us, to point out a more secure path in the trackless deep.

John Smeaton's Canal

ALSTON. Set in a wide and green hollow nearly 1000 feet above the sea, it looks out towards bare mountains looped by roads which climb 2000 feet on their way to the town. The highest point is Hartside Cross. Mounds and ramparts at Hall Hill tell of a Roman settlement; mounds below Tyne bridge tell of a vanished fortress.

From the main street, rising sheer from the river bank, open steep lanes and yards which thread the grey mass of the old town. Some of the houses perched on the slopes have outside staircases clinging to the walls. One, near the church, built in 1691, has a narrow verandah above the pavement. Below the little slanting marketplace with its 19th-century market cross rises a building Alston is proud of, the town hall set up in 1857 with a clock tower like a church tower, its canopied buttresses and oak sprays carved in niches.

The tall spire of the modern church is a landmark for miles. It has a weathercock and pennon from 1770. Fragments of Alston's medieval church are in the porch, small gravestones with shears, pieces of stone carved with flowers. Inside the church there is little of interest except the oak reredos, with its paintings of bishops and saints and the holy lamb.

From the churchyard we have a superb view of the valley, where the South Tyne, shaded with trees, makes its course over rapids and waterfalls. The most interesting spot is Nent Force, a pretty waterfall where, ten years before he built the Eddystone Lighthouse, John Smeaton began an underground canal about five miles long called Nent Force Level. A hundred years passed before it was finished, but it is navigable for three miles still.

The trees by the river shade Randal Holme, a rambling farmhouse of 1746, built round a 14th-century keep with walls six feet thick, and a stone stairway to the roof of which traces can be seen. In the vaulted cellar is a tiny window of which one bar of the medieval grating remains. The oak rafters in many of the old rooms still bear the mark of the adze.

Fifty years after the building of Randal farm there was born in Alston Hugh Lee Pattinson, who became a distinguished chemist. After some years in Newcastle he returned to Alston as assay master in the lead mines, and patented his method of extracting silver from lead ore. Six years before he died (in 1858) he was made a Fellow of the Royal Society.

The Lonely Church Among the Hills

ARLECDON. Its one possession is its lonely church among the hills, with 19th-century walls, a 20th-century tower, and two ancient monuments: the 14th-century font, and the chancel arch. The arch remains from the old church, with a crude head on one side of it; the font has come home after having been astray, for it was discovered early this century lying about in the neighbourhood. There is a fragment of an ancient coffin stone, and we found also bits of carved stone on a windowsill, so old that they may be part of a Saxon cross.

The chancel has fine carving in its stalls, the stone pulpit has elegant tracery, and the beautiful stone reredos has the Evangelists under canopies, with three oil paintings with Gabriel bringing the good news to Mary, the scene at Bethlehem, and Our Lord at supper with the two at Emmaus when the day was far spent. On each side of the chancel arch are paintings of Michael with his flaming sword and St Kentigern with his staff.

We noticed that in this lonely place Thomas Baxter was the shepherd of his flock for 62 years of the 18th century.

The Valley of Eden

ARMATHWAITE. It is in the valley of the Eden, and it seemed to us that it might be the garden of Eden itself as we stood on the fine bridge looking up at the steep hills shaded with the green and brown of bracken and beeches, oaks and conifers, and then down again at the stalwart line of beeches in the shining mirror of the river.

The few buildings gather round the bridge, the oldest a farm called Nunclose, the tiniest a miniature chapel rebuilt 300 years ago after being used for generations as a cattle-shed.

All around this solitude are the everlasting hills, and down by the river is the Castle, a striking house, mainly modern, but with a wall five feet thick and many stones from a Norman castle. A richly carved oak overmantel of 1640 is in one of the rooms, with three quaint heads and a shield of the Skelton family, who lived here till the beginning of the 18th century. From another branch of the family came John Skelton, the satirical poet who sought refuge from the anger of Cardinal Wolsey by taking Sanctuary at Westminster, where he died.

The Happy Teetotaller

ASPATRIA. It has a peep of Scotland across the Solway Firth, a church with Norman stones in its walls, carving older still, and the grave of one of the humorous men in the public life of a serious generation, Sir Wilfrid Lawson.

He was a great teetotaller, and no man in his day made more people laugh at temperance meetings. He lived in the big park of Brayton Hall, and many plots for the downfall of the drink traffic were hatched under the trees by its lovely lake. Here Sir Wilfrid Lawson lived out his long life, dying early in this century, mourned by all who knew him, for he was one of the friendliest and happiest men who ever sat in Parliament. He stands in bronze in the Embankment Gardens looking out on the Thames. His house was burnt down at the end of the war.

There is a fine fountain to his memory at the cross-roads, on which St George is slaying the dragon with his lance; the bronze plaques set in the stone show his portrait with scenes of Temperance and Peace, and the inscription tells us that "he championed the cause of temperance with gay wisdom and perseverance." He lies in a simple grave outside the chancel.

He would see the church made new with its turret and pinnacled tower, its nave of six arches, and its fine chancel arch guarded by kings. On the gates of the chancel screen are the names of the vicars from 1292. In the chancel is a canopied sedilia with a king at one end and a bishop at the other. On each side of the east window are oil paintings given by Sir Wilfrid Lawson in memory of his sister, one showing Our Lord rising from the tomb, the other showing Pentecost in the upper room. In the window itself Christ stands in a red robe on an island amid streams with a great company of prophets, martyrs, disciples, kings, and queens about him. In seven other windows given by the seven children of Lady Lawson, Daniel is with the lions and David is playing his harp, and there is a fine Te Deum with saints and angels.

In a church where so much is new it is surprising to find so much that is very old. The original chancel arch is now the entrance to the tower, refashioned so that it looks like a copy of itself, and a fine doorway through which the Normans passed is now the entrance to the vestry. There is also a Norman font on five pillars, its square bowl richly carved with undercut leaves and with an extraordinary grotesque which has heads at the ends of two tails, both heads busy eating the leaves and branches of a tree, while the proper head is biting at the root. It is a very queer joke 800 years old.

Here also we found stones older still, a Viking hogback four feet high carved with knotwork, a fine example of a Northumbrian cross, and remains of 10th-century stones and crosses carved with spirals and rings, and one carved with a swastika.

Outside are stone coffin lids and a coffin, and in the churchyard is a magnificent memorial carved by the man who lies in a grave close by it. He was the well-known archaeologist W. S. Calverley, who was vicar here, and the memorial they have set up to him is a copy of the Gosforth Cross, one of the best surviving anywhere.

Exit From Lakeland

BASSENTHWAITE. It lies at the foot of Skiddaw, and its lake is the third biggest in Lakeland. "This house done by John Grave 1736" says one little house in the village.

We see the spire of the new church as we ride along by the lake, but only those who turn across the fields see the old one near the water's edge. It is the work of the Normans made new last century, and stands charmingly by a busy little stream. The interior has crooked old arches, and there is a medieval gravestone carved with a cross and a sword. There are several memorials to the Speddings, who lived near by at Mirehouse, where the most famous of their family was born. He was James Spedding, who gave 30 years to the study of Francis Bacon, his edition of Bacon's Life and Letters so impressing Carlyle that he called it "the hugest and faithfullest bit of literary navvy work I ever met with in this generation." Among the friends of Spedding were Coleridge and Thackeray, and it was Tennyson who called him "the Pope among us young men, the wisest man I know."

Bassenthwaite does not rank high in Lakeland scenery. Its commanding feature is the view of Skiddaw, which at some points shows a clear rise from the lake level to the summit. A striking show when we called in June was the array of foxgloves on the wooded fells on the western side of the lake. We found whole hillsides as coloured as the hills of Scotland are coloured by its richest heather later in the year. The finest viewpoint overlooking Bassenthwaite is the bold hill Barff, opposite the head of the lake. Compared with such lakes as Ullswater, Derwentwater, or Hawes Water, Bassenthwaite is just a quiet exit from the Lake Country.

Treasure Trove

BEAUMONT. From its hill above the River Eden we see Carlisle four miles away and Scotland across the Solway Firth. Here still are traces of the Roman Wall, and near the church is a Roman stone found in the river about a century ago.

Where the church stands a Roman mile-castle once stood, and in this simple building are Roman stones that have been used again. Its first builders were the Normans, and some of their masonry is still at the east end of the chancel. The nave has old beams in the roof, and there are two gravestones 600 or 700 years old, one with a flowered cross, the other with what looks like a minstrel's harp. One of the rectors, Thomas Lewthwaite, ended a ministry of 57 years here in 1762.

The village has seen some of the great figures of history passing by, for here came Edward the First on his last journey, before he died at Burgh-on-Sands, and here, a few years later, came Robert Bruce to camp for five days. The village has also seen the discovery of remarkable treasure trove: in 1837 many medieval coins were found at Sandsfield near by, and in 1884 a box containing 6000 coins of the 14th century came to light.

Small Neighbours for 1000 Years

BECKERMET. Close neighbours in this narrow strip of Cumberland between the mountains and the sea, these two little places, Beckermet St John and Beckermet St Bridget, are named after their churches, and each has relics nearly a thousand years old.

St John's is a 19th-century church standing high on a pretty corner, where the Black Beck and the Kirk Beck meet at an old stone bridge before hurrying on to the sea. A neat and simple building it is, in which we found a collection of ancient stones in the porch and on the windowsills. Some are gravestones, whole and broken, big and small, carved with crosses and sometimes with a sword. One has parallel lines branching from the stem of a cross, and another a flower in the centre of three circles forming the head of a cross. There are some big fragments which are perhaps the oldest of all, pieces of crosses carved with patterns 900 or 1000 years ago.

Here as a peace memorial is something modern in the style of the 15th century, an attractive chancel screen with linenfold panels and traceried bays.

St Bridget's church stands lonely and rarely used on one of the rolling hills. It has an old bellcot, and thick walls which tell of Norman days, and its chancel arch seems to suggest alterations in the 13th century. But we do not need to go inside to see its best and oldest treasures, for they are in the churchyard—two shafts of crosses made and carved in the time of the Normans. One is of very worn white stone, about six feet high, and has a plait pattern; the other, of red stone, is shorter, with spirals and cable bands and an inscription no longer readable.

The Victory Column

BEWCASTLE. Here still are fragments of building foundations in a Roman camp that has sent many relics to Carlisle museum; and here too are the gaunt grey walls of a ruined castle built almost entirely of material from Hadrian's wall. There is a massively-built farmhouse which was perhaps a border fortress 600 years ago. Here is Hobbie Noble's Well, reminding us of the Hobbie Noble in Sir Walter Scott's ballads, and an unlovely 18th-century church which does not attract the pilgrim. All these old things has Bewcastle, but they are not what we come here to see. We come to this far-away spot for one magnificent possession, the Bewcastle Cross in the churchyard, one of the most famous in England.

Long before the Conquest it was here, perhaps in the 7th or 8th century. The head which once crowned its 14-ft shaft has gone, but the carving of the shaft is exceptionally well preserved, enough to show at a glance that the sculptor who fashioned it was a master of his craft. Beautifully and boldly done it all is, though some of the detail is worn by time, and on each of the four sides is still something to see. The north face has panels of vine, scrolls, and knotwork, and a chequered panel rather like a chessboard. The south face includes a line of runes, about the meaning of which scholars differ, and part of a sundial dividing the day between sunrise and sunset into 12 parts. The east face is a long panel filled with many devices, bold vine-scroll patterns with clusters of fruit, two delightful squirrels, birds and strange animals, one eating the grapes.

But most interesting of all is the west face, where three of the four panels are carved with human figures. One shows John the Baptist holding a Holy Lamb; another Christ standing on a lion and an adder, with his right hand raised in blessing; while the third shows a man holding a hawk on his wrist, his hair falling over what looks like a cape on his shoulders. The fourth panel is the key to it all, for its inscription tells us why the cross is here; it was set up as a victory column, long before the days of Alfred.

In Sight of the Great Wall

BIRDOSWALD. It is little more than a farm, yet Roman Cumberland is all about us. Here on the steep cliffs above the River Irthing, with a magnificent view of the river in its deep wooded ravine, was the fortress the Romans called Amboglanna, the biggest of all their camps near Hadrian's Wall. It extends over more than five acres, and parts of the dry ditch can still be seen.

But more interesting still are the remains of its Roman buildings, which include among many others a kiln for drying corn. We see walls six feet high and five feet thick, many of them finely preserved; on some of the stones are the marks of Roman chisels. The stones of the Romans were used by the builders of the farmhouse, and a host of Roman treasures have come to light on this remarkable site, including statues of Hercules, altars, pottery, and coins, most of which are in the safe keeping of Carlisle Museum. A neighbouring farm also has Roman stones in its walls, and there is a magnificent Roman gateway through which Cumberland men and women still pass today.

The Great Wall is plain here for all to see, like a raised road; and not far away are the remains of a considerable tower. Equally thrilling are the inscriptions on the rocks at Gait Crags, thought to have been written by the Romans using the quarry.

About a mile from Birdoswald is Triermain Castle with its two towers, another old house built of stones from Hadrian's Wall.

Two Towers of Long Ago

BLENCOW. Three roads run from its little green triangle, and along one is the old fortified Hall of the Blencowes, a sorry but impressive sight. It has towers of the 15th and 16th centuries, one with a yawning rent and the other with its top gone for ever. What was once a mansion fine and strong is now a homely farmhouse joining these two ruins together.

From Queen Elizabeth's time until 1913 Blencow had its own grammar school, now merged in that of Penrith. Among its famous pupils were the great Quaker George Whitehead, who did much to improve the status of the Friends, and the great lawyer Edward Law, who was leading counsel for Warren Hastings and became Lord Chief Justice, raised to the peerage as Lord Ellenborough.

Cousin Westmorland's Church

BOLTON GATE. It stands above the little River Ellen on a slope facing Skiddaw, and we found its church appealing to us because it is thought to have been built by that Earl of Westmorland who comes into Shakespeare on the eve of Agincourt with that little band of brothers to whom King Henry comes, hearing one of them wish that they had with them one ten thousand of those men in England who do no work today:

What's he that wishes so?
My cousin Westmorland? No, my fair cousin:
If we are marked to die we are enow,
To do our country loss; and if to live
The fewer men the greater share of honour.
God's will! I pray thee, wish not one man more.

The earl gave his church two stone porches, two little transepts, and windows with fine tracery. Most attractive outside, its most striking feature indoors is the stone vaulting of the roof of the nave, which suggests that perhaps the earl was thinking of churches on the Continent when he planned one for himself.

Victory for Sir Hugh

BOOTLE. An ancient village between the fells and the sea, its dull grey street is gladdened by the little River Annas flowing by the wayside under pretty bridges. By the wayside, too, is the imposing tower of the church, which, though modern, is lit by lancet windows and has a chancel arch in the style of the Normans. The modern oak stalls and pulpit are finely carved, and among the glass are scenes of John the Baptist preaching and in prison, a figure of his father Zacharias, and a richly coloured scene of the Nativity with shepherds and angels.

The tall 15th-century font has shields round the bowl carved with initials and old lettering signifying the Trinity, and on one of these shields are the arms of the Huddlestons, whom we meet elsewhere in the county. A fine little brass portrait is shining on the chancel wall. It shows Sir Hugh Askew who was knighted by Edward the Sixth at the battle of Pinkie, when Protector Somerset marched against the Scots, slew thousands of them, and gained nothing by his victory. But Sir Hugh gained his knighthood, and here he stands in armour with his hands in prayer and with flowers in the grass at his feet.

On a pedestal in the churchyard is a sundial which only the very tall can read, and close to the church a modern granite cross marks the site of Bootle's ancient market cross.

Rising up in swelling lines behind the village is Black Combe. Its 1970 feet, easily climbed from here, reward the climber with one of the most magnificent panoramas in the country. On some days no less than 14 English and Scottish counties come into view, as well as the Isle of Man, Snowdon, the Irish coast, and the Mourne Mountains beyond it. Wordsworth, coming this way, saw it all with the poet's eye, and in a poem that is not one of his best described this spectacle:

Of Nature's works,
In earth, and air, and earth-embracing sea,
A revelation infinite it seems.

A little link with the England older than Chaucer is still at Seaton Hall a mile from Bootle. Here by the farm buildings are some ruins of Seaton Nunnery, founded in the 13th century, and there are three fine lancet windows in what was once the east wall.

The Loveliest Valley in England?

BORROWDALE. Those who call it the loveliest valley in England cannot be far from the truth, for in a very few miles it has all the beauties of our Lakeland paradise. Here are smooth fells and rocky crags, wooded slopes and rich pastures, the majesty of great mountains seen afar, the music of running water, and the rare magic of Derwentwater that is never twice the same.

From the lake to the natural gateway called the Jaws of Borrowdale, and on to the farthest end where only lonely passes take us out, it is all pure Cumberland delight, with nothing we would change.

The five hamlets in Borrowdale have all their character and charm.

There is Seatoller, whose cottages begin to climb up the hill to the Honister Pass; Rosthwaite where the valley divides; Stonethwaite with its little roads going in and out and leading nowhere; Grange, with a bridge that attracts the artists, a simple church with a fine cross to four who fell in the war, and the viewpoint of Peace How, given by Canon Rawnsley in memory of the Keswick men who fell; and at the very end of Borrowdale is Seathwaite, one of the tiniest and the very wettest inhabited places in England. Here, on the same hillside, with a silvery waterfall and the deserted plumbago mines, are the old yews of which Wordsworth wrote, calling them

Those fraternal four of Borrowdale,
Joined in one solemn and capacious grove;
Huge trunks, and each particular trunk a growth
Of intertwisted fibres serpentine
Up-coiling and inveterately convolved.

Alas for the four brother yews! One has vanished and one is now a twisted wreck. Time and storm have made them what they are.

Borrowdale church stands near to the road, white and lowly. The first minister on its list was here 56 years, and the three fonts seem to have been quarrelling with each other for more than a century. The oldest, small and simple, was thrown out in 1825 in favour of the second, a little more elaborate. The second went in 1875, in favour, we suppose, of the third and grandest; and now all three are here again together.

Many of the delights of this valley belong to the nation for ever. One such is Castle Crag (an ancient fort), standing within the Jaws like a sentinel and having on the top a stone with the names of the Borrowdale men who died for us. Another is the curious Bowder Stone, an immense boulder of about 2000 tons, 60 feet long and 35 high, which, after rolling down the fell-side, has remained balanced on an edge so narrow that through a hole in it two people can shake hands. A third national possession is the fell whose summit is called King's How, in memory of Edward the Seventh. From it the mountain scenery is magnificent, and on the top is an inscription telling how King Edward's sister dedicated it as a sanctuary of rest.

Here may all beings gather strength, and
Find in scenes of beautiful nature a cause
For gratitude and love to God, giving them
Courage and vigour to carry on His will.

Close to Derwentwater are two falls, one famous. In Barrow Falls the water comes down about 120 feet in two jumps; in the Falls of Lodore it is hemmed in by high wooded cliffs and pours grandly over mighty boulders when there has been a heavy rainfall on the Watendlath Fell and High Seat above them:

Retreating and beating and meeting and sheeting,
Delaying and staying and playing and spraying,
Advancing and prancing and glancing and dancing,
Recoiling, turmoiling and toiling and boiling,
And gleaming and streaming and steaming and beaming,

So Southey said, but in simple truth the Lodore Falls usually have no resemblance to the poet's fantasy, though in imagination they go tumbling and splashing all over the world.

The obvious way of approach to Borrowdale, the most beautiful dale in England if variety in scenery is the test, is from Keswick by the highroad alongside Derwentwater, which many people think the most beautiful English lake. The lake is the continuation of the dale, filling the whole trough of the River Derwent which makes the lake. Between picturesque crags on the eastern side and the graceful Cat Bells range on the western side it lies smiling, with a strip of woodland on its margin nearly all the way.

Those crags, Castle Head and Walla Crag, rising from woods, and Falcon Crag standing more clear, all have lovely views of Derwentwater, Borrowdale waiting beyond, and a medley of mountains as backgrounds all around. More woods hide Lodore when the vale is reached beyond the lake, and more crags make a draped border for the vale, and presently, always wooded, rise from the floor of the dale itself and seem to block the way, while the fells on the other side rise into mountains. Straight ahead the dark mass of Glaramara gives the warning that soon there will be no ways out of this paradise to the still loftier heights beyond except by toilsome passes, available only to the human rambler or the sure feet of the mountain pony.

Beyond Rosthwaite the one main road turns westward, and at Seatoller begins the climb out of the vale by Honister Pass, perhaps the ruggedest main highroad in England. But this is not the end of Borrowdale, except to people who only travel on wheels. On each side of Glaramara, east and west, comes down, past that lofty wilderness of rocks, a narrow upland glen, bringing the headwaters of the

Derwent, and giving access to the highest cluster of peaks in England: Scafell Pike, Scafell, Great End, Bow Fell, and Great Gable. These two lonely valleys draw their highest waters from within a stone's throw of each other on Esk Hause, the hub of the Scafell range, behind Glaramara; and the traveller who knows Cumbria from above as well as from below never forgets the Borrowdale Fells whence its waters come, and where the grandeur of England culminates.

Roman England Round the Corner

BOWNESS. Proud memories it has of its place at one end of Hadrian's Wall, for here, on this headland looking over Solway Firth to Scotland, are many relics of the big Roman station whose ramparts enclosing five acres can still be partly traced. Among these grey stone houses, huddled together in narrow winding streets, we are not surprised to see a fragment of Roman England round any corner.

Built into the village walls are relics and stones both from the Wall and from the Roman camp, one of them a tablet of the 3rd cohort of the 2nd Augustan Legion; and in a roadside barn wall near the King's Arms Inn is a small inscribed altar. The Roman guard-room was near the school; though it has been exposed to view in our own time, it was covered when we called. We found two stones from it standing by the rectory.

The Roman ruins would be a wonderful quarry for the Norman builders who came this way in the course of time and it is not surprising to be told that much Roman material was used in the raising of the modest church on the edge of Bowness. There is Norman work still to be seen in the leaning walls of the nave and chancel, in some of the windows, and in a simple nave doorway. Another doorway, now built-up, has Norman capitals carved with little trees; but the greatest Norman treasure is the fine font bowl rescued from a garden about a century ago. It has four sides tapering off to eight, and its carving is of elaborate lattice pattern and trees with quaint leaves.

We have heard that the pulpit and the eagle lectern are made of old roof timbers, but, however that may be, they are both attractive, the pulpit with traceried panels and the lectern with three lions at the foot and three saints holding books as they stand on pedestals. The best glass is in a peace memorial window showing Mary with a fallen soldier at the Cross, but there are also pictures from the life of Our Lord, St Michael with two saints, and a scene of St Columba landing at Iona and blessing the men in a little boat.

Resting in the porch are two old bells, one of them made in the year Shakespeare died, and though their tongues are silent they have a tale to tell. They take us back to the days of a border raid, when the Scots came over the Firth and carried off the two church bells from Bowness. Pursued by the men of Cumberland, the raiders could only manage to reach their own shore by dropping their stolen trophies in the sea, at the place since called Bell Pool; and there they lie to this day. But the story did not end until the English had made an avenging raid into Scotland, bringing back as hostages these two bells in the porch, which are waiting, we imagine, until the other two lying deep in the Firth are restored. We were told here that one of the Scotch bells came from Middlebie and the other from Dornock.

At Drumburgh, four miles from Bowness, is the site of the smallest Roman station on the Great Wall, a few mounds being left to mark it. Here too, amid the houses clustered on the hillside, rises a tall, gaunt farmhouse that was once a castle, with a fine flight of steps leading outside to the second storey where an ancient doorway has kept its old studded door. Over the doorway is a coat-of-arms, and on a small parapet of the roof are two stone eagles keeping watch above the hamlet.

Deep in the sand of the beach at Bowness have been found early English coins; and beneath the peat in Bowness Flow men have come upon many of the old piles forming a palisade.

Caesar's Standard-Bearer

BRAMPTON. It has treasures of its own, and it is set in a captivating corner of the hills.

It has the great Roman wall a mile or two away and hills about it clothed with trees; it has not far away the lovely lake called Talkin Tarn, and it is within half an hour's walk of the romantic spot called the Written Rock, by the River Gelt. Here, about 50 feet above the water, is the rock with an inscription thought to have been carved by a Roman soldier in the first years of the third century. It may be that the stone for Hadrian's wall was quarried here, and this was the inscription as it could be read when Tennyson drove over to see it about the middle of last century:

> VEX · LLEG · II AVG · ON · AP · APRO · E
> MAXIMO CONSULIBUS SUB AGRICOLA OP ·
> OFICINA MERCATI

Tennyson thought the inscription very pathetic as the sole record of a standard-bearer of the sacred legion. Today only a few words can be made out of the letters, which come into Tennyson's story of Gareth and Lynette as left "crag-carven o'er the streaming Gelt."

Crowning a steep hill known as the Mote, above a triangular green, Brampton has raised a bronze statue to the seventh Earl of Carlisle; it is by J. H. Foley who has another statue of the Earl in Phoenix Park, Dublin. Lord Carlisle was Irish Secretary in Lord Melbourne's Government, sat in Lord John Russell's first Cabinet, and was a man much beloved.

Not far away is a plain cross known as the Capon Tree which recalls a much less noble man, for it was set up in memory of the followers of the Young Pretender who were hanged from a tree on this spot. In a narrow street is a house where the Young Pretender stayed for a week, and it is said that here he wrote his terms for the surrender of Carlisle, receiving the keys from the mayor, who came with the corporation and gave up the keys on bended knee.

At a cross-roads is another monument, a marble pedestal with a bronze portrait of George Johnson, a quaint old man who won little fame beyond the borders of his county, but who, when he died in 1896 at 80 years old, had earned an epitaph which tells us that "plain patient work fulfilled that length of time."

The town itself is clustered round the market square. It has an octagonal Moot Hall set up in 1817 with a clock tower, and two flights of stairs to an upper room, and standing by it are the iron stocks. By the marketplace is one of the finest modern churches for miles around, built on the site of an old hospital chapel. It has a splendid west tower and a tiny lead spire, and has much beautifully carved oak in the sanctuary and the stalls.

But it is for its magnificent Burne-Jones windows that travellers come to Brampton from afar. They have a wealth of colour and a noble series of portraits. The great east window glows with red and purple, blue and gold, in the finest Burne-Jones style, with 14 dazzling figures against a rich background of flowers and leaves. Our Lord himself is shown as an unconventional young man in a purple cloak, wearing sandals and carrying a lamb. St Martin in glowing armour is cutting his crimson cloak with a sword to give half of it to a beggar. St George is in flaming red, the Madonna is in blue, and St Dorothy in a purple cloak is carrying a plate of fruit.

In a charming series of little windows are scenes with children in them. The memorial chapel to Brampton soldiers has Our Lord on the way to Calvary, and Michael slaying the dragon. Other windows have a really beautiful Charity dressed in white with children hiding behind her gown, and a series of 12 lifesize portraits in which Adam is leaning on a spade, Abraham is shown as a man of war wearing Cromwellian armour, and John the Evangelist has an eagle over his shoulder.

Alone among its graves is the chancel of Brampton's old church, a grey building a mile out of the town. For 150 years it has stood solitary, and we may hope it will endure, for it was largely built by the Normans with stones from the Roman wall. The light still pours into it through two Norman windows, and in a recess outside the south wall is an ancient gravestone with a cross. There is an inscription to Richard de Caldecote, a vicar who died 600 years ago, and an old rhyme to an 18th-century vicar, Richard Culceth, which tells us a sadly familiar truth in its own way:

Man's life's like cobwebs.
Be he ne'er so gay;
And death's the broom
That sweeps us all away.

We remember that here it was very charming to find lovely beech hedges lining almost every road and lane.

Richard Made It

BRIDEKIRK. Standing together in the churchyard here are the ruined chancel of a Norman church and a dignified new church in Norman style. Open to the sky in the ivy-covered ruins is the pathetic grave of a little one who lived and died on the same day a few weeks before Trafalgar.

The new church has the two good Norman doorways (one with a carved tympanum) from the old one, and a collection of medieval coffin stones ranged round the apse outside. Its treasures include a fragment of a Roman altar, a piece of a stone cross about 900 years old, and a rare and beautiful font finely carved on four sides with strange animals and little scenes. One side shows the baptism of Jesus, and another the expulsion of Adam and Eve from the garden. On a third side we see the sculptor with his chisel and mallet, an artist's portrait of himself we do not remember in any other font, and a band of runic writing which has been deciphered in these words:

Richard he me wrought,
And to this beauty eagerly me brought.

It is generally believed the carving was done about 800 years ago by a famous architect and sculptor, Richard of Durham, and this piece of his work is notable for showing how the Scandinavian influence lingered on for several generations after the Normans came. The inscription has puzzled many experts and without doubt the font is one of the most interesting in the country.

The famous font would almost certainly have been used at the baptism of two men on Bridekirk's roll of fame, both sons of vicars, and both born at the vicarage in the 17th century.

One was Sir Joseph Williamson, who became Secretary of State in 1674 and four years later, in the scare of a popish plot, was shut up in the Tower by Parliament, only to be let out again by the king a few hours later. He gave Bibles and prayer-books and plate to his father's church, and £500 for the poor of Bridekirk.

The other vicar's son was Thomas Tickell, friend of Addison, whose works he edited. He is remembered for his lines on the death of Addison, in which, writing of the funeral at the Abbey, he gives this fine description of the scene:

Can I forget the dismal night that gave
My soul's best part for ever to the grave?
How silent did his old companions tread,
By midnight lamps, the mansions of the dead,
Through breathing statues, then unheeded things,
Through rows of warriors, and through walks of kings!
What awe did the slow solemn knell inspire;
The pealing organ, and the pausing choir;
The duties by the lawn-robed prelate paid;
And the last words that dust to dust conveyed!

This poem, the work of one of our minor poets, was described by Dr Johnson as the grandest funeral poem in our language.

The Saint of the Candles

BRIDEKIRK keeps alive the name and fame of St Bridget, or St Bride. A lovely story is told that when Bride was a girl she went to Palestine and became a serving-maid in the inn at Bethlehem. She would be there when Joseph and Mary arrived; she would see the shepherds and the wise men and the little donkey in the stable.

It is said that she helped Mary to nurse the Child, and that when Mary was able to walk to Jerusalem carrying the Child with her, Bride walked before her with a candle in each hand. So it is that we associate St Bride with Candlemas, the second day of February, the day on which all candles were blessed in the days when churches were lit by candle light. The story goes that though the wind was rough Bride always walked where it was so still that the candles did not go out.

Ever after this St Bride was the friend of mothers and babies. In the western islands of Scotland the nurse will say when a baby is born, "Come in, Bride."

Bride always wore a mantle of blue, and when she found a lost child crying for its home she would comfort him and put her mantle round him, singing this lullaby:

O, men from the fields
Come softly within.
Tread softly, softly,
O men coming in.

Wordsworth's Son John

BRIGHAM. It lies near Cockermouth, with a great quarry abandoned in its very midst, and a 13th-century tower rather spoiled by a little gabled roof.

The restorers have taken distinction from the church as well as from its tower, but they have left the three Norman arches, with carved capitals separating a fine 14th-century aisle. This aisle was the chantry of Thomas de Burgh, who was rector before he died in 1348, and in it he sleeps. His tombstone is carved with an elaborate cross, a chalice, and a missal, and lies below a beautiful traceried arch in the wall. Next to it are three sedilia and a pretty piscina from which three faces look out.

Many old carved stones lie in the church, some believed to be fragments of a church standing here before the Normans came. One is the base of a cross 900 years old, carved with twining patterns.

The font is 13th century; and let into the wall is an old coffin stone bearing a fine cross.

The glass of the east window is in memory of Wordsworth's son John, who was vicar here for 40 years, but does not come into fame in any other way.

History off the Beaten Track

BROMFIELD. Lying off the beaten track, its ancient church has a fine view across the lowlands and the Solway to the magnificent mass of Criffell, towering above the Scottish hills coming down to the sea. It is said that a church stood on this spot in the second century, that the Romans built another, and that still a third was here in the sixth century when St Mungo came, perhaps baptising his converts in the Holy Well, which we see in a field close by. The well is called by his name, and so is the church, St Mungo of course being none other than the great Cumbrian apostle Kentigern. It was a hermit who nicknamed him Mungo, meaning My Darling.

The church as we see it takes us back no farther than Norman days, but it has possessions older than itself. In the porch are two fragments of 10th-century crosses, and part of a worn cross-head which may be 1700 years old.

The church the Normans built was much changed in the 14th century, when it was given chapels and a new chancel. But there is still an arcade of the 12th century, and a high and narrow Norman doorway with chevron ornament. Its tympanum has a chequer pattern, and is thought to be part of one of the hogback monuments the Normans would find here when they came. The chancel has walls richly panelled in modern oak and a traceried reredos with panels of wheat and grapes. By the chancel arch are a worn head and a smiling boy.

There is a wealth of fine coffin stones six and eight centuries old, many found in the churchyard where they were buried by the 14th-century builders. Some are in fragments, some whole. Some have shears by their cross-stems, others swords; one has a very beautiful fleur-de-lys head, and one in the chancel is richly carved on the edges. In the north chapel, under an arched recess, is a fine stone engraved with cross and shield in memory of Adam Crookdake, a celebrated warrior in these parts 600 years ago. He lived at Crookdake Hall, two miles away. On the chapel walls are many memorials to the

Ballantines and their descendants, one a coloured heraldic brass on which we see a griffin with a sword and a green lobster.

Very charming in a chancel recess are the tiny marble figures of two little boys sleeping on their dainty bed, twins who lived for only a few hours about a century ago. Also in the chancel is a stone with an intricate mass of lettering in memory of Richard Garth of 1673, a vicar turned out by Cromwell. A massive cross on the old steps in the churchyard is a tribute to Richard Taylor, who was vicar 46 years in our own time, and an attractive cross by the gate is in memory of the men who died for peace.

About a mile from Bromfield is The Gill, an old home now a farm. It is still owned by the family of Reay to whom it is said to have been given by William the Lion, the Scottish king who died the year before Magna Carta, and this gives it one of the longest records of tenure in the north of England.

Education, Ninepence

BROUGHTON. It is Great and Little, two grey hamlets of winding ways set pleasantly on the slopes of a hill above the hurrying Derwent, here crossed by a fine stone bridge.

A stone a mile away marks the site of the ancient church which has vanished like the mill which once stood beside it. In the fields between the two parts of the village is a 19th-century church with little to show of its own, but with a splendid view of the Cumbrian mountains. Two centuries ago the almshouses were founded for four poor women, and three centuries ago the Baptists built a chapel here and the Quakers a meeting-house.

It is Little Broughton which can boast the greatest son, for here Abraham Fletcher was born in 1714. It is said that his education cost ninepence, and certainly the only thing he did not have to pick up for himself was his father's trade of tobacco pipemaking. Reading, writing, and arithmetic he taught himself, and it was the lure of arithmetic which drew him up a rope to the cottage loft at the end of the day in his father's workshop, there to study till he could no longer keep his eyes open. By 30 he was a schoolmaster with a gift for mathematics, and a wife who discouraged learning as an unprofitable thing. But again he was able to turn knowledge to profit by studying the medicinal properties of plants and selling herbal mixtures till all the people spoke of him as Dr Fletcher. His proudest moment was when he held in his hands the first of his two mathematical books, called the Universal Measurer, a survey of every theory of measurement. He died at 78, having many years before accurately predicted his length of life to within 16 days.

Here Died a Great King

BURGH-BY-SANDS. Here was once a castle belonging to Hugh de Morville, who kept back the crowd with his sword while Thomas Becket was murdered in Canterbury Cathedral; but not for this is Burgh famous. It is famous for its memories of our great king Edward the First, who died here within sight of the country which feared his very name. He was on his way to crush the redoubtable Robert Bruce, and, reaching Burgh, he would see this Norman church and these spacious views of the Solway Firth. The church was to see him again, for it was not long before they brought his body back from the marshes to lie in state.

It is fitting that such a historic building should have kept its fascination down the centuries, for this church with its striking tower and its old yew near by is indeed a fascinating place. We have called it Norman, but parts of it are thought to be Saxon, and plainly to be seen in these walls are Roman stones from Hadrian's Wall, which is still traceable hereabouts. The site of the church was once a Roman station.

There are big Norman beak-heads at the north door, and another one high up in the chancel, while near the altar is the grim stone face of a man with a beard and a drooping moustache. The nave has a 13th-century aisle, some of the capitals of its massive pillars being simply ornamented.

The great west tower, built in the 12th century, is like a Norman castle. An immense square of masonry, it is set back two-thirds of the way up, and heavily embattled. There is no ornament, and no buttresses other than thickenings of the wall. Big round-headed windows at the top leave the belfry open to the weather, exposing its bells, which are said to be 600 years old.

This well-nigh impregnable village fortress must have played its part in the incessant warfare of the border. Its only entrance is by an immensely strong iron gate in the nave, turning on two hinges and protected by three great bolts. It reminds us of the door into Great Salkeld's tower. Beyond is an inner doorway without a door, over it three curious carvings perhaps of animals. The inside of the tower is lighted by three little windows with sills seven feet deep, and the stone roof is vaulted. A spiral stairway leads up to the belfry, and altogether it would be hard to find a queerer tower anywhere.

The church is curious for having at its east end something like another tower, so old that it may be Saxon. Outwardly it does not show us a tower, for the very thick walls do not rise above the chancel roof. It is reached by a door in the east wall, leading to a little room where a priest is thought to have lived. Very interesting at this end of the church are marks made by the sharpening of arrows, perhaps intended for Edward's hammering of the Scots.

John Stagg who was born in this village in 1770 lived to set his name securely in the county's roll of fame. He was the son of a tailor and such a promising lad that it was intended he should be educated for the church. But tragedy came early to rob him of his sight and he was forced to eke out a living by selling books and playing the fiddle. His wanderings gave him a great knowledge of the country folk, and this found expression in various volumes of verse. He will for ever be known as the Blind Bard of Cumberland.

A mile or two from the village, on Burgh Marsh, is a pillar with a canopied head of the king, the 19th-century successor of a 17th-century memorial put up by one of the Dukes of Norfolk. It stands on the marshes where King Edward died.

Great of stature, invincible in courage, with a real love for his people, Edward was of powerful and subtle intellect, and sometimes in his necessity observed the letter rather than the spirit of his laws. But, although he cruelly hanged 200 Jews in London and banished the remainder from the realm, and though he oppressed the Scots with a heavy hand, he was in his violence only a son of his age.

He it was who first established the principle of no taxation without national consent; he instituted the Customs and originated our import duties; he maintained the common law against the Church and advanced the people at the expense of feudal tyrants.

Regarding himself as King of Scotland, he was provoked by Robert Bruce's rising to organise his last war. He was a majestic white-haired old man, a Hercules in decline, but with spirit unflagging. Too ill to ride, he was borne by horses to Carlisle, where in a last fury he mounted his steed, rode two miles a day, and reached this place only to die.

He took leave of the worthless Edward the Second, bidding him send his heart to Holy Land with 100 knights, and not to bury his body until the Scots were utterly subdued. His bones, he said, were to be carried before the army from battlefield to battlefield until the end, so that he might still lead his forces to victory. Then, with the name of God on his lips, he sank back and died.

The Village of Two Lakes

BUTTERMERE. Tucked in between Crummock Water and its own lake of Buttermere, it lies in all the splendour of Lakeland scenes, with little but a church and an inn to turn our thoughts from nature back to man.

Yet the Fish Inn has a poignant memory, for it was the home of a Cumberland girl whose fame once went all over England and found its way into verse and drama. She was Mary of Buttermere, known everywhere for her beauty and the cruel tragedy of her marriage. Her story belongs to Caldbeck, where she lies in the same churchyard as John Peel.

The small plain church of Buttermere is very attractive, with much fine woodwork. The font cover was given by the children; the ceiling has 16 angels looking down, the altar rails are delicately carved, the pulpit has traceried panels and a vine frieze, and there is a reading-desk given by the old boys of a Southampton headmaster who died on his way to this church.

Small as it is, the village serves for the two beautifully-placed lakes of Buttermere and Crummock Water. It is the only place hereabout where there is room for a village, so immediately and steeply do the mountains rise from the shores of the lakes. Between lake and lake is about two-thirds of a mile of flat ground, across which Buttermere Lake sends its outlet waters by a brook's course to Crummock Water, and Crummock sends them on by the River Cocker to the Derwent.

There is so much of beauty and interest about these closely neighbouring lakes that it is impossible to see them adequately in a few hours. Everyone compares them. Buttermere, the smaller, is much the better wooded on both sides, and its woods give it a softer charm. Both are hemmed in by mountains close at hand; but Crummock Water seems the more overhung, though with one exception the Buttermere mountains are higher.

We cannot boat on Buttermere, but we can on Crummock. The general views over Buttermere are the more extensive and the best. They include the Buttermere Fells, Honister Crag, and the descent from the pass; and southward over the lake the bold summits Red Pike, High Style, and High Crag. Down Red Pike come the white, tumbling, vociferous waters of Sour Milk Gill, seen from afar. Red Pike, after a rugged climb, has the best view from these Buttermere hills; and over that way, under High Crag, goes the walking path to the central cone of English mountains, Scafell Pike and his peers.

Buttermere possibly has the preference over Crummock Water, for Crummock looks harder, with Mellbreak, a most aggressive hill for its height, rising abruptly from the shore on the one hand, and Whiteless Pike and massive Grasmoor, farther back, frowning wild and rugged. But Crummock Water takes on a softer beauty at its lower end, while at its upper end it gives passage across its waters to whoever will see Scale Force, the waterfall with a sheer leap of 120 feet. And, lastly, there are for the pilgrim here the attractions of the mountains on either side of Newlands Vale, most easily seen from Buttermere.

A Man Who Should be Famous

CALDBECK. An old church, a lovely bit of nature, a memory of a beautiful girl and her tragedy, and a memory of an old man more famous than he deserves to be—all these has Caldbeck.

Its little gem of natural beauty has the odd name of The Howk, a wooded glen where a stream runs and tumbles between the rocks. Standing across it and somehow adding to the picture is one of the biggest waterwheels in England, 42 feet across and looking far too immense ever to have been turned by this little stream. Now idle for ever, we suppose, it once worked the machinery of a mill.

The waters that splash along in The Howk run on past Caldbeck church and were busy working another mill when we called. A great deal of the church was built in 1512, but some of it looks older and some is very new. An old piscina and a stoup were uncovered in 1932, and a medieval coffin stone with a finely carved cross is standing in the chancel. "This steple was builded in the year 1727" we read on the wall.

Thousands come here to see the grave of John Peel, and their feet have worn a path in this churchyard where no path was meant to be;

but there are very few who give a thought to the man who made Peel famous, the man who, if poets are to count at all, should count far more than Peel. He was John Woodcock Graves, who was born in Cumberland at Wigton, worked for a while at Caldbeck, and died on the other side of the globe. After John Peel's death in 1854 he told the story of how the famous words of the song came to be written. He and Peel were sitting, he said, in a snug parlour at Caldbeck while the snow was falling outside:

> We sat by the fireside hunting over again many a good run, and recalling the feats of each particular hound, or narrow breakneck scapes, when a flaxen-haired daughter of mine came in saying, Father, what do they say to what granny sings?
>
> Granny was singing to sleep my eldest son with a very old rant called Bonnie Annie. The pen and ink for hunting appointments being on the table, the idea of writing a song to this old air forced itself upon me, and thus was produced, impromptu, D'ye ken John Peel with his coat so gray?
>
> Immediately after I sung it to poor Peel, who smiled through a stream of tears which fell down his manly cheeks; and I well remember saying to him in a joking style, By Jove, Peel, you'll be sung when we're both run to earth.

He was right. Of Peel himself there is little to say except that he was a clever huntsman (though rather a pitiless one) who kept his pack of hounds for 55 years. But neither he nor the poet's words would have lived on had not a third man transformed the old rant to which they were being sung into a tune which will go lilting down the ages. It is more than time that John Peel's real immortaliser should have his share in his fame known. He was William Metcalfe, a Norwich man who for 50 years sang in the choir of Carlisle Cathedral and was conductor of the Carlisle Choral Society. It was in 1868 that he heard John Peel sung to the old rant of Bonnie or Cannie Annie, and at once realised what a rollicking song could be based on this air. He sang his own version at an important dinner in London the next year, and it was met with wild enthusiasm. From that time it was Metcalfe's version which was sung; it is his song we sing today, and he who would make a pilgrimage to the man who brought most fame to the name of John Peel must go to Carlisle, where William Metcalfe was laid to rest in 1909.

In a grave in this churchyard lies a woman whose tragic adventure in her girlhood was the talk of England.

Tragic Mary of Buttermere

THE Buttermere Beauty, Mary Robinson, was the daughter of an innkeeper to whom a gallant came wooing in 1802. She was in her girlhood; he was 44, with a lurid past of which she knew nothing. John Hatfield was one of the most extraordinary impostors of the age.

Born of humble parentage about 1758, he was educated at his native Mottram, Cheshire, began life as a commercial traveller, and married a daughter of Lord Robert Manners, who made him a wedding present of £1500. This he squandered, and then deserted his three children and their mother, who died of grief.

The impostor lived by representing himself as a member of the family of the Duke of Rutland, and while imprisoned for debt induced a credulous clergyman to bespeak for him the sympathy of the Duke of Rutland, who redeemed him from prison, gave him money, and paved the way for him to abuse his patronage in a way that brought him into prison again.

His imprisonment at Scarborough lasted seven years, and during that time he managed to get in touch with a Devonshire lady named Nation, who lived with her mother opposite the prison. Although there had been no meeting between them, she eventually paid his debts, married him on his leaving prison, and went to live with him at Dulverton, in Somerset, where a child was born. More impostures followed, and Hatfield fled, abandoning his wife, to appear at Keswick with carriage and horses, pretending that he was a member of Parliament and brother of Lord Hopetoun. Fraud and forgery and the pillage of new friends maintained him until he heard of beautiful Mary of Buttermere, whom he married in the name of Hope. Being challenged by a judge who knew the brother of Lord Hopetoun, whom he had impersonated, Hatfield was arrested, tried for forgery, and, less than a year after his marriage to Mary, was hanged.

Mary was made the heroine of ballads, books, and plays, and a public subscription was raised for her, so that she was able to marry an honest farmer and retire from the scene of her tragedy.

The Ruined Abbey

CALDERBRIDGE. A charming village of grey houses lining a busy road, it lies in the delightful valley where the River Calder comes down from the fells. Its 19th-century church, standing on the bank by the old bridge, is more pleasing outside than in. It is in 13th-century style, and has in the churchyard a tall peace cross, with horses and twining serpents among its decoration.

But it is for another and far older shrine that the pilgrim comes to Calderbridge, the fine ruins of Calder Abbey, founded 800 years ago. Along the valley and through a stately beech avenue we come to it, sheltering in its hollow under the fells. A place of much fascination and beauty it is, an almost roofless ruin of ivied walls, doorways and windows, and lovely arches rising from velvet lawns. It was colonised by Furness Abbey monks, and nearly destroyed a few years later by the Scots. Its monks fled back to Furness, were refused admission, and eventually founded the abbey of Byland in Yorkshire. Some years after it was colonised again, its endowments being greatly enriched, and by 1180 Calder Abbey had completed the building of a proud stone church.

All that is left of this 12th-century church, beyond a few loose fragments, is its fine west doorway with a round arch of three rich mouldings; it has foliage capitals, but has lost the shafts each side. Nearly all the ruins we see belong to the 13th-century abbey built by Thomas de Multon of Egremont: a square cloister court with the church on the north, the chapter house on the east, a convent on the south, and a house for lay brethren on the west which has quite disappeared.

The most striking remains are of the abbey church, the five lofty bays of its north arcade, the splendid tower arches on their clustered piers, and the tower itself which is still 64 feet high and was once half as high again. The transepts have fine arches opening into vanished aisles, and the north transept has a beautiful doorway with deeply cut mouldings, through which the monks carried their dead to the cemetery on the east. The south transept has at one corner a spiral stairway leading to a passage high up in the thickness of the wall. It has openings in the window splays, and along this passage the monks would pass to the tower, where another stairway led up to the belfry.

Part of the chancel is here still, with three sedilia, and with an arched entrance to a side chapel where there are fine arches and lovely double lancet windows. The chancel has also the interest of three old figures lying on tombs not so old as themselves, battered stone knights of the 13th century in chain mail with their shields; one of them, with his hands clasped and his legs crossed, is said to be Sir John le Fleming, lord of Carnarvon Castle at Beckermet, who may have been buried in the abbey as one of its benefactors. A head carved on a big fragment of another stone is thought to be the portrait of his son and heir Sir Richard le Fleming.

The chapter house contains fragments of carving and parts of ancient coffin stones, and high up in its west wall are fine lancets. Below them are two beautiful arches between the chapter house and the cloister court. The library is a corner of the chapter house, and contains among its many old fragments some heads of saints and two inscribed stones. Between the library and the court is a lovely double portal.

Two houses hereabouts have their connection with the old days of the monks. The first, standing on part of the abbey site, has the dining-room foundations belonging to the old refectory. The second, Sella Park, on the other side of the village from the abbey, is a modernised Jacobean house standing in what was once an abbey deer park. Close to the road, it is picturesque with many mullioned windows; and still in it, from the house Darcy Curwen built in the 17th century, are fine fireplaces, a newel stair, and a broad staircase with old oak balusters.

Black Tom and Black Diamonds

CAMERTON. Black Tom lies in the little church, King Coal rules in the village, and the River Derwent bends and doubles between them in its swift course from lake to sea.

The church is deep in the lovely valley, as far from the village as it could get, with only rough roads and field paths leading to it, and the racing stream looping round it; but it cannot hide from the mountainous tip of the pit-head, reaching higher than its leaning tower and spire of the 19th century.

Through centuries of rebuilding it has grown into a plain little church of neat panelled pews with bobbin ends, but still it clings to its Elizabethan silver chalice and the knight in black armour on his red stone tomb.

Black Tom of the North, as Thomas Curwen was called, belonged to a family powerful in these parts in medieval days. This statue of him came here about 1500, but it is said that he himself was buried in Shap Abbey. He makes a bold figure in his black armour, with his long hair resting on a crested helmet, and holding one of the biggest double-handed swords we have seen, nearly five feet long.

The Capital of Cumbria

CARLISLE. By the serene River Eden, in the arms of her tributary streams the Caldew and the Petterill, the romantic warrior town of border ballads has settled down to a peaceful old age, with a castle of grim memories, a house rich with Roman sculptures, a fragmentary priory, and a cathedral little more than a choir—but what a choir! It has medieval pictures and carvings by the hundred, and the grandest window (they say) in England.

The city was born under Mars on the highway of war, close to the Scottish border, closer still to the Great Wall which Hadrian stretched from Solway to the Tyne, the farthest outpost of Caesar's British Empire. It has watched Romans fighting Britons, Britons fighting Picts and Scots, Celts and Saxons; it has seen Danes and Normans quarrelling round its walls, which the Danes knocked down and the Normans built up again. It has seen English noblemen surprised by Scottish chieftains, and chieftains chased by noblemen, farmers arming against Border thieves, Royalists defying Roundheads, and the rising tide of the Jacobites flowing into its castle. Even in the cathedral we found a wife beating her husband over the head with a kitchen pan, one of hundreds of quaint carvings. "I am the King of the Castle" has been a favourite game since Carlisle had a castle; and once there was a Queen of the Castle, but she was a prisoner. Legends of Arthur and his knights haunt the ramparts still.

Hadrian built his wall on one side of the Eden, and a city grew up round the Roman camp on the opposite bank, where later William Rufus built his castle keep. A priory and a cathedral rose on the second highest point in the city, watched over by Henry the First, who made his own confessor Carlisle's first bishop. Then in the procession of kings came Henry the Second and the King of Scotland to confer on their rival claims. Edward the First held his last parliament within these walls, and at the cathedral door mounted a white horse and rode out of the city, a dying man intent on conquering Bruce and Scotland, but defeated himself by Death before he could cross the border. Some years earlier Robert Bruce had sworn a fickle loyalty to Edward before the cathedral altar. Richard the Third and John of Gaunt (his contemporary portrait is in the east window) stayed here as governors of the castle; Mary Queen of Scots stayed as its prisoner. Here came 15-year-old James

Parnell to visit another famous prisoner, George Fox, who won the lad to a faith for which he died in Colchester Castle four years later, the first Quaker martyr and founder of the Quakers.

The castle surrendered to the man Scotland calls Bonnie Prince Charlie, that most honourable of the Stuarts who outlived his better nature and died a poor drunkard. Carlisle watched him march out of its gates on foot at the head of his recklessly brave 4000 to conquer England to the tune of the bagpipes; and when the tide of the last invasion of England had turned, when the last battle had been fought on English soil, the Young Pretender returned to Carlisle, no longer on foot but riding listlessly, a dispirited youth. We have seen the chair he rested in that night; it is in Carlisle's museum. After he had passed King George's men came to batter down the city walls with 18-pounders, to pack 300 of the prince's pitiful garrison into the cathedral and 96 more into the castle dungeon.

Through the din of battle comes the song of the ballad, of Kinmont Willie and the bold Buccleuch, who went to his rescue and

Wi' the stroke of a sword instead of a file
He ransomed Willie in Auld Carlisle;

or that other famous ballad of William of Cloudsley who, outlawed for stealing venison, stole back to the town one night to kiss his wife and was rescued from the very gallows in the market square.

The din died down, and Carlisle's poets sang on, mostly in dialect of homely things, and none more charmingly than Susanna Blamire, whose "And ye shall walk in silk attire" travelled far beyond the Cumberland border. She died here in 1794, ten years after Bernard Barton was born here. Robert Anderson, whose poems laugh and weep with peasant folk, has his memorial in the cathedral, where John Brown, a more sophisticated poet, was a minor canon, and where Walter Scott, the poet who only wrote novels to pay his debts, came for his marriage on Christmas Eve with the raven-haired Charlotte Carpenter, the French refugee's daughter. Carlisle can point out the house from which they were married, and a dull place it is for the beginning of such a romance.

War and poetry—and Carlisle has its share in peace too, perhaps in a great world peace, for President Wilson's mother was the daughter of the Carlisle minister Thomas Woodrow. Thomas Woodrow Wilson, President of the United States, called to see his grandfather's Congregational Chapel in Lowther Street before going on to Versailles to lay with his famous Fourteen Points the corner stone of the League of Nations.

It is a mock warlike front with which Carlisle greets those who come from the south, by train or by the Penrith road, for they pass between two great round towers with overhanging battlements and projecting walls, an impressive entry to the city, but of the 19th century and serving not war but the law, as assize courts and civic offices. Near by stands William Lowther, Earl of Lonsdale, sculptured by the Carlisle artist Musgrave Lewthwaite Watson. The earl was the patron of art to whom Wordsworth dedicated his Excursion.

The road between the towers leads to the centre of the city, the Green Market with its 17th-century cross, a stone pillar on steps bearing a rampant lion and a sundial, and the town hall of 1717 with a clock tower and a double flight of steps outside, but with little dignity. The 14th-century Guildhall, on the contrary, is charming, its rooms lit by tiny windows. From its weathered beams a grotesque wooden fellow looks down into the square. More old houses huddle round St Alban's Row and other old alleyways. The looming walls of castle and cathedral draw us all the time, but there are two more doors to enter first, Tullie House and St Cuthbert's church.

Tullie House is 17th century, enlarged last century to make room for the library, art gallery, and museum. Here are the stocks and the pillory, the city's treasure chest with five locks, and a show of plate belonging to the Guilds (mostly 18th century and with a lovely Neptune and Aphrodite drawn by sea-horses on the Shoemaker's Salver). Here is the armchair covered with a tartan where Prince Charlie rested on his way back to Scotland, persuaded from the march on a panic-stricken London by the advice of his leaders, and sure in his sick heart that had he not listened to them he might have been sitting on the throne of England that night instead of in this chair—and well he might, though it could hardly have been long before the head which rested here, the head no Scot would betray for £30,000, would have been forfeited. King of England he is called by a falsehood on his tomb in St Peter's in Rome, and king he might have been, for perhaps a day.

There are thrilling sculptures here—gravestones, milestones, and altars, left behind with pottery, coins, and other relics by the Romans who made and manned Hadrian's Wall 1800 years ago, the great wall which passes to the north of the city. Here is the torso of a Roman soldier, and here a little lady with a fan, carved by a Roman in England not much more than a century after Christ was born in Bethlehem. She sits in a chair on a gravestone four feet high, caressing a little hunch-backed boy as he plays with a bird, a concave canopy like a shell over her head, and over that two lions crouching. There is another seated figure in fine robes, and on a stone over seven feet high stands a man 1700 years old, wearing a crown and high boots. With his robe caught loosely over one arm, he seems to be pouring an altar oblation from two horns.

St Cuthbert's church (the saint was once given all Carlisle as endowment for his monastery at Lindisfarne) is a quaint 18th-century place with a most surprising pulpit, a massive thing which slowly slides from its place by the wall and takes up its stand for the sermon in the middle of the church. The sermon over, the preacher back in his seat, the pulpit moves off again, drawn by ropes attached under the floor to a handle turned in the vestry. We were interested to find the bust of a vicar who for more than 2500 Sundays had waited for this lumbering thing to reach the middle of the church before he stepped into it. He was John Fawcett, who died in 1857. In a window is a bright oval panel of a preacher who used no pulpit at all for his sermons, the brown-robed St Cuthbert on his hermit island of Farne, looking like a St Francis of the sea, with an otter at his feet and seabirds on thc rocks. A window near him has a mosaic of 14th-century fragments of heads and canopies in red and gold.

Other churches and chapels there are, and a magnificent wooden reredos richly carved and gilded in the Roman Catholic church of Warwick Square.

In a garden near Sir Robert Smirke's handsome Eden Bridge stands a warrior saint in memory of Robert Creighton, twice mayor of the city and younger brother of Bishop Mandell Creighton, another of Carlisle's famous sons, looking so stately in bronze in St Paul's. The placid river flows on through a park of fine trees, past Carlisle's cenotaph, and above the pleasant gardens strangely called The Bits the castle walls rise from their steep bank 60 feet above the river, the city's highest point. It is a red sandstone fortress covering three acres, impressive still, though the Victorians knocked even more of it down than the Commonwealth army did in a whole year's siege.

In the outer walls is the tower where Richard the Third stayed as governor, called the Tile Tower because of its unusually small bricks over the Norman foundations. Here are two brick vaulted rooms and a Tudor fireplace.

A deep grass-grown moat guards the castle on the sloping city side. In place of the old drawbridge, a stone bridge now steps across the moat to the gatehouse, where a barbican with a portcullis of massive spikes like giant teeth threatens our head. Under a vaulted archway, through two more massive doors, and we are in the outer ward where soldiers drill and have their modern barracks. The inner gateway, called the Captain's Tower, has Norman and medieval work in its walls, and leads to a small courtyard where are fragments of the Elizabethan barracks for the soldiers who guarded Mary Queen of Scots. Of her prison tower only a panelled stair with 14th-century mouldings is now left, but we may look down from the great ramparts with their giant buttresses to the Lady's Walk, where the Queen took her exercise and hatched a plot or two. Even she, inveterate plotter that she was, must have shuddered at the sight of these rampart walls, 18 feet thick in places, her first experience of an English prison. They brought her water from a Roman well, and we found it flowing still in the keep built by William Rufus, with low walls 15 feet thick on the Scottish side, and with an entrance which looks little more than a hole in the wall. We climb up instead by Henry the Eighth's stairs, to find the first and second floors given over to the relics of the famous Border Regiment, a fascinating military museum.

Still higher we climb to MacIvor's Cell at the top of the keep, knowing that here again we are treading in the footsteps of Sir Walter Scott, for behind a heavy door with four locks, in a dark chamber with only a three-inch slit for light and air, lay the original of Fergus MacIvor of Waverley. He was Major MacDonald of Kippock, captured at Falkirk because his English horse pricked up its ears and carried him willy-nilly into the English lines. He left this cell to be executed on Harraby Hill in 1746, and for weeks his head hung over the city's English Gate.

The outer room to MacIvor's cell has more to show in its few square feet than any other part of the castle, for its walls and its door are covered with curious carvings, some quite beautiful though done with nothing but a nail, the beguiling of many a prisoner's dragging hours. A quaint scene shows cocks watching a fox climb into a bag. The leopard and the fleur-de-lys of France are here, the shields of famous Border families, a Scotsman in kilts, Justice with her scales, a dramatic stoning of Stephen, the Crucifixion, and more.

Below are the dungeons, terrible as ever, stone tombs for living men, stone walls, stone roofs, stone floors, and only a glimmer of light from the air shaft to show the glint of water on a stone worn smooth with the tongues of prisoners, who licked its miraculous dampness like drought-maddened animals. In the walls are holes for the iron staples which held them with chains, 96 of them in one dungeon on that night when 300 more of Prince Charlie's garrison were packed in the cathedral choir. Most of them left only to die; the rest were transported, all for the crime of being carried away, against their better judgment, by the charm of this young prince in his better days.

We walk along the remains of the city walls, past the Deanery, to an arch leading to where the cathedral stands on its small green, with one of the busiest streets of the city to one side and to the other side all that remains of the priory where men withdrew to contemplate eternity, a fragment of medieval peace grouped round with the Deanery, an ancient gateway, and the houses of the clergy.

The Deanery is made from the prior's lodging, and has a 15th-century tower often used as a refuge in war. Here in the tower is the most beautiful room in Carlisle, the prior's old dining-room, with a lovely oak overmantel and a far-famed ceiling of richly carved panels and moulded beams, and with the prior's painted inscription to tell us that he, Simon Senhouse, set this roof here to the intent that within this place they shall have prayers every day of the year. In every third panel two birds hold scrolls with verses in old English characters. An inscription over the arch of the monastery gatehouse proclaims that it was built by Prior Slee in 1528.

It was Prior Gondibour who built the handsome refectory 500 years ago, a single room over a vaulted crypt, 80 feet long and nearly 30 wide, with a most delightful little pulpit at one end like a tiny room. The pulpit has a delicately carved stone ceiling, and through its unglazed windows the sound of the reader's voice reached the monks at their meal. Here we found the priory's only link with its Saxon predecessor, the monastery inspired by Cuthbert. It is the head of a Saxon cross. With it is a small gravestone marked with shears. Other treasures are a Miles Coverdale Bible of 1550, a pair of tusks said to have been given by Henry the First, founder of the priory, who is believed to have laid the tusks on the altar of the cathedral as proof of the grant of tithes. Here is also a red cope of Venetian velvet, and a blue one of 16th-century silk embroidered with portraits of eight saints. Half the windows of the refectory look into what were once the cloisters but are now only fragments. The prior's tithe barn has managed to keep a little of its old timberwork.

The cathedral itself is a strange mixture of red sandstone and old grey stones, impressive in its strength, yet with a nave little longer than a Manx cat's tail, and all its glory in the choir. The nave, with stones in it from the Roman wall, was sadly battered down in the Civil War when after a year's siege the soldiers used its stone for rebuilding the fortifications, some of the Roman stones going back to their old home after many centuries. Only a scrap of the Norman nave was left, just two bays, boldly buttressed at the abrupt west end, and with a row of old heads looking out from over the clerestory. We found the people of Carlisle anxious to restore the nave to its old and true condition, and who does not wish them well?

The central tower was made new at the beginning of the 15th century on the Norman piers. It has no great beauty, and a beacon turret does its best to make up for its lack of inches. Warning flares have been lit here, generally to tell of Scots advancing over the border. In a niche below stands an angel with drawn sword, and a bell still calls the folk to worship as it has called for 600 years. The south transept has a wall like a fortress eight feet thick, and a most elaborate copy of a 14th-century doorway.

From the outside we see the two Norman bays, two partly Norman transepts, the insignificant tower, and then comes one of the loveliest choirs in England, starting in the 13th century with a triforium and three arched clerestory windows of flowing tracery, and with its last bay ending in the 14th with two graceful buttresses. They rise on each side of the gabled east end, with pinnacles and canopies and niches for James and John, Peter and Paul. Between the buttresses stretches the mighty east window, with glass so precious and tracery so glorious that it is said to have no equal in the land. In a niche above it a gentle Madonna puts an arm round her little Son as if to shield Him from the evil gargoyles round the corner. A three-corner window gives light to the triforium passage which crosses in the wall over the east window, and then the gable is finished off with nine crosses and a border of leaves. It is all so beautiful that no one minds that the gable is not symmetrical, and that the builders had to hide the fault with a small addition to one side.

We come upon much worse faults when we enter the new-looking Norman doorway copied from the 800-year-old window over it. First we notice the absurdly short nave, only 39 feet long, for it lost 100 feet in the Commonwealth, and then we notice that the tower piers have settled, distorting the arches round so that they seem to be crushed by the masonry. The smaller arches of the clerestory have not fallen out of shape but have been deliberately made with one side longer than the other, a proof that by the time the Norman builders reached these upper windows the settlement had taken place and they built to allow for it. Their faith that no more settlement could occur has been justified through 800 years. The two Norman arches of each arcade rest on pillars of prodigious girth, and over them the triforium arches gape like caves. From the walls hang the colours of the First Border Regiment.

On the top of the tower piers, whose faulty foundations caused so much damage, 15th-century piers as long again as the Norman piers have been added, making four lofty arches, one with curious unglazed tracery at the top. On each side are the Norman transepts.

When the 13th-century builders pulled down the Norman choir to build a bigger one they found that the width could only be increased on the north side because of the priory buildings on the south. The centres of the nave and choir are therefore out of line, but this effect is partly hid by the organ and the canopied stalls blocking the view through the tower arch, while a small door has been made at the side of the arch to lead into the centre of the choir.

We leave the imperfections of the nave, the crushed arches and the gaping stones, and pass into a choir where all is perfection. It is higher, broader, and more than three times as long as the nave, is lined with stately canopied stalls and graceful arches, is filled with little carvings in stone and wood and painted panels 500 years old, and is lit by as grand a window as we have seen. Over the triforium are graceful three-arched clerestory windows of flowering tracery, the walk between them railed with a stone balustrade of singular charm. There are aisles on each side, with arcaded walls and vaulted roofs, perfect 13th-century work ending in a richer bay of the 14th to form a passage behind the altar. Here are quaint stone figures, one man holding his knees and doing his best to hide a mistake of the builders where the roof ribs fail to join their corbels. The south aisle has its original Norman arch for entrance from the tower, but the added north aisle has a rich 13th-century arch, and also two recesses with a curious ornament like stone fingers set slantingly round their arches. A door from this aisle leads to a spiral stair with a lovely stone roof, one of the rarely-seen gems of a choir packed full of treasures. At the east end of the aisle is the modern altar of St Michael's Chapel, with four oak figures on posts. They are Cuthbert, with the King who granted him Carlisle as an endowment for Lindisfarne; Ethelwulf, Henry the First's confessor (first bishop of Carlisle), and Henry himself, holding the White Ship in which his son went down. Behind the choir are two big oak cupboards 500 years old, with doors on long iron hinges and painted with thistles.

It happened, just as the 13th-century's new choir was being roofed, that fire destroyed it all except the aisles and the arches of the arcades. These lovely moulded arches, eight each side, were shored up and new clustered pillars built under them; and so it is that we find 13th-century arches on 14th-century pillars. The exquisitely carved capitals of these pillars have formed a fascinating peepshow for 600 years. Set in deep-cut foliage is a complete series of the occupations of the months, the most perfect stone calendar in England. Round the year with medieval England we go, down the south arcade and up the north, while queer faces in medieval headdresses watch from higher up the arches, and weird creatures lurk in the foliage of the half-piers at the end.

The first in the peepshow is a three-faced Janus, looking back to the Old Year and forward to the New, and toasting them with deep draughts while the third face keeps an eye on the present. In February a man crouches over the fire, the picture of misery, emptying the water from one boot while he holds his foot nearer to the flames. A hooded man digs by a leafless tree in March, while birds, a squirrel, a bear with human hands, and a bishop with an animal's body gather round. The gardener is busy pruning a tree in April, while two creatures, half-human, half-animal, throw their arms round each other for joy that Spring has come. Who the droll little woman is who gives a bunch of leaves to a young man in May, while three winged creatures look on, we do not know; but June is plainly the month of the chase, a vigorous picture of a mounted man with a hawk on his wrist, roses in his hand, and musicians and mythical creatures crowding round. Owls swoop through the hot July evening with mice in their beaks, and we wonder why the mower with the scythe does not throw his close hood back. A cripple with a crutch works in the harvest field in August. September is another harvest month, and in October a man with a handkerchief tied round his head gathers grapes, and a fox runs off with his goose. The sower goes forth in November, and a stag and a horse are here for the hunting. In December, the month of feasting, an unpleasantly dramatic scene shows a man holding an ox by the horns, while another heaves the pole-axe, a form of medieval butchery still too common today. Close by a man tends the pigs.

By the first year of the 15th century the fire and its damage had been forgotten; the roof was on a still finer choir; the glass was in the wonderful east window. Then began the final glory of the woodwork.

Like rows of little spires pointing to the sky are these canopied stalls, with pinnacles rising towards a blue roof spangled with stars, where painted angels sit astride projecting hammerbeams. The beams carry no weight except the angels, for the 14th-century builders changed their minds and left the lovely curving roof free of the open timbers they had intended to support on these projections. The fine bosses are modern, but are copied from the old.

Gone are the angels which once hovered over the pinnacled stalls, and gone the figures from the niches, except for one old old man, a grave monk with flowing beard and rosary, who bows to the altar. But angels with their heads tossed back are on some of the arm-rests between the stalls, and under the seats is a world of quaint creatures, 46 misereres superbly carved. Here are lions and griffins, dragons and storks, eagles and foxes, feeding, fighting, and struggling; men and angels, a mermaid with her glass, a feathered Michael with an expiring dragon, and, most lively of all, a woman like the Ugly Duchess holding her rueful-looking husband by the beard and striking at him with something like a frying pan. In front the stalls are cut roughly with knives, the work of some of the 300 Jacobite prisoners packed in this choir 200 years ago. Some of them left their initials here before they were taken out to die, pathetic scratchings.

Between the choir and the north aisle is a wonderful oak screen put here in the middle of the 16th century by Lancelot Salkeld, Carlisle's last prior. Dragons and fishy looking monsters curve all over it, and three hold up shields along the cornice. In the lower panels are 12 medallion portraits thought to be Flemish.

From the aisles we see the pictures on the backs of the choir stalls, 70 paintings 500 years old, fading but fascinating. Those to the north tell the stories of Anthony and Cuthbert, those to the south of Augustine, all with explanatory rhyming couplets such as Chaucer might have written, and between them are portraits of the Apostles, each with the sentence he is said to have contributed to the Creed.

Of Anton story who lyste to here
In Egypt was he bornt and doyth aper.

So begins the story of St Anthony, and in quaint pictures and rhymes we learn of his hermit life and temptations in the wilderness. Next comes a charmingly naïve account of Cuthbert. We see him as a child forbidden to play with his toys, then healed by an angel, guarded by an eagle, and fed by a dolphin. We see his house thatched by crows. He stands in the sea with waves up to his chin reading his book of devotions (perhaps the very book buried with him, which we have seen in the library at Stonyhurst). An angel comes to visit him riding on a donkey, and then we see him dying in his island hermitage with a green rug over his knees.

On the opposite side is Augustine as a child at school, greeted by a master with a birch. We see him sailing away from his mother in a tiny boat, studying, listening to St Ambrose, weeping and dreaming and racked with toothache; and then comes his baptism in a font, his mother's death, and later his own at evensong. In the last he is being drawn in a cart by four white horses.

From faded pictures on wood we raise our eyes to vivid pictures in glass, the gems in the branching tracery of the east window, that triumph of 14th-century stonework, about 50 feet high and half as wide. Only York has anything to compare with it, but this is grander in design. It has nine tall lights, more than any other 14th-century window has in England, filled with modern glass showing the life of Christ; but it is the 600-year-old pictures in the unique tracery which draw all eyes with their vivid colouring and scenes. At the top Christ sits in judgment, a rainbow at His feet and angels blowing trumpets,

Derwentwater

The Derwent River

A Cottage in Borrowdale

Rydal Water, smallest and shallowest of the Lakes

Haweswater, highest of all the Lakes

Daffodils by Bassenthwaite

Derwentwater and Causey Pike

Cattle on the Banks

Looking across to Lancashire

The Ferry Boat

Lovely Windermere

A Shepherd with his Flock near Carlisle

Derwentwater and the Vale of Keswick

St Bees Norman Doorway

Calderbridge Calder Abbey

Abbey Town Holme Cultram Abbey

Greystoke The Chancel

Bridekirk
The Wonderful Font

Lanercost
Clerestory Arches

Penrith
An Ancient Cross

The Magnificent East Window

The Norman Doorway

The North Aisle

Ancient Doorway, Aisle, and Chancel of Carlisle Cathedral

Carving on a Choir-Stall

Carving on 14th-Century Capitals

Screen of St Catherine's Chapel

Prior Salkeld's Screen

Thomas Sheffield's Monument

Alabaster Carving of the Crucifixion

On the Salkeld Screen

Wood and Stone Carving in Carlisle Cathedral

An Autumn Glimpse of Skiddaw

Wythburn Church

Mungrisdale Church

Alston Market Place

Lanercost Priory

The Ring of Stones near Keswick

On Cleator Moor

Long Meg and her Daughters, near Little Salkeld

Prehistoric Stone Circles of Cumberland

Greystoke The Stately Castle

Dacre The Castle Keep

The Valley of the Esk

Ennerdale Water

The View from Castle Head

Scarfclose Bay

The Charm of Derwentwater

Buttermere and High Crag

Thirlmere and Helvellyn

Great Heights and Still Waters

Loweswater and its Wooded Shores

On the Banks of Crummock Water

Bewcastle Cross

The Ruskin Monument on Friars Crag

Gosforth Cross

Norman Pillars at Kirkby Lonsdale

Wordsworth Memorial at Grasmere

Ancient and Modern Monuments of Lakeland

while Peter stands in white at the gate of heaven welcoming the redeemed. The silver towers and turrets of the heavenly city appear in the distance. An angel looks out of a window over Peter's head at an old man, a priest, a youth, and a maiden waiting at the gate. Below are the lower regions, like a terrible picture from Dante, and next comes the resurrection.

More 14th-century glass is in a Norman window over a nave door, a medley of fragments through which wanders a lonely little pilgrim. One window in the north transept has a pathetic interest, for it is to five children of a dean who died within five weeks from scarlet fever. Another honours John Heysham, who founded Carlisle's first dispensary for the poor, and drew up the famous population statistics known as the Carlisle Tables, long used by insurance companies for calculating the average length of life. The finest modern glass is a small masterpiece in the gracious little 14th-century St Catherine's Chapel entered by a Norman arch. It is by Christopher Whall and shows in rich colouring the Shepherds and Wise Men bringing their gifts, while, like a shadow of what was to come, loom the three crosses of Calvary, reminding us of the wooden crosses of Flanders and the men who lie under them, in whose memory this window is.

An exquisite pair of 15th-century oak screens is in this chapel, with linenfold panelling and faces peeping out from the moulding. Here also is a dainty fragment of alabaster with Christ on the cross, a host of people crowding round, and an angel kneeling. An arch leads from the chapel into the transept where, covered by glass, is a stone with faint scratchings of a rare Norse inscription 900 years old. The bishop's pastoral staff is in the crossing between the nave and the choir, an astonishing piece of modern craftsmanship, with a spiral stem of ivory and a head of silver, its base rimmed with topaz and amethyst set in pearls. The bishop's throne, also modern, has an oak canopy 30 feet high.

Six bishops and a dean have brass portraits or statues in their cathedral. On the floor of the choir, near the stalls new in his day, is 15th-century Bishop Bell, his brass portrait a little worn under its canopy, but with some of the rich detail of his robes still clear. In a quaint small brass of 1616 on the north aisle kneels Bishop Henry Robinson with his crozier in one hand and a lighted candle in the other, and three dogs to help him keep the wolves from the sheepfold.

A wolf is lying down with a lamb, and scattered about are broken weapons of war (not prophetic, for the Civil War was soon to arm neighbour against neighbour). In the background is Queen's College, Oxford, whose provost the bishop had been, and above is the cathedral with a man receiving benediction at the door.

The other bishops are in stone and bronze, the oldest nameless, but smiling still after 700 years. Near him is Bishop Barrow, a curious worn animal at his feet; he died in 1429. Together in the south aisle of the choir are three fine figures from last century, Bishop Samuel Waldegrave in white marble, peacefully asleep after his kindly work among the poor; Bishop Harvey Goodwin, handsome in bronze by Hamo Thornycroft, under an oak canopy with cherubs at his head and a mitre at his feet; and Dean Francis Close in marble, the founder of Dean Close School. Other authors among Carlisle's clergy were Bishop Law and Archdeacon Paley, whose writings and personality made a deep impression on his generation, and whose pleasant optimism helped the world along. The bishop's memorial is the statue of a woman representing Religion leaning on the cross; the archdeacon's is the pulpit with alabaster scenes from the New Testament. He died in 1805 and lies with his two wives under the north aisle. Prior Senhouse, whose beautiful room in the deanery tower is his best memorial, has his altar tomb in the north transept.

Poet, business man, sculptor, and little child have their memorials in the south transept. The child is Elizabeth Dunbar, and the artist who sculptured her smiling in her sleep was her own father. The sculptor whose medallion portrait is near her is Musgrave Watson; Carlisle has many of his works, and one of his reliefs is on the pedestal of the Nelson Column in Trafalgar Square. The business man with a marble bust on the wall is George Moore, the traveller in lace nicknamed (for his success on the road) the Napoleon of Watling Street, who gave his money away, and was killed in the streets of Carlisle in 1876 by a runaway horse. Also in this transept is a pleasant relief of Thomas Sheffield, a 19th-century citizen, sitting reading.

The poet died in 1833, and all Cumbria mourned, for Robert Anderson's dialect poems were of the homely kind that touch the heart and lighten it with a rare humour. His portrait is in marble on the wall, and a simple pedestal is over his grave in the cathedral's green space. It is said that his first poem (on Lucy Gray) gave Wordsworth the inspiration for the famous Lucy Gray.

Through new hammered iron gates of great beauty and dignity, with the arms of the city on one side and of the cathedral on the other, we pass out of the green close. We cross the Eden bridge, and then, looking back from Stanwix at the best view of the old town, we see the last of its solid mass of castle wall and the lovely line of the cathedral choir set round with the distant hills, and we say Good-bye to its bold fighters, brave builders, and dear poets.

Preaching at Ninety-Four

CASTLE CARROCK. It is beeches, beeches nearly all the way from Brampton to this village below the fells which give us so grand a view of Solway Firth.

Men whose history is only written in the surface of our land left their pit dwellings in the highlands of this neighbourhood, and an earthwork known as Halsteads close to the village. Their cairns have been opened, and in one at Greenwell was found the skeleton of a man with a drinking cup.

Among a small group of stone houses is the simple little church, with an outside stone staircase leading up its tower to the belfry. It is no great age, but it stands on the site of a church said to have been built from stones of a vanished castle, and on the sanctuary floor, cut with a flowered cross and a chalice, is the gravestone of a rector who preached his first sermon the year Crecy was fought, six centuries ago. Another rector, Richard Dickenson, preached his last sermon when he was 94.

Tolled Through the Centuries

CASTLE SOWERBY. All we could find of it was a church and a farm, standing together on a hill looking across at the fells of Lakeland. The church is long and inviting, and is a Norman building lengthened in the 13th century and altered since. Of the two bells we see hanging, one has been here at least 600 years, and the other is just old enough to have rung out the news of the defeat of the Armada.

The nave has five Tudor arches to mark off an aisle, and the view of the chancel with its kingpost roof is very charming. A touch of colour comes from the east window, and great dignity from the panelled pulpit and the low screen. There is a tablet to Dr Joseph Hudson, who knew this church in the 18th century and laboured in his 92 years to free this and other places from the payment of tithes.

King Coal's Country

CLEATOR. It lies on the edge of the great hills, in a countryside rich in iron ore and dotted with mines, and its chief attraction is a very neat little embattled church with the unusual feature of a fine shelter built on the north side like an aisle outside. It rests on two arches and brings us to the porch.

Though mostly modern, the church has still a good deal of Norman masonry in its chancel walls; some of the stones at the bottom may even be Saxon. There is a Norman window, a 15th-century one, and an old square-headed doorway. The chancel has a modern arch well panelled in Tudor style, and the nave has a fine hammerbeam roof and pews with bobbin ends. The lectern is an oak eagle finely carved; and the stone pulpit projects from a little bay in the wall. There is a font perhaps 300 years old with a rich modern cover, and an old cross-head carved with a shield.

The windows make a pleasing display of colour, among them St Leonard with manacles and a book; Faith, Hope, and Charity; Christ appearing to Mary in the garden; the adoring Shepherds; and figures of Justice, Mercy, and Humility. A window by the font shows Our Lord with the children, another shows the lady of Egremont and her husband meeting St Bega at the castle gate, and two more show the crucifixion and a knight receiving his crown from Christ. These two are a peace memorial, and between them is a brass plate on which two soldiers are engraved.

Between the villages of Cleator and Cleator Moor stands a lofty Roman Catholic church designed by Pugin in 13th-century style, with fine arcades and rich capitals, and with a rose window in the west wall. Fine, too, are its altars, with saints and Bible scenes under intricate pinnacled canopies. More saints are under canopies on some of the pillars.

The hamlet of Cleator Moor has an ancient stone circle and a modern church. The church is imposingly built in Norman style, with a massive tower, and a fine doorway opening into a striking interior with arches great and small. The chancel roof is vaulted, and the lectern is a splendid oak eagle.

A Little Picture Gallery

CLIFTON. It is Clifton Great and Little, with a church between them on a steep ridge above the road. In its new walls is the arch of the Norman doorway of the vanished church and a coffin stone engraved with a cross, and the vestry treasures an old carved cross-shaft.

The sanctuary has fine oak carving in the richly-traceried panelling and the reredos where four angels watch over bronze panels of the Nativity, the Shepherds, and the Wise Men. In the windows are the Good Samaritan and the Good Shepherd, and there are modern pictures by the chancel arch of St Kentigern and St Bega. But the artistic treasure of the church is a Crucifixion believed to be the work of Guido Reni, and there is also a copy of Correggio's Descent from the Cross.

This little building has its pathetic memory of our own time in seven wooden crosses from Flanders set along the churchyard path, but it lifts up its eyes to distant snow-capped hills across the deep valley with its rippling stream.

Wordsworth's First Memories

COCKERMOUTH. One of the old Cumberland towns, it has seen much fighting round its proud castle on a little hill; it has seen three churches rise in succession on another hill; and it has a great name standing out in its list of sons, the name of William Wordsworth.

In the ceaseless border warfare the castle played its part for centuries, and in the Civil War it was first besieged and then dismantled. Some of its foundations are Norman, and some of it was built with material from the Roman station a mile away.

Most of what we see was built in the 13th and 14th centuries, and the structure is divided into two wards by a group of buildings in the middle. The lower ward has the flag tower and the great gatehouse, with its barbican walls seven feet thick, and its arms of famous families. The ruined walls of the upper ward are shaped like the bows of a mighty ship, with three storeys of windows at the tip looking out over the Derwent far below. The central buildings include an inner gatehouse and a roofless tower with two storeys. The upper storey was the kitchen and has still two wide fireplaces. The lower seems to have escaped damage and is the best complete room in the ruins, with a finely vaulted ceiling supported by a single column in the middle. There are also two little vaulted dungeons.

Full of history these broken walls and towers seem to be, but they are not quite all the history written in stone in Cockermouth. From the marketplace we can step aside into a little cobbled courtyard to see what is left of the house called The Old Hall, with its memory of the most tragic figure in Elizabethan England. Here came Mary Queen of Scots, fleeing with 16 followers from her defeat near Glasgow; and here she was received by the wealthy merchant Henry Fletcher, who gave her 16 ells of rich crimson velvet to replace the poor clothes in which she stood. With Darnley murdered, Bothwell taking refuge far away, her throne gone and her cause lost, we may think of Mary's visit here as among her last days of freedom before the long years of imprisonment.

Two things take our interest in the wide main street of the town. One is the statue of the Earl of Mayo, for ten years M.P. for Cockermouth, who became Viceroy of India and was assassinated on an official visit to the Andaman Islands. The other is the house of many windows where William Wordsworth opened his eyes in 1770 and his beloved sister Dorothy the year after. In memory of their childhood here is a fountain in the park above the town, with a charming sculptured figure of Dorothy as a child.

Many times in Cumberland we think of Wordsworth, but never more intimately than here where his first years were spent. He grew up to remember the joys of the castle, to tell us in The Prelude how the Derwent,

The finest of all rivers, loved
To blend his murmurs with my nurse's song,

and to write in the magic music of the Intimations of Immortality his recollections of early childhood here.

A few months after Wordsworth died the church he had known in Cockermouth was destroyed by fire. On its foundations the new All Saints rose up, big and high and dignified, with a Wordsworth memorial window showing Our Lord with prophets and evangelists. The glass is unfortunately in the glaring style of the middle of last century, and much better as a window is that in memory of the town's last M.P., which has good figures of eight saints.

The churchyard is a place of many memories. It has the grave of Wordsworth's father John, and the gravestone of an old hand-loom weaver has the name of the weaver's clever son, who died across the globe. The boy was Fearon Fallows, whose friends sent him to develop his genius at Cambridge, and who in 1820 became the first

Astronomer Royal at the Cape of Good Hope. He planned the first observatory there and saw it built; he made a catalogue of southern stars; and he died far from home at only 43.

And there is a third stone we can see, full of the quaintness of the 18th century, with an inscription already crumbling away. It was put up by Joseph Gilbanks in memory of the three faithful and affectionate wives he hoped to meet again in the next world, all three having died within 11 years. He was minister here for a generation, and schoolmaster for many years of an old grammar school close by. Some of its famous pupils he taught, and the list of those who came here as boys is a remarkable one. Within a few decades there were William Wordsworth, Fearon Fallows, and Christopher Wordsworth (who became Master of Trinity at Cambridge). There was Fletcher Christian who led the mutiny on the Bounty. There was the father of the three Queketts, of whom two are remembered in science and the third in Dickens as a model London curate. And there was John Walker, who was blacksmith, engraver, schoolmaster, and doctor, and has been called the Apostle of Vaccination.

Pioneer of a Great Idea

HE was born here in 1759, educated at the grammar school, and followed his father's calling as blacksmith until he was 20. Then he turned schoolmaster.

Before he was 30 he had published a volume of geography and history, the success of which led to his travelling widely to prepare a Gazetteer. This ran through six editions in 20 years. Publishing having brought him to London, he studied at Guy's Hospital, after which he took his medical degree, and in 1800 visited Naples with an English doctor and helped to introduce vaccination there.

Jenner had been experimenting with vaccine for a quarter of a century, and had been violently opposed until 70 physicians and surgeons signed a declaration in his favour. Walker, having in the meantime accompanied Sir Ralph Abercromby on his Egyptian expedition, settled in London in 1802, and began a campaign for the new treatment, to which he gave the rest of his life. Eventually a national vaccine board was set up, with Jenner as president and Walker as director, and for 17 years the two men worked together in amity, twin stalwarts in a great work for a pest-ridden nation.

Admitted to membership of the College of Physicians, Walker, a man of simple earnest character, devoted his whole strength to the task, and was able to boast that he had vaccinated more than 100,000 people. A man of liberal ideas, he was among the pioneers of the anti-slavery crusade, and did much to awaken public opinion to the horror of sacrificing widows on the funeral pyres of their husbands.

Good Work Brings its Reward

CORNEY. Coming to its little church on a lonely hilltop we are rewarded by a splendid view of this fascinating countryside. Far in the valley below a mountain stream chatters under a tiny bridge, and here and there among the hills the farms are dotted. Over the lowlands we look to the sea, and inland rise Black Combe and the rocky crags that guard the lakes and dales.

The church, refashioned last century, has two 17th-century bells in the bellcot, but it has little to show of its Norman predecessor founded by Lord Corney and given to the Priory of St Bees. Yet its people must be proud of their length of days, for we saw here on a gravestone that Richard Pullin was 97 when he died, and we have heard that John Noble, who was buried here in 1772, reached the great age of 114, his life stretching from the end of Cromwell's to the beginning of Napoleon's.

He would be only about 95 when there was born at Wellcome Nook near here Edward Troughton, famous for the scientific instruments he invented and made in the 18th and early 19th centuries. Many were astronomical instruments for observatories, but it seemed that everything Edward Troughton touched he improved, from telescopes to sextants and barometers. He invented a new and far better way of marking the graduations on the circles so vital in many instruments; he made telescopes for the most accurate work at Greenwich Observatory; he supplied the precision instruments for several famous surveying expeditions; he made compasses and theodolites and pendulums; and altogether his beautiful workmanship and clever ideas found their way into half the countries in the world.

Though colour-blind and deaf, he let no misfortune deter him, and one of his proudest days was when the Royal Society gave him its coveted Copley Medal. At the end of his life he would sit in his dingy parlour in Fleet Street with a huge ear-trumpet waiting by, wearing his old snuff-stained clothes and a dirty wig. They laid him to rest in 1835 in Kensal Green cemetery, and Sir Francis Chantrey made a sculpture of him for Greenwich Observatory; but the fame of his firm (Troughton and Simms) has lasted on into our own time.

Wordsworth and the Stream

CROGLIN. Its very attractive modern church is in Norman style, as if to remind us that the Normans built a church here 800 years ago. The chancel when we called was gay with the flags of many nations hanging from the roof.

The churchyard has two relics from the long ago, both much worn by wind and weather. One is a gravestone with a cross in relief, and with part of an inscription to a Bishop of Carlisle in the 13th century. The other is a badly weathered sculpture of a 14th-century lady, her hands still clasped but her features gone. Older than either is a memory the village has of Richard Lionheart, who gave some of its land to an old family as a reward for the bravery of one of them at the Siege of Jerusalem in the Third Crusade.

Croglin is one of the many Cumberland places which come into Wordsworth's poetry. He wrote of its stream, called Croglin Water, as fearful of its fate at the hands of a new generation:

Down from the Pennine Alps, how fiercely sweeps
Croglin, the stately Eden's tributary!
He raves, or through some moody passage creeps.
Plotting new mischief—out again he leaps
Into broad light, and sends through regions airy
That voice which soothed the Nuns, while on the steeps
They knelt in prayer or sang to blissful Mary.
That union ceased; then cleaving easy walks
Through crags, and smoothing paths beset with danger,
Came studious Taste; and many a pensive stranger
Dreams on the banks, and to the river talks.
What change shall happen next to Nunnery Dell!
Canal, and Viaduct, and Railway tell!

Two Pulpits From One Tree

CROSBY-ON-EDEN. It is High and Low Crosby, the one high up with a handful of farms sheltered by beeches, the lower one with the church. Both lie by the River Eden with views of the meadows and woods on the way to Carlisle. We can trace the Roman wall close by.

Eight centuries after the Romans went away the Normans came

and roughly carved the small square bowl of the font that has been much battered by the hand of Time; and eight centuries after the Normans there was cut down hereabouts a tree which was made into two pulpits. One of the pulpits is here in this small church of red sandstone. It is a square pulpit with panels admirably carved with pomegranates, wheat, and vines, an uncommon piece of craftsmanship keeping company with an equally fine oak lectern, on which is an angel with spread wings. The rest for the Bible is actually a canopy over a beautifully carved figure of the Good Shepherd.

The other half of the tree from which this pulpit was made was fashioned into a pulpit for Liverpool's new cathedral; we imagine that it would be the first pulpit made for the cathedral and we have seen it in the lady chapel there.

The church which has these treasures is still in its first century. Its nave windows are curious for having cut-glass stars in the tracery. The memorial to Crosby men who did not come back is a triptych of oak from the training ship Britannia, with a copper cross from the same ship bearing bullet marks.

A Tragic Family

CROSSCANONBY. Half a mile from the coast of Allonby Bay, it has a little church built by the Normans, who used Roman stones in some of the walls. The 13th-century builders added an aisle, opening from an arch which has a carved face each side and cuts through a Norman window at the top.

Most interesting are the stones which were standing as memorials before the Normans came. One is a hogback gravestone (shaped to imitate a little house of the dead). Of the others the best is a stone carved with a tall cross and a very crude human figure, thought to be St Lawrence, from the gridiron above his head. Among some fragments is part of a carved cross-shaft of red sandstone.

The Norman font has a square bowl strikingly sculptured with curling leaves and stems, and stands on pillars. There is fine old woodcarving in some of the new seats, and a collection of old tablets to the Senhouses who lived in Maryport, where their house Netherhall treasures a great collection of Roman things found close by.

The little windows of an aged farmhouse overlook the churchyard, seeing among the graves a family stone full of human sadness. Though her name is not the most prominent, the tragic story of this grave centres round a mother who lived to be 80 and died in 1827. She was married to a ship's captain. Their little son died three weeks after he was born. Sixteen years later, in the prime of his life, the husband vanished at sea, with all his crew. Another 19 years, and a daughter died at 26. Then, as if she had not borne enough, this old lady at 72 had to bear the news that her son of 37, called after his father and a ship's captain too, had also perished with his men.

The Lady 600 Years Old

CUMREW. It is on the Pennine slopes, with the fells rising suddenly from the doors of its farms. In the very shadow of the mountains and almost hidden by farm buildings is its simple church, refashioned a generation or two ago with a tower where a 14th-century bell still rings. It was then that they found under the floor the chief treasure of Cumrew, a 600-year-old sculpture of a lady in a long flowing robe with loose sleeves. She wears a kerchief and a wimple, and with her are two dogs, one a spaniel, above her head. The figure is nearly eight feet long, and is thought to represent the widow of William Dacre who lived not far away in a fortified house whose site can still be seen.

The church has two 17th-century possessions, a silver chalice and a finely carved altar table in the vestry. In the wall of a barn near by are some stones carved by the Normans, reminding us of their church which stood where the modern one stands today.

CUMWHITTON. Past farms and trees and a little hill crowned with Scotch firs goes its one wide street; but the church calls halt to the lover of Old England, for here are stout walls and three simple arches built by the Normans 800 years ago, and in the north wall is a small window which may be Saxon. The tower with its outside steps is 19th century, but when the chancel was made new its 13th-century masonry was used again.

In the churchyard are fragments of gravestones 600 years old.

Old Stones

DACRE. It is guarded by the castle that defended it from border raids, and has a beautiful church that was here before the castle as we see it was built.

Something of a surprise it is to find in a quiet village this massive keep with turrets and battlements and walls seven feet thick. Except for changed windows and doorways, and the fact that it is now a farmhouse, the keep is as they built it in the 14th century, though the moat has become a muddy ditch. Over an entrance are the arms of an Earl of Sussex.

The tower of the church was made new two years after Waterloo, and under it we go through a Norman arch into a fine nave and chancel. The arches in the nave are over 500 years old, and some of the pillars from which they rise are two centuries older. The 15th-century clerestory windows light up the ancient beams of the roof.

The spacious chancel with its lancet windows is 13th century, and has a priest's doorway with carved capitals but no shafts. Sleeping in the sanctuary is a knight in armour, probably a Dacre who died 700 years ago; and on the wall is one of Chantrey's beautiful women, mourning for Edward Hasell, who died in 1825.

Many times in this church we are reminded of the Hasells, who have been at the great house Dalemain since 1665. A monument carved with cherubs tells of Sir Edward of 1707, and there is an inscription on the floor to his wife, whose father lost his head for his loyalty to Charles Stuart. There are 17th-century altar rails, a bell that was here before the Reformation, and communion plate made by Elizabethan craftsmen.

The churchyard has a quaintness all its own. Standing among the gravestones are four stone figures representing a story in the life of a bear. First we see him asleep; then with a cat clinging to his back; then trying to get rid of the cat; then happy again, with his annoying visitor safely swallowed. It is thought that these carvings (now rather worn) were pinnacles of the castle walls in its great days.

One of the tombstones covers the family grave of the Troutbecks, and on it, every Easter Day, the money one of them left 150 years ago is distributed to the poor.

Among the treasures of Dacre are two stones in the church. They may well have come from the lost abbey, of which no sign remains unless we count these fragments. The bigger of the two stones is about 1000 years old and part of the shaft of a cross. It is carved with quaint animals and two scenes, one being Adam and Eve with the tree and the serpent; the other two figures are shaking hands. The figures are supposed to be King Athelstan of England and King Constantine of Scotland agreeing over a treaty they made at Dacre in 926.

The other stone is a smaller fragment of a cross and its detail is very fine. The chief figure on it is the Anglian Beast, a remarkable creature with an almost human face, beautifully chiselled about 1100 years ago.

A mile or two from Dacre is Hutton John, one of the old fortified manor houses of Cumberland, with a Tudor wing and a Stuart wing added to a tower 600 years old. The gardens are charming. There are two Tudor terraces, with eight magnificent yews. For generations they grew in a great hedge, and they have been clipped to their present shape for over a century. A natural curiosity is a rockery of limestone formed by the hard water of a hillside spring. Inside a little grotto the water is turning moss into stone before our eyes.

A Treasure in Oak

DALSTON. Very pleasant in itself, and with memories of several interesting people, its church and its low stone houses gather round a little square. As beautifully situated as any in this countryside is God's acre here, trim like a garden; and lovely is the scene where paths and lime trees border the River Caldew as it falls over a rocky weir and goes winding down the valley.

The story of the church begins with the Normans and ends with much restoring and rebuilding in the last two centuries. At the bottom of some of the walls is 12th-century masonry, and among the 13th-century remains in the chancel are lancet windows, the priest's doorway, and a low window near it. An old stone seat runs along the south aisle wall, and in the wall of the modern porch is part of an ancient coffin stone with shears and four circles as well as a cross. Here, too, is a richly carved Norman capital.

The spacious interior has panelled walls, trim benches, and stout timber arcades supporting a fine modern roof. The reredos is attractively carved and painted, with figures of St George and St Michael under canopies. The front of the altar, also coloured and gilded, has fine scenes of the Annunciation, the Nativity, and the Baptising. There is an old chest bound with iron.

One of the treasures of the village is a font cover designed by Sir Robert Lorimer, an exquisite piece of carving in oak. On four pinnacles it has the signs of the Evangelists, the fifth and tallest pinnacle being crowned by a fine St George, resting on his sword after slaying the dragon. Round the edge of the base are charming scenes depicting the four ancient elements: Earth, where rabbits are busy nibbling in the grass, Air, where an eagle is among the sun and moon and stars, Water, where we see a dog swimming and a graceful swan with cygnets, and Fire, represented by tongues of flame. A window in the baptistry is aglow with a fine figure of Hugh de Lilford, a hermit here 600 years ago, wearing a red robe and carrying a book and staff. There are two memorials with portrait heads, one showing Isaac Sheffield of last century, the other, designed by Musgrave Watson, to Walter Fletcher, who was vicar for 52 years.

It is not surprising to find in this churchyard the graves of two Bishops of Carlisle, for we are but three miles from Rose Castle, their chief seat for seven centuries. Here lies Edward Rainbowe, bishop for 20 years after the Restoration and famous as a preacher, his grave marked by an upright stone on the south wall. Bishop Hugh Percy of last century has a fine cross.

From the churchyard is a charming view of the great house, Dalston Hall, in its park a mile down the valley. We see the buildings of its main front, irregular and delightful, and chiefly built in the 16th and 17th centuries. The house has still its defensive tower of the 15th century, with coats-of-arms and an inscription in reversed lettering telling how it was put up by John Dalston and his Elizabeth.

By the roadside about a mile from the village stands Cardew Hall, with stone walls and a stone-tiled roof. It is a farm now, but was once the home of John Denton who wrote a history of Cumberland in the 16th century. It was the birthplace in 1747 of Susanna Blamire, who wrote songs in Scottish dialect and delightful poems of Cumbrian country life. She has been called the Muse of Cumberland, and she sleeps in the churchyard at Raughton Head.

Here was born Musgrave Watson, a sculptor whose genius needed only time and whose work is seen where London's millions pass it every day.

A Sculptor of the Nelson Column

HE was born at Hawksdale Hall here in 1804, son of a yeoman who, although the boy showed a genius for carving and drawing, articled him to a Carlisle solicitor. It chanced that the lawyer was an art connoisseur, and encouraged him.

Left fatherless at 19, Watson went to London, where he was encouraged by Flaxman to study at the Royal Academy schools, and at 21 to go to Rome. There he maintained himself by carving, etching, and watercolour painting. Returning to London he served as modeller to Chantrey. His first original work of note was a beautiful little sculpture of Death and Sleep carrying off the Body of Sarpedon, which was followed by a delightful marble sculpture symbolising Literature.

Commissioned to make a statue of Lord Eldon and his brother Lord Stowell, he produced a splendid model, but before he could finish the carving he was laid low by death. The work was completed by George Nelson, and stands, a noble monument to arrested genius, in the library of University College, Oxford. Among his other achievements was a statue of Queen Elizabeth, a fine monument with scenes from the battle of Culloden (afterwards destroyed by fire); a splendid seated figure of Flaxman, and one of the reliefs on the pedestal of the Nelson Column in Trafalgar Square.

Watson had great gifts as a sculptor, but lingering ill-health prevented the full development of his genius, and he died when only 43, with fame and fortune within his grasp. He sleeps in Highgate cemetery. There is a medallion of him in Carlisle cathedral by his sculptor friend George Nelson.

John Dalton and John Milton

DEAN. A quaint turret with two hanging bells draws us at once to the church with its weird gargoyles. Some of it is 13th century and there are windows made in the 15th. An old font with interlacing arches stands by the new one. Let into the wall is an old stone lightly carved with an ornate cross, and in the windows are figures of St Oswald and St Aidan, richly robed.

Standing in the churchyard on its pedestal of steps is the base of an ancient cross; and against the chancel wall is a memorial to William Hetherington, known in Cumberland for his writings in prose and verse. His home was half a mile away at Branthwaite Hall, and round it he wove a story of life in feudal times. Now a quiet farmhouse, it has a wing built in 1604 and a big square tower 40 feet high.

At the vicarage was born in 1709 the less famous of the two John Daltons of Cumberland, a man who won a little renown by his poems and sermons and more by his adaptation of Milton's Comus for the stage. It was joined with the delightful melodies of Dr Arne, whose reputation it established at the same time.

Chancing to hear that Milton's grand-daughter Elizabeth was in need, John Dalton arranged a special performance of Comus at Drury Lane, with Garrick speaking a prologue written by Dr Johnson. This raised £130, and enabled the poor lady and her husband, Thomas Foster, to start a little business at Islington. Probably the last descendant of the poet, Elizabeth died in 1754; she was one of Deborah Milton's ten children.

Roman, Saxon, and Norman

DEARHAM. A village in the Cumberland coalfield, it bears the mark of industry and attracts us only to the church where it has rare treasures. Here is Roman, Saxon, and Norman.

The church has Roman material in the walls, including part of a Roman altar in the vestry. Its nave is the size and shape of the church the Normans built; its chancel is 13th century; and its massive tower was raised over 600 years ago as a place of protection for men and beasts when the raiders came over the border. Built into the walls of the porch and the modern aisle are a number of medieval coffin stones and memorials, many carved with elaborate crosses.

There is a Norman doorway, and a fascinating Norman font carved with patterns on two sides and with imaginary creatures on the other two. One defies description; the other is a flying dragon. In the first, the vicar suggested, we see the devil coming in before baptism, and in the second he has grown wings to fly away.

The special treasures of Dearham are older than anything the Normans built in England, and one at least was used by them as building material. It is called the Adam Stone, and stands about four feet high in the window where it is mounted for us to see. Its carving is a piece of symbolism supposed to refer to the fall and restoration of man. Three little figures seem to be Christ and Adam and Eve standing hand in hand above two serpents. Below are many symbols, including tongues of flame, thunderbolts, and the endless twining band of Eternity. At one end of the stone is the word Adam, and at the other is an inscription in runes thought to mean, "May Christ his soul save."

A second stone is part of a cross apparently illustrating the legend of St Kenith, a 6th-century hermit brought up by seagulls. We can make out among the patterns a bird and a figure on horseback.

Finest of all is the great complete cross now in the church, though it stood outside for centuries. Rather higher than a man, it is in splendid condition, and its carved pattern is said to be an illustration of Yggdrasil, the great world tree in Norse mythology.

These three rare pieces of carving are all at least 900 years old, the Adam stone being perhaps the oldest. Each would be part of a memorial to someone who died before the Normans came; and it would seem as if Dearham were a favourite burying-place for those who could afford a rich monument to their memory. When the church was restored in 1882 several of the actual graves were found. In all of them were hazel wands, and the oldest are thought to have been dug for people who died at the beginning of the 9th century.

Here in 1866 was born John White, founder of a college in Africa.

A White Man Beloved in Africa

HE was only 26 when he went out to the Transvaal to follow in the steps of those who fought for justice for the natives, sometimes in the face of strong opposition from white men.

Twice he journeyed 500 miles through tropical valleys and swamps and across unbridged rivers to a village in Northern Rhodesia, once in response to a call for a missionary, and again to accompany James Loveless, who started a centre there.

Back in Southern Rhodesia John White gathered a few Africans round him in a mud hut and taught them so that they might become missionaries to their own people. So began the Waddilove Training Institution, of which he was the head for 14 years. He translated the New Testament into the language of the tribes around.

He was never too busy to help whoever came. The Africans loved him so much that they begged him never to leave them, and it is difficult to say who was most distressed when he fell ill after 40 years of work and the doctors insisted on sending him to England. He died at Birmingham in 1933. Courteous to every man without thought of race or colour, he was a hero of whom Dearham and England may be proud.

Where St Cuthbert Stood

DISTINGTON. It has one long street in a countryside of coal and iron, but it is redeemed by its place between the sea and the Lakeland mountains, and by its fine 19th-century church above the village.

Built in 13th-century style, it has a fine chancel arch, splendid lancets, and lovely arcades with shining granite pillars whose capitals have foliage. The oak altar has four angels under canopies; the low chancel screen is of wrought iron with the signs of the twelve disciples on brass shields; and the oak pulpit is richly carved with scenes of the Baptism of Our Lord, His preaching in a boat by the sea, Peter sinking, the calming of the storm, and the miraculous draught of fishes.

It is thought that this church stands on one of the places where St Cuthbert stood preaching 1300 years ago, and that it is the fourth shrine to be raised on the site. The first would be a wooden structure built by the early converts, and it is thrilling to think that the parts of the broken Saxon cross now treasured here may have stood beside it. They are crudely carved, one piece having a three-legged cross.

The second church was a Norman one which lasted until the 17th century, and some of the things it treasured are still to be seen. There are ancient gravestones, a piscina found in the rectory garden, an Elizabethan silver chalice, two bells known to have been here before 1552, and fragments of stones, one carved with a monk's head. A similar stone is in one of the farm walls at Hayes Castle, the ruined home of the old lords of Distington, and other ancient stones are in old houses in the village.

Of the third church, built in the 17th century, there is one relic in the chancel arch standing solitary in the churchyard. Another is the font of 1662 now in the Mission Church two miles away at Pica. It was in this third church that Henry Lowther was rector for no less than 63 years last century. His only memorial is the memory of his good works, especially what he did for the Sunday school here, which has a little fame all its own. It was started before his day, as long ago as 1787, and was one of the earliest in all England, in one of our remotest villages. Robert Raikes had started a few years before at Gloucester.

Two miles away at Gilgarran we saw in a farm wall by the roadside a stone to a 17th-century man said to have been buried in his own orchard. The inscription tells us that, having cast his trade from port to port, he at last reached the haven.

A Haven for the Birds

DRIGG. A long village of scattered houses near the coast, it has fine views of the mountains towering up to the east. Its great salt marsh between the River Irt and the sea is one of our sanctuaries for birds, and can be visited at nesting-time.

Here on a little hilltop the Normans built a church which was added to by 13th-century builders; but what we see is a plain little structure refashioned last century, in which ancient masonry was used again. It has a steep black-and-white roof, an arcade in 13th-century style, and attractive woodwork in the door and the reredos.

John Dalton and the Atom

EAGLESFIELD. Lying between the mountains and the sea, it has given to the world three men whose names live on.

Here, six centuries ago, was born Robert Eglesfield, who as a priest heard the confessions of an English queen. Going to Oxford, he bought a few buildings and founded Queen's College, beginning with 12 fellows and 70 poor boys, and finding his own rest at last in the college chapel.

Very different is the story of Fletcher Christian, who was born about 1753 in the house called Moorland Close. Here he passed his first years, going to school not far away at Cockermouth. The sea called him, and Fletcher Christian is for ever remembered as the leader of the mutineers in that amazing drama of the ocean, the Mutiny of the Bounty.

These two men went from here into the world, one to add something to a university, the other to stir England with a story. But the third and greatest son of Eaglesfield made no such stir, and even here as a boy his adventures were those of the mind. We think of him as we see his humble cottage, proud of the tablet which records his birth; we think of him as we see the Quaker meeting-house where as a boy he ran his own little school; and we think of him in the church, which is called after him and has a memorial put here by the Royal Society of London. He was John Dalton, immortal in science and the founder of the Atomic Theory.

Destined to make Chemistry a science, John Dalton was born in 1766, of Quaker parents who eked out the profits of a tiny farm by weaving. The boy left school at ten, but was helped in later years by John Gough, the blind philosopher, to a knowledge of mathematics and languages.

While still a boy Dalton noted that the colours of military uniforms at a review did not differ in his sight from the colour of the grass. He pondered the problem, and in early manhood was able to reveal to science a physical disability not guessed at till then—colour-blindness, a subject of immense importance where signals are controlled by light.

He became a schoolmaster at 12, with a barn for a school and babies for scholars, and in due course equipped himself so well as to be appointed Professor of Mathematics and Natural Philosophy at New College, Manchester.

He made important discoveries in relation to gases, the force of steam, and the elasticity of vapours, and was only 37 when he communicated to the Manchester Philosophical Society the first results of his inquiry into "the relative weights of the ultimate particles." A year later he startled the world with his famous theory of Atomic Weights.

Taking hydrogen as the unit, he gave 21 atomic weights, each expressed in atoms of hydrogen. When at last appreciated and accepted, the discovery was declared to be the greatest scientific advance of the age. Dalton and the great chemists who followed him went to the grave believing they had found in the atom the ultimate and indivisible form of matter, though in our own day their successors have split it into electrons, whose mass and velocity they have recorded. John Dalton discovered a new realm for scientific research, a universe teeming with lesser worlds.

The philosopher's experiments were carried out with the most primitive instruments, and even of these he was not complete master, but such was his unwearying application, his unfailing memory, and his careful systematising, that he triumphed over all difficulties. He died at Manchester in 1844, and in four days over 40,000 persons filed past his coffin.

Farewell the Luck of Eden Hall

EDENHALL. It has a bit of Saxon England in its church, but it lost its famous Hall, the home of the famous legend, at the beginning of last century. A new Eden Hall was built, and now that has gone too. We stood and watched a man with a pick knock down one of its last walls.

And so the old legend has proved doubly false. The precious glass goblet whose shattering, the fairies said, would bring about the fall of the house, is safe at South Kensington, but the luck has gone out of Eden Hall. It was a fairy goblet, the legend tells us, stolen by the butler from the fairies he surprised dancing round the well in the sunken garden. We found the sunken garden a wilderness and the well a dark pool domed with evergreens, and we thought we heard a fairy weeping for the desolate scene. A giant cedar in the park sloping down to the River Eden must have seen the passing of both houses.

On the way to the church in this park we pass an ancient cross with a pierced wheelhead; no one knows quite why or when it was first put here.

It is believed Saxon masons laid some of the stones of the chancel and of the north of the nave, that the slit of a window seen from the outside, and the priest's door now blocked up, may also be Saxon. Ancient gravestones have been used as building material in the north and south walls of the nave. Much has vanished in restoration, but much remains to delight us in this tiny place with its great porch.

The Normans raised their own church on the Saxon foundation, but their chancel arch is hidden and only the rough font looks Norman. The 13th century put an almost square window into the chancel, and the 14th dotted other windows about at odd levels. The 15th added the small quaint tower wearing a tiny spire like a nightcap, its buttresses needlessly massive, and the top-heavy parapet sitting on the tower so badly that daylight shows between them. Over the west window are five shields, one with a niche. More shields, some with the arms of the Musgrave family, are on the 17th-century gallery, approached by a stone staircase inside the tower. Other steps from the nave lead up to a vestry.

Still more shields of the great families of the neighbourhood are in old glass in the windows, and the east window is bright with vine-leaf fragments in blue, green, and yellow, with saints and angels and two little men it is possible to name, Ceolwyn in a brown hat and cloak, and Cuthbert in a purple gown and green surplice. Most of this old glass is Flemish.

The tongues of three bells hang in the nave, but the bells themselves, two older than the Reformation and one of 1665, still hang in the tower.

Beneath the beautiful panelling of the chancel roof, and between Tudor stalls with linenfold, lie the brass portraits of William Stapleton and his wife, who lived at Eden Hall in the 15th century and must have used the famous goblet and known its legend. She is a tiny figure, barely 27 inches, with a fly-away headdress, while he is three feet long with a tiny waist encased in intricate armour, a peaked helmet, and flowers in the grass at his spurred feet.

Many are the inscriptions to the Musgraves who followed them at the Hall, including one to Sir Philip, the M.P. who declared for the king and commanded the royalist forces in Cumberland and Westmorland when the Civil War broke out. He fought for both Charles Stuarts, a price on his head which he risked valiantly, living to see the son back on the father's throne.

Eden Hall has gone, pulled down by the house-breakers because no one would buy it for a home; but the Luck of Eden Hall has survived.

The Luck of Eden Hall

THE Luck of Eden Hall is the name given to the precious glass cup which has for centuries been in the possession of the Musgraves who lived for as many centuries at Eden Hall. According to an old superstition, the cup was stolen by their butler from some fairies he found dancing round the garden well. Enraged, they warned the thief:

If e'er this cup shall break or fall
Farewell the luck of Eden Hall.

But these fairies never lived in England, for the goblet is of Syrian or Persian glass, and was fashioned by some eastern glassworker at least a century before a Musgrave was fighting for Edward the Third against the Scots. When Sir Nigel Musgrave, who inherited it from a long line of ancestors, went to India a few years ago, he deposited this 700-year-old cup in the Victoria and Albert Museum where it remains, a thing of beauty with its eastern origin plain to the antiquarian. Over six inches high, it spreads out like a trumpet at the top, and is decorated with rich enamel work. It has a case of stamped leather made for it by a Musgrave 500 years ago. Now Eden Hall has fallen before the fairy cup, a fall which shatters also the foundations of Longfellow's poem, a translation from the German of Johann Uhland, in which he told (in none too good verse !) the end of the legend:

As the goblet ringing flies apart,
Suddenly cracks the vaulted hall;
And through the rift the wild flames start;
The guests in dust are scattered all,
With the breaking Luck of Edenhall!

In storms, the foe, with fire and sword;
He in the night had scaled the wall,
Slain by the sword lies the youthful Lord,
But holds in his hand the crystal tall,
The shattered Luck of Edenhall.

The Ruin Above the River

EGREMONT. It has outlived its powerful lords and their great castle, the stones of which are now a romantic ruin on a hill which rises steeply from the swirling river.

Very impressive it must have been in its great day, with walls 20 feet high and a tower rising 80 feet. Now little walks thread round the hill and climb to the gatehouse, set in a corner of a ruined wall with Norman herring-bone work intact and a dry moat below. The gatehouse is the finest part of the ruin, and we walk under its archway with part of the old vaulted roof above our heads. Across the courtyard is the ruin of the postern gate with the roofless court house near it, and a grim square hole looking like a huge well or a dungeon.

Between the inner and outer courts is the stern ruined front of the great hall which has stood since about 1270 and has still a row of open windows and a doorway, the most effective part of the castle seen from the town, silhouetted against the sky. From this meagre fragment of a great stronghold is a fine view of the town and the distant mountains. By one of the paths bringing us down from it is a piece of a cross 700 years old.

Down in the little marketplace stands a fine bronze soldier, the town's remembrance of those who did not come back. Among the old houses in the narrow streets is one with a stone doorway of 1580.

The new church stands where the Normans built their church, close by the marketplace. It has fine arcades and lofty roofs and a chancel with a precious fragment of the 13th-century church in four beautiful lancets divided by double columns. The transept arches have in them rich mouldings worked in the 13th century, saved from the old church, and the old stone seats for the priests are in the vestry. We found the old font near the doorway. The striking oak reredos is richly panelled and has a lovely cornice with four bands of carving and saints under canopied niches. The alabaster pulpit has figures of Our Lord, the Madonna, and the Archangel Michael, and the striking font has a great shell borne by a kneeling angel.

Egremont's castle has a story fitting its romantic appearance.

The Horn of Egremont

THE tradition is that in crusading days Sir Eustace de Lucy, lord of Egremont, and his brother Hubert went together to Palestine. As they left the castle Sir Eustace blew on the horn which hung at the gate:

> *Horn it was which none could sound,*
> *No one upon living ground,*
> *Save he who came as rightful heir*
> *To Egremont's domains and castle fair.*

"If I fall in Palestine," said Sir Eustace, "do thou return and blow the horn and take possession, that Egremont may not be without a Lucy for its lord," and Hubert promised to do this.

But when they reached the Holy Land he began to covet his brother's estate, and from desiring he came at last to planning that Sir Eustace should die, employing assassins to drown him in the Jordan. The ruffians assured him their work was well and truly done.

Or, according to another version of the story, it was fate that played into Hubert's willing hands; Sir Eustace was taken prisoner by the Saracens and asked his brother to return home and collect the large ransom demanded.

Whether or not Hubert had murder on his conscience he came to Egremont alone and secretly, not daring to blow the horn at its gate. Time passed without news of Sir Eustace, and Hubert's feeling of guilt at usurping his brother's place gave way to a sense of security. Openly and unashamed he exercised the rights of lord of the manor, passing his days in cheerful hunt and generous feast.

As he sat at a banquet one day the doubts he had lulled to sleep sprang upon him, for suddenly came the blast of a horn at the castle gate. It was the horn of Egremont, which none but Sir Eustace could or would sound. Escaped from his prison, he had come to claim his lands. The miserable Hubert dared not face him, but fled by a postern gate while the rightful lord was welcomed to his own.

The story says that long afterwards Hubert crept back to beg forgiveness, and, being pardoned, spent the rest of his life in a monastery doing penance for his sin.

The Solemn Beauty of the Grey Heights

ENNERDALE. It is Ennerdale Water and the climbing mountains about it which bring us here, tempting us along the rough and winding paths. We are told that it is the least frequented of all the Cumberland lakes, and we wonder that it should be so, for it has a solemn beauty, with the grey gaunt heights and the gentle slopes mirrored in its depths.

Under Bowness Knott and Great Borne's 2000 feet is a sunny slope with a patchwork of fields like a green coverlet running down to the lake. There are grey houses at the foot of the fells, and a little inn on the edge of the lake, which is between two and three miles long and a mile wide.

Its beautiful setting is all the village has for us; it lies in a pretty valley where the River Ehen and the Crossdale Beck meet near their bridges as they come from lake and fell.

The church was built in Norman style last century, and has nothing that is old except a bell which may have belonged to the ancient priory. We come for the glorious view from the churchyard. It was one of the lakeland scenes that Wordsworth loved, and it is the churchyard of the poem he wrote in the spring of 1800 about the Two Brothers. We should like to see all our churchyards kept as sacred fields or gardens as Wordsworth found this then.

He found it a beautiful green field so free from monuments that "an orphan child could not find his mother's grave," and in talking it over with the poet the priest was made to reflect that stone-cutters might beg their bread if every English churchyard were like this. And yet, said the priest:

We have no need of names and epitaphs,
Nor symbols, sir, to tell us that plain tale:
The thought of death sits easy on the man
Who has been born and dies among the mountains.

The Delectable Mountains

ESKDALE. It is one of Cumberland's delightful valleys, full of interest and beauty, with little hamlets dotted along it, and with great rocky crags crowning lovely wooded slopes. Running part of its way up the dale, and ending at Boot, is one of the smallest railways in the world, bringing us from Ravenglass on lines only 15 inches apart. It is man's work in miniature where nature has been lavish, for bordering on Eskdale are Birker Force, a fine waterfall to see after heavy rains, and Dalegarth Force, one of the county's gems, a waterfall leaping over 60 feet of rock into a wooded ravine. Not far away is Devoke Water, the small lake a mile long and half as wide, high up in the fells nearly 800 feet above the sea. It is famous for its trout.

Those who follow a track leading north from Boot, up the fell and across Eskdale Moor, will come upon stone circles and other prehistoric remains which must be the oldest signs of humanity hereabouts; a branch track is the old Funeral Road along which bodies were borne from Wasdale to Eskdale.

But it is more thrilling to make for Hardknott Pass, over which the Romans drove a remarkable road connecting their settlements at Ravenglass and Ambleside. Halfway between the two they built their fort known as Hardknott Castle, guarding one end of the pass from a commanding position on a crag 800 feet up, and glorying in some of the finest mountain scenery in the country, with a magnificent view of Scafell Pikes less than four miles away. The Roman fort has been excavated, and the remains show it to be roughly a square of 125 yards, enclosing just over three acres, with the base of a tower at each corner and a gateway at each side. The north tower on the highest point was perhaps a signal station, and the walls or rampart of the fort are five feet thick.

At Eskdale Green is a little modern chapel of St Bega, but the old church of the dale is hidden away at the end of narrow lanes at Boot. It is a trim little place, prettily set among the fields near the prattling Esk, and is said to have been founded by Randulf le Meschin, who became Earl of Chester when his kinsfolk were wrecked with Henry the First's son in the White Ship. It is St Catherine's church, and more than once we think of her here. Her name is on a bell, perhaps 500 years old, which keeps company with a 17th-century one in the turret, an old tradition saying that this ancient bell used to ring out from a big oak tree on a hill near by. And we see her under an elaborate canopy on the reredos, wearing a crown and holding a book and a sword, her companion under the other canopy being St Bega holding a church. The panelling of the Sanctuary has its canopies too, under which are fine figures of St Peter, St Andrew, and the Good Shepherd with His hand on a child.

Other possessions which are new and fine within these ancient walls are the fine oak benches, a splendid eagle lectern, and a black-and-white roof with stout oak timbers. The altar rails have panels of open tracery, and the altar table has arches carved with vine and grape. The east window is 14th century, and so is the font bowl, lightly carved with varied tracery and perhaps the largest we have seen in this countryside. It has come back to the church after being used for about 60 years on a farm.

All the windows are filled with stained glass, one a Last Supper with Judas holding his bag but having already lost his halo.

Standing in the churchyard is a striking memorial to a huntsman who died full of years, Thomas Dobson, Master of the Eskdale Foxhounds for more than half a century. At the top of a tall block of rough granite his portrait is carved, and there are other carvings of the things he knew so well—a fox and a hound peeping out from the inscription, a whip, a horn, and a brush.

Not far away is still another reminder of St Catherine, an old well dedicated to her memory.

One of the old homes of Eskdale is carrying on as a farm, though much of it was pulled down in the 18th century. It is Dalegarth Hall, once the ancient manor house of the Austhwaites and later the home of the Stanleys until John Stanley built himself Ponsonby Old Hall at the end of the 17th century. It is a massive and pleasing house, with quaint round chimneys, great beams and stairs of solid oak, and a room with a plaster ceiling adorned by hounds and stags.

The Stone by the Wayside

FRIZINGTON. It was one of the stricken places when we called, with its iron mines closed, and its people saddened by long unemployment. On a brass in the church are engraved two angels and the names of 54 men who did not come back, the men this village gave to the war which ended its prosperity.

The tiny spire rises above the red-stone church like a sharpened pencil. It is all new from the 19th century, and the best possession of this bare little place is a fine oak altar and reredos with rich canopies and borders of vine.

Half a mile away, near the lodge of a fine modern house hidden in trees, is a plain stone which has lost its cross. Here in olden days they would rest a body on its way to St Bees for burial, setting it down at the foot of the cross while a monk read the burial service.

In the Deep Ravine

GARRIGILL. Far beyond civilisation it lies, one of the most remote villages in the remotest corner of Cumberland. With the mountains rising on every side, its little group of old stone houses stand in a very deep hollow where torrents come leaping over the rocks, some of them through underground channels.

The churchyard is in the deepest part of the ravine, and in this setting the church itself seems fittingly severe. Refashioned in the 18th century, part of it is 700 years old; its bell is said to have been the dinner bell at Dilston Hall, in Northumberland, in the days of the Jacobite Earls of Derwentwater.

The simple nave is as broad as it is long and has only three windows. The chancel arch opens into a plain chancel. The very rough font was dug up after being long buried, and so was the square holy-water stone, each side of which has a circle with a cross in it. Preserved in the vestry is the base of an ancient cross.

The Saxon Cross

GILCRUX. It is a prosaic grey village of wayside farms and cottages, but has a distant view of Scotland's hills across the sea, and one of the few ancient churches surviving in this part of the country.

Set low on a bank near one of several springs, it is a sturdily-buttressed place, with a miniature arcade of two round-pillared arches with square capitals, a chancel arch with a crudely-shaped peephole on one side, and a rough font, all hewn in the days of the Normans. Some of the windows are 13th century, others are 15th; oldest of all are the fragments of a cross carved with knotwork in Saxon England.

Great Caesar and Great Scott

GILSLAND. What sights it has seen! Great Caesar and Great Scott! Caesar's legions manning the Great Wall of England; Walter Scott walking with his heart's delight.

Down where the River Irthing struggles over rocks and under trees we come upon fragments of Hadrian's Wall, creeping across England from Solway Firth to the mouth of the Tyne.

But there were Depressions in those days, too. In the vicarage garden is a wall which the Romans obviously intended to be much wider, and we can see how their plans were restricted and the wall made narrower, perhaps for economy's sake. Two Roman altars here have inscriptions still clear after 1800 years, one in praise of Jupiter, one with an interesting reference to Hadrian's own cohort.

The bell in the vicarage is a child in comparison, in spite of its 500 years. It is so small that it may have been carried by hand from its old church at Over Denton. Gilsland's own church is modern.

To the romance of this place is added the romance of Walter Scott, a road taking us uphill to the house where he is said to have met Charlotte Carpenter. Here they must have stayed to admire the view of the wooded valley, and tradition makes of the Popping Stone, which juts out of the stream farther along, a platform for Scott's proposal to Charlotte. It is not surprising that Gilsland had a place in his heart and another in his books. He describes it in Guy Mannering. A simple stone house within sound of the river was even pointed out to us as the meeting-place of Meg Merrilies and Dandy Dinmont.

In any case it seems beyond all human doubt that the meeting here was the turning point in the life of Scott.

Walter Scott is Saved for Literature

IN 1797 Scott was 26 years old, had been five years an advocate, and in these five years had earned £400. In spite of his lameness he was a fine horseman, and an ardent member of the Edinburgh Light Horse, raised to resist threatened French invasion.

With two companions he rode through Tweeddale to Cumberland, meeting on the way David Ritchie, who now lives secure as the Black Dwarf; and finally arrived at Gilsland, which had been chosen for the holiday. The wound in the poet's heart due to his rejection by Margaret Stuart had lost its poignancy, although he loved her till the end, but here at Gilsland a new romance came into his life, one of abiding consequence to literature.

Holidaying here was the daughter of a French immigrant, Charlotte Margaret Carpenter.

And the young couple fell in love; and Scott went off to Jedburgh Assizes to sit up late at night with a friend, "sair beside himself about the lady, raving about her till one in the morning." The course of true love did not run smooth, for the rigid prejudices of the Scotts were all against Walter's marriage to the daughter of a Frenchman, and this, coupled with the grim record of his paltry five years' earnings at the Bar, moved Scott to a stern resolution: he made up his mind to emigrate to Jamaica.

Jamaica, ancient lure of languishing hopes! Had not Burns, eleven years before, packed his small belongings and set out for port to take passage on a Jamaica-bound ship, with only a beggarly dozen of his masterpieces written? Scott was to leave, in a similar paroxysm of despair, with exactly nothing written. But the lady of Gilsland saved him from himself for eternal fame. In her pleasant English she wrote him an ultimatum.

No wonder, she said, that his father and uncle called him "a hot-headed young man"; she agreed with their description, and she would not go to Jamaica. "I must believe that when you have such an idea you have determined to think no more of me. I begin to repent of having accepted your picture. I will send it back again if ever you think again about the West Indies."

It was enough. Three months later Scott and Charlotte were married, on Christmas Eve in 1797.

The Old Church in the Pines

GLASSONBY. Just a handful of small houses and barns, it has a lonely church completely hidden by pines. It is known as Addingham church, but there is no Addingham, for the village was washed away in the 14th century, and much of its church, which had been desecrated by bloodshed shortly before the flood came, lies in the River Eden. The 14th-century building we see contains some of the original stones from it, and is a simple structure of a nave, a chancel, and a porch. In its walls we noticed many stones unusually large. The chancel has a remarkably wide and low arch, and a tiny window little more than a foot square. The other windows are mostly 15th century, and, though they have two lights each, the arches are hollowed out of single stones. In the nave is the base of an old stone cross.

The most notable possessions of the church are the old relics from its predecessor, found in the river bed and brought here for safety. In the gable of the porch is a fragment of a Norman stone, and in the porch itself are several pieces of carved red sandstone, including parts of 11th-century cross-shafts with excellent knotwork. Here also are two old gravestones with crosses and swords, and one of the interesting old gravestones called hogbacks, long and very massive and shaped like the roof of a house for the dead person.

The churchyard also has its relic from the river bed, a curious ancient cross with an immense head on a small shaft. It has spiral ornament, and the head has four holes and a raised central boss.

A near neighbour of the village is Gamblesby, where the iron stocks are still on the green, though hard to find. It was on Gamblesby Low Fell last century that someone found a stone chest containing human remains.

The Precious Stones of Long Ago

GOSFORTH. Here, among the foot-hills of the west Cumberland fells, is one of the greatest treasures in the county, the famous Gosforth Cross, which takes a high place among the ancient monuments of England. We find it near the fine lychgate, with the remains of another cross for company.

Worn but very fine, it is a remarkable sandstone monolith nearly 15 feet high; the tallest ancient cross in the country, it is thought to be a relic from the Scandinavian settlement here in the generations just before the Norman Conquest. The slender tapering shaft is partly round and partly square, and is crowned by a fine four-holed head carved on the arms with the triquetra, the emblem of the Trinity. The cross-head is said to be unique in Northumbria for not being carved with a crucifix.

The round part of the shaft, with its carving, is thought to represent the trunk and branches and leaves of the World-Ash, the sacred tree believed by the Northmen to support the universe. The square part has on its four sides figures and devices symbolising the Northmen's belief that their new faith, Christianity, would ultimately triumph over paganism. It illustrates myths told in the Edda, and the four sides can perhaps be interpreted as the four parts of a 10th-century poem which became one of the classics of the north. Known in the Edda as Voluspa, or the Sibyl's Prophecy, it told the story of the world in a way the Northmen could understand, and expressed the poet's belief that Christianity would prevail.

The south side of the cross shows dragons and plaited snakes, a horseman, a wolf, and a hart; the west side has dragons attacking one of the gods, a horseman upside down, and a little figure apparently emptying a cup above another figure bound by a serpent; this is probably Loki's wife saving him from punishment by catching the snake's poison directed at him. The north side has a horseman attacked by another and a winged dragon, and on the east side, above a scene of the Crucifixion, is a figure, probably Odin's son, rending the jaws of one of two dragons plaited together.

Part of another ancient cross forms the pillar of the sundial; and in this churchyard we remember a treasure of a very different kind, a fine and shapely cork tree said to be the most northerly one in England.

There has been a church standing here for at least a thousand years, and the pleasing little building we see was originally Norman. After much alteration it has still a simple Norman doorway now blocked up, and some curious Norman capitals to the chancel arch, where the carvings show three peeping faces perhaps meant for the Trinity, a man's face with a long moustache, another with curious foliage coming from its mouth, and a tiny face with two arms reaching up to touch its beard. In the churchyard wall are some fragments of zigzag and a Norman capital.

But if there were no Gosforth Cross this church would still be a great place for the pilgrim, for it has a priceless collection of ancient stones. Some are older than the Conquest; one is an old boundary stone, others are medieval gravestones carved with crosses and other emblems. One of these in the porch is a very fine coffin stone deeply cut with what looks like a vine trailing about a cross, and with two tiny pairs of shears in odd places as if they were an afterthought. Still more remarkable and much rarer are two of the hogback monuments which covered the graves of long-forgotten chieftains perhaps a thousand years ago. Rescued from the foundations of the Norman church, they are both elaborately carved, and shaped like houses of the dead with their roofs clearly defined, one roof as if with tiles and the other with crossing bands. The bigger hogback is called the Saint's Tomb and shows human figures wrestling with the serpents of evil, some of which have heads like wolves; at the end a worn crucifix suggests the triumph of Christianity. The smaller one, called the Warrior's Tomb, is said to be unique, being carved on one side with interlacing patterns and on the other with two opposing rows of quaint little soldiers whose leaders seem to be making truce. The end shows an armed figure who may be the Warrior himself.

One of the most extraordinary pre-Norman sculptures we have seen is on the archway at the end of the north aisle. Known as the Fishing Stone, it was once part of a churchyard cross. Its top panel shows a Holy Lamb trampling on the serpents of paganism, and we see the conquered serpent with hanging head. The lower part illustrates the story told in the Edda of how Thor fished for the World Serpent, and here we see him sitting with Hymir in a boat and using an ox-head for a bait on his line.

The church has two old chairs, each carved with two eagles at the top. There is a neat modern font with traceried panels, and there are some curious old oak collecting boxes in the vestry. A most unusual treasure we found on one of the window-sills is a Chinese iron bell, perhaps the only one of its kind ever to ring in an English church. Though cracked, it is finely ornamented in Eastern fashion, having a mass of scroll work, a horrible dragon, a fish in water, three inscriptions, and water lilies. It was given to Gosforth by Lady Senhouse after her husband, Sir Humphrey Senhouse, brought it from a fort he captured on the Canton River in 1841, and a tablet tells of his death on board H.M.S. Blenheim after Canton was taken. By the bell are two old stone cannon balls from forts in the Dardanelles.

A stone on the nave wall tells of Christopher Denton who was rector 50 years, and who lived in the village street at a quaint old house which has a tablet with the names of John and Margaret Shearwen, who built it in 1628. Nearly as old is Gosforth Hall by the church, a farm which includes much of the house built by Robert Copley in 1658. His initials are on the head of the original doorway now built into a barn. Here still are the fine stone pillars of the gate, a fine old fireplace, a newel stair, and some splendid old beams in the roof. In a corner of the field above the Hall is the site of an ancient chapel built over the Holy Well whose cold clear water never fails. The foundations have been excavated in our own time and found to be those of an oblong building of a type rare in Cumberland, perhaps medieval.

The Medieval Fortress

GREAT CORBY. High above the Eden, in a lofty bower, stands Corby Castle, its oldest walls, made by Norman builders, rising sheer from the steep cliff. In the heart of the superb house which the Howards, owners for the last 300 years, have made of this medieval fortress is still a spiral staircase trodden by 12th-century mailed feet.

We can imagine how it was loved by Lord William Howard, the famous Belted Will whose portrait, painted 300 years ago, stands out among the Correggios, the Gainsboroughs, and other pictures by

English and Italian artists in the castle gallery. Two of the Howard lions stand on the imposing modern parapets. Venerable trees surround the old walls, the oaks on Castle Hill rivalling the beeches in the grove. From the lawn, shaded by a great cedar, we can stand and look down on the river, broad and deep, winding away in its wooded gorge, with its shady walks that lead to the salmon coops and caves.

Then we step down to enjoy the wonderful sight of the stone grotto below the lawn. It is a curious place of mermen and mermaids, gods and goddesses, of huge mouths bristling with teeth through which water pours in a joyous cascade, into a pool about 80 feet below.

Between the mermen and the river a stone Polyphemus stands by himself, looking at the world through his one eye, Pan pipes in his hands. He is ten feet high and has been given the trunk of a young tree for a staff.

The stripling village of Corby, looking across the Eden to its beautiful sister-village Wetheral, is content to be overlooked for the castle's sake. Among its little houses is a relic of the past, the great sandstone arch of the forge, resting on two pillars. The place seems to have grown up anyhow, with a lane slanting up the middle of the street, so that the villagers look through their front windows on the bushes of the hedge.

The Happy Schoolmaster

GREAT ORTON. It has been through great adventures, for many Roman causeways and foundations have been found about it, and it is known that the village was once surrounded by a rampart and a ditch, and that the road through it was barred by locked chains at night. We may see Roman tiles in the walls of the church, which stands on a long road lined with red and white houses.

From an enclosure west of the village, known as Parson's Thorn, we looked on a magnificent panorama of 30 miles and saw 15 churches, some of them in Scotland.

Almost as small as a church could be is this simple oblong place with a stone roof sheltered by limes. Its walls are three feet thick and most of it is from the 12th century. The chancel walls are built to lean outwards like a ship. There are two Norman windows in the chancel, and part of an ancient pillar piscina.

One of the bells hanging in the gable summoned the people to church in a Roman Catholic England. In a window is St Kentigern preaching to the people of Cumbria, who are dressed as in the 6th century. The modern font has an effective cover on eight arches and pillars.

In the years between Trafalgar and Waterloo there died in this place the Richard Dixon who was master of the old school for nearly half a century, and was known as Happy Dick. They laid him in the churchyard and this is the epitaph they gave him:

Seven times seven he taught this school
And canvassed many a tedious rule:
Five times seven, as you may mark,
He served here as parish clerk.
He was a just and upright man,
As far as we his life could scan:
But now he rests beneath this clod,
Till called upon to meet his God.

The Stones of the Old Invaders

GREAT SALKELD. A famous little place near the River Eden, it has a fascinating church with much in it to see, and an ancient rectory full of memories of celebrated men. One of its old farms, at Burrel Green, treasures a 16th-century brass dish nicknamed the Luck of Burrell, the story being that it was stolen from the fairies, like the famous Luck of Eden Hall.

Not unlike a Norman keep is the splendid 14th-century tower of the church, so massive and strong that it was evidently meant as a stronghold or a refuge during the border wars. Immense for the size of the church, it has an embattled parapet, a square turret all the way up, and windows which are little more than slits. Near the bottom outside is a little opening with an iron shutter, intended to ventilate a dungeon down below where prisoners may have been kept.

The only way in to this medieval fortress is by one of the most wonderful old doors in Cumberland, set in a little arch in the west wall of the nave. This door is really a massive iron grating, with a tremendously strong lattice of uprights and cross-pieces, and with oak baulks between the bars helping to make this one of the strongest doors we have seen. The ironwork was marvellously made by a 14th-century smith, together with three huge hinges and two great bolts two feet long.

Opening the door, we find within the tower a vaulted room lit by three windows in the thickness of the walls. Above two of them are old gravestones adorned with crosses and such symbols as a sword, a horseshoe, and shears. The dungeon is below, and a spiral staircase leads to an upper room which has a fireplace and an old gravestone carved with a sword, a bell, and a hunting-horn.

The chancel is 15th century, and so are many of the windows; but the simple chancel arch is a fine piece of Norman work. It is not so fine, however, as the gem of a Norman doorway in the porch, one of the best in the county. Less than a yard wide, it has three shafts at each side, and three mouldings, while the arch has three rows of deeply-cut zigzags with five queer heads, one rather like a man with an eye closed, and another a creature wearing a crown. The rich carving of the capitals includes flower and leaf designs, and little faces among winding stems, but the most striking capital of all is one showing a lamb-like animal with a dragon rearing above it, and a bird attacking the dragon.

In the porch is Great Salkeld's oldest treasure, a Roman altar found in the churchyard in 1890, one of the few we have come upon. Here, too, is a fragment of Saxon stonework, and one or two more old gravestones, while outside the porch a weathered gravestone tells of the Dalstons, who lived in a 17th-century house near by.

The church still shows the hand of the Normans both inside and out, and the walls of the nave are exceptionally thick. The panelling of the sanctuary is enriched with Tudor woodwork, and on the nave wall are several pieces of armour of Shakespeare's time, a helmet, a sword, and two breastplates: one of them has apparently had a heavy blow on the shoulder. Lying near the altar is the worn and mutilated stone figure of Thomas de Caldebec in his priest's robes of 600 years ago; and on the chancel floor is a long gravestone with a cross and a sword, thought to be that of Stephen Close, a rector who may have built the chancel. A lovely window in the nave has a fine portrait of St Cuthbert and two scenes from his life, one showing him as a shepherd boy watching the angels carry away St Aidan's soul, and the other showing him preaching to a company of peasants.

The ancient rectory is a simple but very beautiful house, with thick walls. Partly 600 years old, it underwent much change in the 17th century. Here lived two men who became Bishops of Carlisle, and one who became Bishop of Lichfield.

The Pitiless Judge

IN the rectory was born Great Salkeld's fămous son, Lord Ellenborough. He was born in 1750, when his father, the future Bishop of Carlisle, was rector here. Educated at Cambridge, he was called to the Bar at 30 and in seven years was chosen to conduct the defence of Warren Hastings before the House of Lords.

Throughout the trial he combated with great skill the declamatory eloquence of Fox, Burke, and the other distinguished accusers, and at last secured an acquittal. At first a Whig, he was converted by the French Revolution to reactionary Toryism, and in every reformer saw a dangerous anarchist. In the trials in which he figured as Attorney-General his bitter language recalled that of the Courts in Stuart days. He was made Chief Justice and raised to the peerage as Baron Ellenborough, though retaining his seat in the Cabinet of the ministry of All the Talents, a dangerous linking of politics with justice which aroused public resentment. It was he who tried Lord Dundonald and inflicted what has always been considered an outrageous penalty, a fine of £1000 with a year's imprisonment, in addition to the disgrace of the pillory—a sentence which Parliament afterwards expunged.

He fiercely resisted all the humane legal reforms introduced by Romilly. When William Hone the publisher was prosecuted for blasphemy, Ellenborough was apparently determined on conviction, and as the judge took his seat one morning Hone exclaimed from the dock, "I am glad to see you, my lord; I know what you are come here for; I know what you want." The Judge answered: "I am come to do justice; my only wish is to see justice done"; whereupon Hone dared to cry out: "Is it not rather, my lord, to send a poor bookseller to rot in a dungeon?"

To his deep mortification Ellenborough heard the jury return a verdict of Not Guilty, followed by applause it was impossible to quell. He took the verdict as a personal affront, and, although he showed indomitable courage in facing the mob which acclaimed the verdict, the result of the trial appears to have broken his heart.

Church, Castle, and Queer Houses

GREYSTOKE. It stands out among its simple neighbours like a gem, not only for the charm of the houses round the green, but for the magnificence of the great house and the church.

The ancient cross on the green was talked of as a landmark 300 years ago; the great house is a stately castle; and the church has something of cathedral dignity.

Greystoke Castle stands in about 6000 acres, and its park is said to be the biggest enclosure in England without a road or a right-of-way running through. Its wall runs for miles, but of the castle itself we see little more than a flag. It is not old as castles go, having been burned down intentionally in the Civil War and by accident since, but it is old in family history and has been built up again as a noble structure. Here lived the proud nobility of Cumberland, the Greystokes, the Dacres, and the Howards who were here when we called.

But if the castle is private, the great church is open for all to see, and to admire. Approaching it we pass a stone which has stood in the path for centuries and is now railed off with an inscription to tell us about it. It was the Sanctuary Stone, marking the boundary within which anyone fleeing to the church was safe.

The impression, as we step inside the church, is one of spaciousness. The oldest thing we see is the chancel arch, which, with the wall above it, was built when the Norman style was changing into English. Nearly all the rest is 15th century, having been built anew after the church was raised to high dignity with several chantries, several priests, and a college of secular canons. The tower and chancel were rebuilt last century.

Here still are the 20 stalls of the canons, with some beautifully carved misereres, including a pelican, a little scene with a unicorn, an angel killing a dragon, three men with a horse, and many odd faces. Here still are some parts of the 15th-century screen attached to a rood beam older than themselves; an altar stone with five crosses; and the four bells that were ringing before the Reformation.

One of the aisles has a fine east window, and the chancel has a finer one still, for its collection of old glass is only rivalled in Cumberland by that in the great east window of Carlisle cathedral. In the upper halves the pictures include a saint standing on a little red demon, two family groups of the Dacres from their chapel in the castle, the five wounds of Jesus, and a priest kneeling on a cushion. In the lower halves are ten scenes from the legend of St Andrew, who went to rescue St Matthew from the city of the cannibals. We see him addressing the people, sitting by a boat, standing by a church, looking at the flood which came to the wicked city, and restoring the drowning people; and we see Matthew speaking from a prison window. Two of the scenes show Jesus in glory between Peter and Andrew, and Jesus appearing to the disciples beside the sea. The glass high up in the tracery is modern, except for some beautiful little heads and figures at the top.

Several old monuments recall the family history of the castle and the great days of the collegiate church. There is an alabaster figure of the 14th Baron Greystoke who founded the college and built the first castle, and whose grave in the chancel has an inscription in brass of "the good baron." He died in 1359. Also in alabaster is the 16th Baron, who asked to lie here and left to the church his horse and armour. Earlier than either is the carved tombstone (by the altar) of the 10th Baron, who died in 1306.

There is a brass inscription to two old masters of the college, and two little brass portraits side by side of Richard and Winifred Newport, who died in the middle of the 16th century. A third portrait is under the choir stalls, and a fourth (of Margaret Moresby) is in the vestry.

Very touching is a modern brass tablet to a soldier who fell in France, showing that humanity does not perish even between enemies in war. At Christmas time in 1914, we read, Henry Askew was laid to rest by the Germans, who raised a cross to him with the words, *Here Lies a Brave British Officer*.

One who perhaps knew this church as a child has no memorial in it. She was Isabel Foster, who was born at Greystoke, married a Fleet Street cutler, and was burned for her faith with six others at Smithfield in the bitter reign of Mary.

On the edges of Greystoke Park are two attractive old houses, Johnby Hall, chiefly built in the 16th century, and Greenthwaite Hall, built in the 17th. More freakish than beautiful are three old farmhouses seen from the Penrith road, each built by a strange whim to look like something else. Two looking like forts are called Bunkers Hill and Fort Putnam; the third, like a church, is Spire House.

Roman Altar and English Church

HAILE. It stands on a hill, blown by the winds of the sea, and its church is in a lovely hollow where we forget the works of the iron mine on the opposite hill. With a thousand years of history behind it, the church is seen as a simple modern building, with little to show of its great antiquity; yet not quite all has gone, for here as elsewhere there are ancient stones full of interest, some inside the church and some out. Leaning against the churchyard wall are four broken ones carved at their edges with knotwork, and looking out from the south wall of the nave is part of a 10th century cross with good scroll carving. Older still are two stones in the vestry; one with Roman lettering is said to be from a Roman altar, and the other, with a circle round the head of a cross, may be Roman too. Here also is part of an old window moulding built into the wall.

Far younger, though it has seen many generations of human life, is a little low screen by the font. On one panel it has a fine castle with an imposing gateway, and on the other the arms of the Ponsonbys, who lived at Haile Hall above the village. One of them, John Ponsonby of 1670, lies close to the west wall of the church, where we see his gravestone with its crude and confused lettering.

Haile Hall has a lovely avenue of beeches leading to a fine stone gatehouse; over the archway are the Ponsonby arms again, with their three double combs. Looking through the arch we see the house itself, which has 1591 over one door and 1625 over another.

Grey Hamlet in the Hollow

HALLTHWAITES. The grey hamlet lies in a hollow almost hidden from the church, which stands alone by a highway, winding along the slopes of the fells, with delightful views of the Lakeland hills.

It is a lofty 19th-century church in the style of 700 years ago, with a steep black-and-white roof and two fine windows showing St Margaret giving bread to the poor, and St Bega, in nun's robes, serving the men who are building her nunnery. A simple font of 1727 stands in a corner unused, and also from an earlier church are two richly carved chairs held by pegs so that they may be folded flat for carrying. There is also a fine pewter flagon of 1705, over 13 inches high. The last century put a sundial in the churchyard, and this century added a cross of peace, carved with the knotwork Saxon masons were so fond of.

Lower down the road is another churchyard, all that is left of the old chapel of St Anne; and among the fells two miles north is a circle of about 50 stones put here before there was a church in the land, before the first page of our history was written.

Bootle
Hugh Askew, 1562

Carlisle: Bishop Bell, 1496

Greystoke: Margaret Moresby, 1540

Westward: Truth and Fame with the shield of Richard Barwis, 1648

Crosthwaite (Keswick): Sir John and Lady Radcliffe, 1527

Edenhall: William Stapleton and his wife Margaret, 1458

CUMBERLAND BRASSES

Here was a Roman Shrine

HARRINGTON. It grew from a village to a small flourishing port in less than a century, and the church from its hill watched that growth of grey roofs in their cleft by the sea. For eight centuries a church has been here, but men have made many changes in it, as wind and rain in twice eight centuries have levelled the fortifications of the Roman camp in which it stands. We have seen a Roman altar from here in Newcastle Museum.

Of the old church only a Norman doorway and an unused font of the end of the 12th century are left in the tower. Other old stones are a coffin lid marked with a cross and shears, two fragments of lids (one with a sword) in the nave walls, and part of what must have been a fine cross nine or ten centuries ago. It was found in 1924 buried ten feet deep.

It is a long plain church with a hammerbeam roof, and many pictures in its windows. One showing Christ comforting the old and healing the sick is to a man who followed in His footsteps as rector here for 57 years, A. F. Curwen, who died in 1920. On a brass panel are the names of 118 men who did not live to see the peace they fought for.

A Cumbrian in America

HAYTON. Round a long and wide green gather the inn and the church, the cottages and the farms, for a fine view over Solway Firth. The tall plain church of last century has a wagon roof supported over the nave and chancel by 118 small hammerbeams. The chancel screen is in wrought iron with scrolls and leaves; the pulpit was carved by a woman in memory of her father, and she carved the litany desk in memory of her sister.

On a bluff among trees at one end of the village is a substantial farmhouse, all that remains of Hayton Castle, besieged in the Civil War, built up again the same century, and for 300 years the home of the Musgraves.

Here in 1735 was born Sir William Musgrave, one of the early trustees and benefactors of the British Museum, to which he left some valuable biographical tracts. Better known was Sir Thomas of his house, born two years later, for he made a great name for bravery during the War of American Independence. Once at Germanstown, the British outpost near Philadelphia, he was surprised by a large force of Americans, but, entering a stone house with his few soldiers, he held it till help came. A military medal was struck showing this house, and it appears again on his engraved portrait in the British Museum. Sir Thomas was the last British Commandant of New York. He became Colonel of a West Riding regiment raised for India, where he served under Cornwallis, and he died a General, and was buried in 1812 outside the famous London church of St George's, Hanover Square.

The Stubborn Archbishop

HENSINGHAM. It is a close neighbour of Whitehaven, but high enough above it to have a very fine view of the harbour and of the town deep in the hollow and wreathed in smoke.

The neat little church on the hill was built in our time when the 18th-century church was pulled down. A sturdy red-stone pile with embattled tower, light and airy within, its chief interest lies in the gallery of pictures in its windows.

The east window glows with colour in a crowded scene of Christ with the children. In another is the Nativity and the woman with the alabaster box of ointment. Four west lancets have the Annunciation and three scenes of the Crucifixion. A window of golden tone shows Charity giving bread to the poor. Gleaming with colour is a window with John baptising Our Lord under a sky with blue-winged cherubs, and in another we see a red-robed Christ holding a crown to a soldier who died in France in 1917.

There is beautiful work in the oak peace memorial of a panel with richly carved and gilded borders of roses and vine, crowned by a lovely St George on his horse rushing at a green Dragon outside a castle.

Here was born Edmund Grindal, who became Bishop of London in 1558, and later was appointed Archbishop first of York, and then of Canterbury during the perilous days in which Elizabeth was re-establishing the Protestant faith in England.

After a distinguished career at Cambridge he was in close touch with Ridley, whose chaplain he was, but he fled from Mary's fires, which consumed Ridley, and returned to England on the accession of Elizabeth. A prominent figure in the religious life of the times, he touched history at many points, and not always judiciously.

Both at Canterbury and at York, where he was a firm but not

unkind suppressor of Romanism, he failed to justify the faith his scholarship had induced the Queen to place in him. He insisted on private meetings of clergy for what he called prophesying, and this, Elizabeth said, led more to division and heresy than unity, whereupon he addressed her in a famous letter of over 5000 words, rebuking her and refusing to forbid the meetings. In answer he was removed from his office, although not actually deposed, and went blind before he could either resign or become reconciled. It was this strife which caused Spenser cordially to take up the cudgels for Grindal and to celebrate him in the Shepherd's Calendar as the wise Algrind.

The stubborn Archbishop is best remembered as a good friend to learning, for, in addition to founding his famous grammar school at St Bees, he left benefactions to the universities.

On the Roman Road

HESKET-IN-THE-FOREST. It is two villages in the old forest of Inglewood, High Hesket on a hill and Low Hesket in a hollow. They have little to show us, but much for us to remember.

Between them by the wayside is a stone platform with a hole in the middle through which grew what is called the Court Thorn, marking the spot where for centuries tenants assembled at the manorial court. The old tree has died, but we found a stripling growing up through the hole to keep its memory green.

But far beyond these feudal days runs the story of life hereabouts, for we are here on the Roman road to Carlisle with the traffic of the Great North Road running ceaselessly by, and here must have come Roman soldiers and merchants of Gaul bringing perhaps the first tidings of Christianity to our island. Here Agricola and Hadrian must have been; here St Kentigern and St Ninian are supposed to have come crusading. It is written that a hundred years ago a hoard of Viking arms, all richly decorated, was found in a mound not far from the inn.

It is said that the church, which crowns the hill at High Hesket, was built 400 years ago when victims of the Black Death were brought here for burial from Carlisle. There is a black-and-white roof, an 18th-century bell, a stone to a Royalist officer of the Civil War, and two sundials and a Flanders cross on the wall outside.

A Nunc Dimittis window with Mary and Simeon in the Temple is to a vicar for 46 years who died in our time, and the east window has a scene of Calvary and portraits of four Bible figures, Hannah and Samuel, Eunice and Timothy.

HOLME ST CUTHBERT. Looking across the lowlands and the sea to the hills of Scotland is this scattered village with a red-stone church of last century in place of the chapel it had before the Reformation. It is plain and spacious, with a simple tower and turret. To the north are the scant remains of Wolsty Castle, made strong in 1250 and used by the Abbots of Holme Cultram as a safe for their treasures. Last century pottery and coins and other everyday things of the Romans were found here.

HUTTON-IN-THE-FOREST. Its simple church is all alone with nature, and its great house still hides in something of a forest. From the Penrith road we catch a glimpse of the mansion, its turrets and battlements contrasting oddly with the part designed by Inigo Jones. Like other Cumberland houses, it has grown up round an ancient tower, and was added to in Elizabethan and Jacobean times.

In the church is a medieval coffin stone, carved with a cross and little pictures of a chalice and a missal. The oak lectern is in memory of a man who ministered here for 56 years last century, and there is a memorial to Sir George Fletcher of 1700, who was "Knight of the Shire near 40 years" and built part of the great house.

Dying in the Fields

IREBY. It has shrunk from a little market town to a village, with its old Moot Hall still here and its old market cross restored after being long in ruins.

More pathetic than the decay of the town is the decay of a small building in the fields a mile away, a hollow place that sends our voices echoing as we look in through its broken windows. It is the chancel of a Norman church, a simple place to which they must have walked for centuries, left to die a lingering death among the graves of who those worshipped in it.

Happily rescued from the poor ruins, and now in the new church in the village, are an ancient font with four carved roundels, and two old stones built into the walls of the porch. One stone is carved with a pair of shears and some crosses; the other has an ornate cross and a sword, the memorial of John de Ireby who lived 700 years ago.

The Norman Mason and the Roman Stones

IRTHINGTON. A thousand years after Hadrian built the Great Wall of England Norman masons stole stones from it to build Irthington's church.

Sandwiched between the Wall and the Irthing, the church was greatly altered last century, but we may plainly see the Roman stones in the chancel. Not far off are the quarries in which the Romans hewed these stones 1800 years ago, while the remains of one of their forts were found last century at a spot known as the Nook.

Into the Norman chancel we came through a fine Norman arch, rich with deep mouldings and with foliage on the capitals. From the wall beside it a bearded face has been staring wide-eyed into the nave for 800 years. The arches of the arcade are either Norman or early 13th century.

For the rest the church is severe and plain, but it has a chalice made the year Shakespeare died, and in the chancel is remembered a vicar here for half a century, John Stamper, who died in 1811. To the north of the churchyard is a stone cut with a flowered cross, a book, and a chalice, possibly 600 years ago.

The villagers will tell you that an old man of 119, Robert Bowman, lies in this churchyard; but it is a very old tale and we feel it has gained in the telling. All round are hills loved by the beech and the oak, and the roads to the village are sheltered with beech hedges.

The Eager Little Middy

IRTON. Its views of the mountains are glorious, but we come to it for its church and its Hall, and more especially for one of Cumberland's oldest and greatest treasures.

Not so old as some flints and spear-heads found here, the remarkable churchyard cross of Irton is old enough, for it was probably carved out of the red sandstone 1000 years ago; and for its beauty and preservation it ranks second only to the wonderful cross at Gosforth. Tapering gracefully to a fine head, it is ten feet high, and is richly ornamented. Beyond the fine timber lychgate it has a new companion on the little green, a graceful cross to the Irton men who died for peace.

The stolid little church was refashioned last century and has a fine tower with an imposing turret above the battlements. Its eight bells must echo far and wide among these hills and vales. The tower archway is screened by attractive wrought iron gates, and the attractive chancel arch has black marble shafts.

The interior is dimmed by its coloured windows, two of them are to a 19th-century admiral; but two we liked better show St Agnes with her lamb and St Paul at the altar to the Unknown God. Among many memorials there are fine brass tablets with rich borders to Sir Thomas and Sir Richard Brocklebank of our own century, and there is a marble tablet with cannon and anchor in memory of Skeffington Lutwidge, who commanded a ship in an expedition of polar discovery in 1773. We read that he was distinguished by his sweetness of manner; but his voyage has another distinction, for serving under him on H.M.S. Carcass was an eager little midshipman of 14 whose name was Horatio Nelson.

Another marble tablet links the church with the Hall about a mile away, for it is dedicated to Samuel Irton of 1866 who was the last of a family line of 800 years. In all the generations of the Irtons there were many notable figures. One went on the Crusades and saw the Holy City captured by Godfrey of Boulogne. Another fought and was knighted at Flodden Field. Others were High Sheriffs in Cumberland, and one sat in seven parliaments.

We get a peep of their fine house from the roadside, in front of it a mighty oak which must have shared most of its story. Once a border castle, the Hall had still its embattled tower and some other remains of the 14th and 16th centuries.

In a lovely hollow farther down the road is Santon Bridge, where the crystal waters of the River Irt come rushing over a rocky bed to pass under a fine stone arch.

General Wolfe's Elizabeth

ISEL. It has the Derwent looking lovely from an old bridge; it has an attractive old church; and it has Isel Hall, with a tower 500 years old, and the rest of it as magnificently Elizabethan as anything for miles around. About a score of stone windows look from the Hall on to a charming walled garden, and the gateway on the road has two stone faces held up by pairs of hands.

It was the home of the Lawsons, two of whom have memorials in the church. One was Sir Wilfrid of 1632; the other was Sir Wilfrid of 1688, who was evidently proud of having married off his four sons and eight daughters, for the fact is recorded on his tablet. There were several more Sir Wilfrids before the direct line ended, one of them the father of Elizabeth Lawson whom General Wolfe wanted to marry. The general was then only a gallant young major, and she had gone from Isel to be a maid of honour at Court. His mother killed the plan but not his love, and years later Wolfe said that the very sight of Elizabeth's picture on the wall took away his appetite for dinner.

The church was chiefly built by the Normans, and has still their doorway, their chancel arch, and several of their little windows. Another window pierced in the 15th century has three sundials on it. There are two stones carved before the Normans came, one being part of a 10th-century cross and the other having the rare three-armed symbol called the triskele, one of the earliest devices found on Christian monuments.

A brass inscription tells of a man who died in the year of Agincourt, and another is in memory of a lady of last century who was born at the vicarage and "lived her life among the people." Her father was vicar 50 years, and she married his successor. In the century before John Kendall had been vicar for 53 years.

Along the road to Cockermouth we pass Hewthwaite Hall, one of the old houses that have become farms. The striking doorway of 1581 is carved with a coat-of-arms and with little figures like dolls under canopies.

Two Griffins Keeping Watch

IVEGILL. Its finest possession is a private house, High Head Castle, crowning the sheer edge of rock overhanging a deep glen and looking away to the fells. Long ago it was a tower to which a chapel was added in the 14th century, but as we see it it is mainly an 18th-century house, with a balustraded parapet and a pediment on which are carved a mermaid and a merman. Two stone griffins keep watch on the gateway of this fine place.

Not far from the castle is a simple 17th-century chapel which has been made new, and has a fine brass engraved with roses to one who lived at the castle in our own time, Herbert Augustus Hill, a Judge of the Court of Appeal of the International Tribunal in Egypt in the days before the war.

The church is still in its first century, and stands as a monument of the energy of Arthur Emilius Hulton, a vicar who built it and died when it was two months old. It has a black-and-white roof, and windows with the Evangelists and the Last Supper.

Poet's Corner

KESWICK. It lies in a green vale with nature lavish on every hand. Above it rises Skiddaw, majestic and famous, and at its door is Derwentwater, the lake beyond compare.

Keswick has for many generations drawn pilgrims to itself. Its streets have the simple attraction of the north-country towns; it has an old church and a new church and a quaint town hall like a third church; it has the Greta flowing through to join the Derwent, and a remarkable museum. It is rich in human interest, and is in reach of most of the beauties in Lakeland.

Is there any wonder that poets come to this place so like a dream? Small wonder indeed that Shelley brought his bride here for their honeymoon, that Coleridge and Southey came with the two sisters they had married amid all the magnificence of St Mary Redcliffe at Bristol; that Wordsworth came, and De Quincey, and Charles Lamb, and John Ruskin.

Still here is the poet's corner in which they gathered, Greta Hall, with its view of the lake they loved. To it in 1800 came Coleridge to live, his best poems already written. To it in 1803 he invited Southey, a far finer man, and perhaps more of a man than a poet. For a little while their two families were together, Coleridge erratic and struggling to master himself, Southey methodical, thinking deeply, writing hard, and revelling in his books; and when the unstable Coleridge cut himself adrift it was Robert Southey who for more than a generation kept this home going, bearing the burden of both families, winning fame as Poet Laureate, and earning the high respect and affection of all. He lies in the old churchyard of Great Crosthwaite, his simple grave where he chose it; and about him are many whom he knew and loved. Here also lie Jonathan Otley, the father of Lakeland geology; Sir John George Woodford, who was wounded by the last shot fired at Corunna, stood by Wellington at Waterloo, and introduced more than one humane reform into the army; and Sir Edmund Henderson, a soldier who increased the efficiency of the police in London at a difficult time, and established the criminal investigation department. The London cabdrivers gave him a silver hansom cab for his interest in their lot and his work in setting up shelters for them.

Great Crosthwaite church is a little apart from the town. It was almost certainly a Christian site before there was any Keswick, and became the mother church of a wide area in Cumberland. It has little bits of Norman work, arches of the 14th century, and much that was renewed in Tudor times, including the west window, with its unusual tracery; and it is said to be unique for having the complete set of 12 consecration crosses outside the windows, as well as some inside. They mark the places where the bishop sprinkled the holy water on consecration day, probably in the terrible reign of Mary Tudor.

Just inside the door is a 14th-century font, finely carved and with an interesting story. It was given, at the end of the century, by two ladies to commemorate the work of a man sent by the Pope to settle a quarrel in Borrowdale between the monks of Furness Abbey and those of Fountains, a man who was afterwards vicar here. Its eight sides are carved with shields and foliage, and the stem has tracery like windows. Near by lie the 15th-century figures of Sir John de Derwentwater and his wife.

On a table tomb are brass portraits of Sir John Radcliffe, who is said to have led the Keswick men at Flodden Field, and his wife Dame Alice, who sleeps in Salisbury Cathedral. He is in armour, and she has a dress with hanging sleeves. On a window-sill is one of the oldest bells in Cumberland, its last peal rung. It is 14th century and came from the little church at Loweswater.

One window has the portrait of Mary Magdalene in old glass, and an old shield with blue lions; another has a 15th-century picture of St Andrew brought here from Furness Abbey, showing him as a preacher with a bell hanging from his staff.

There is a candlestick used before the Reformation, a very old stone carved with a cross, the 18th-century pitchpipe and conductor's baton used here before there was an organ, and one of the quaint old sets of rhyme under the tower telling the bellringers what they would be fined for such sins as overturning a bell, swearing, or coming to ring in spurs or a hat.

But, most striking of all the spectacular possessions of this place, perhaps, is the white figure of Robert Southey, carved by a self-taught Newcastle man and showing the poet looking towards the churchyard he knew so well. Good it is to see this "noblest of them all," and to read the long epitaph, which has the rare merit among epitaphs of being perfectly true. It is by Wordsworth himself, and we take these lines from it:

Ye vales and hills whose beauty hither drew
The poet's steps, and fixed him here, on you,
His eyes have closed! And ye, loved books, no more
Shall Southey feed upon your precious lore. . . .

Wide were his aims, yet in no human breast
Could private feeling meet for holier rest.
His joys, his griefs, have vanished like a cloud
From Skiddaw's top ; but he to heaven has vowed
Through a life long and pure, and Christian faith
Calmed in his soul the fear of change and death.

In this churchyard he loved so much they laid to rest in 1920 Hardwicke Drummond Rawnsley, vicar here for over a generation, with the famous canon who did so much to save England from the spoilers. With Miss Octavia Hill he was one of the founders of the National Trust. Through his watchfulness and enthusiasm many gems of Lakeland are for ever safe, and it is fitting that he should lie almost within sight of some of the great scenes he saved. His tablet in the church links the 20th century with the 6th, for it bears the emblems of St Kentigern, the apostle of Christianity in the north to whom this church is dedicated, and who is believed to have preached on the spot where it stands.

The 19th-century church of St John has an imposing exterior and looks charming in distant views across the lake. It has St John and St Paul in a window next to a scene of Christ blessing the children, and a little roll of fame all its own recorded in tablets on the wall.

There is its first minister Frederic Myers, who preached here 13 years and is remembered for his writings on the Bible; there is his more famous son F. W. H. Myers, born and buried in Keswick, a man of keen intellectual gifts, who wrote on the Survival After Bodily Death; and James Clifton Ward, who as a geologist surveyed this district for ten years and ministered here for a while.

All will want to go to the museum here for its relics of the poets. Among other treasures it has is a model of Lakeland made by Joseph Flintoft, who had to measure the countryside himself and took 17 years to complete it. There is the amazing Rock, Bell, and Steel

Band of Joseph Richardson, consisting of about 60 stones, 60 steel bars, and 40 bells, the longest stone measuring more than a yard and the smallest bell being about two inches across. All are mounted on a huge piece of furniture ready to be struck by hammers, the long stones giving the lowest notes and the small bells the highest. Four men are needed to play this extraordinary instrument. Keswick also has in its safe keeping a fine collection of Lakeland pictures painted by Turner when in his early twenties. They have been given to the town by a generous American, John D. Anderson, who has long loved this corner of the Motherland.

Within a mile of the town are two noble viewpoints belonging to the National Trust. One is Friars Crag, memorial to Canon Rawnsley,

who, greatly loving the fair things of Nature and Art,
set all his love to the service of God and man.

In the place where we stand to look out over the lake is a carved portrait of Ruskin whose earliest memory was of being brought here by his nurse. This scene he must have thought of a thousand times when he wrote and talked of beauty. This view of Derwentwater and the mountains he ranked among the three or four most beautiful in Europe, and there are these fine words from him inscribed on his memorial here:

The spirit of God is around you in the air that you breathe, His glory in the light that you see, and in the fruitfulness of the Earth, and the joy of its creatures.

The other viewpoint is Castle Head close by, a wooded hill rocky at the top. It is all that is left of a volcano, and must have played its part in forming Lakeland. From it the panorama is grand indeed, ranging from England's highest point Scafell to Criffel, 30 miles away in Scotland. On three sides the mountains are magnificent, and below us is Derwentwater looking its loveliest. Among the tree-covered islands helping to make its charm are St Herbert's, home of the saint 13 centuries ago; and Lord's, where once there stood the house of the Radcliffes and the Derwentwaters, before the last earl joined the Jacobites and lost his head on Tower Hill. Across the water are the woods of Brandelhow Park, the first big property acquired by the National Trust.

Still another impressive national possession is the Stone Circle two miles from the town, where 38 stones make a ring about 100 feet across. It is the most important relic of antiquity in Lakeland, unique for having within the circle an enclosure made by ten extra stones. It may go back to the Stone Age; it has pairs of stones pointing to the sunrise at midsummer and midwinter; it was perhaps used by the Druids and even by the early Christians; and it is believed to be from three to four thousand years old. No one quite knows its purpose, or how the great stones were brought and set up; but the imagination is stirred by it and our eyes are delighted by the magnificent scene in which this wonder stands.

Here Robert Southey lived for forty years, best friend of all the Lakeland poets and one of the best of men.

The Three Poets and the Three Sisters

HE was born in Bristol in 1774, his father being a tradesman there. An aunt brought him up and he was a youthful prodigy. At the age of eight he had read all Shakespeare and had the ambition to be a poet. An uncle who lived in Lisbon sent him first to Westminster School and afterwards to Oxford. He was turned out of the school because he wrote an essay making a much-needed protest against the violent thrashing of the scholars.

While at Oxford he met Coleridge. Both were intensely sympathetic towards the French Revolution which was convulsing Europe. At Bristol, they met a friend named Robert Lovell, who, like them, thought a new era was dawning on the world. The three young men set about planning an ideal life; they resolved that they would marry, emigrate to Pennsylvania and start an ideal way of living there. The only part of the plan that was fulfilled was the marrying. They married three sisters, and went their several ways.

Southey's aunt resented the marrying and cast off her nephew; but he sold an epic poem on Joan of Arc to Joseph Cottle, a friendly Bristol bookseller, for £50 and, promptly marrying, left his wife behind and sailed to see his uncle at Lisbon. Before this he had written a three-act drama on Wat Tyler into which he had emptied his revolutionary ardour, a work that was to be used against him maliciously in future years. He wrote solid books of history (Portugal and Brazil); he began a great series of poems on ancient mythologies; and for twenty years he was writing these ambitious poems, all exotic in their character. He barred himself from fame by his choice of subjects. He involved himself in misty studies that could not produce a sense of actuality. He laboured intensely, and the result is that he is not read and never will be read except by those who are interested in his remarkable experiments in rhythm, experiments which he carried on until they cloy. What he regarded as his serious work as a poet is now only a curiosity in literature. The misdirection of his poetic energy is pathetic, for Southey had a passionate belief in his achievements, and did not hesitate to link his own name with that of Milton.

Where the main ambitions of his life were concerned Southey was impractical, but he was not impractical in ordinary life. His travels he always turned to good account by writing of them, and he could write in an interesting way about almost anything. Constantly, too, he was writing verses, simple verses, ballads, odds and ends of poetry, in the simple way that Wordsworth had insisted was the best way. His verses of this kind made him widely known.

Southey now plunged into general literary work, living for cheapness and health in the country, before he made a second journey to Portugal to collect more materials for his massive historical labours. After his return came his final settlement at Greta Hall, Keswick, which he made his home for 40 years.

The Hall was a house made into two houses. Coleridge with his family was in one of them and he suggested that Southey should take the house next door. The Wordsworths had been within walking distance at Grasmere for several years. With Southey came Mrs Lovell and her child, for Lovell had recently died. So the three sisters who had married poets were again gathered under one roof. Presently Coleridge, unmanned by opium, set forth on his vague wanderings, and Southey was left in Greta Hall with three families to support. It is by his work done there in these circumstances that he has won the world's unstinted admiration.

He came there with a library of 4000 books; when he died it had accumulated to 14,000. No man ever loved books more than Southey. They were read and marked and all the family employed in making extracts from them for possible future use. From his Commonplace Books four volumes with 1500 pages have been printed. When he died he left a great mass of unpublished manuscripts.

A turning point, so far as money was concerned, came when he began to contribute to the Quarterly Review, and his articles were so greatly appreciated that he wrote for nearly every number, and received as much as £100 for an article. But this was the kind of writing of which he was least proud.

In 1813 he was appointed poet laureate on the suggestion of Sir Walter Scott, to whom the post had been offered.

Southey's later years were beclouded by the mental failure of his devoted wife. After her death he married Caroline Bowles, whom he had known, chiefly through correspondence, for 20 years. His own mind was failing at the time and that excellent lady, a poet herself, had three difficult years as his nurse. In 1840 Wordsworth called and Southey did not recognise him. He died in 1843. His last year was passed as in a trance. He would walk slowly round his library looking at his books and putting his hand to his brow say "Memory, memory, where art thou gone?" Remembering those last years when his brain was outworn with long labour these lines written by him in his library are surely among the saddest in all literature.

My days among the Dead are past,
Around me I behold,
Where'er these casual eyes are cast,
The mighty minds of old;
My never-failing friends are they
With whom I converse day by day.

My hopes are with the Dead, anon
My place with them will be,
And I with them shall travel on
Through all Futurity;
Yet leaving here a name, I trust,
That will not perish in the dust.

His name will not live in the kind of fame he hoped for in his ponderous books and ambitious poems, but it will live in such perfect little poems as his Battle of Blenheim expressing the irony of War; in an unselfish life of prolonged endeavour; and in a spirit that knew no jealousies. Southey was a true poet, a charming writer, and a good man who wore himself out somewhat fruitlessly because he did not see what were the things he was best fitted to do.

War on the Borderland

KIRKANDREWS-ON-ESK. From the map it seems as though this bit of England north of the Esk should be Scotland, and the Scots were of that opinion for centuries.

To the north is the long straight Scots Dyke made to stop their invasions; in the meadows by the church is the massive square tower of the defenders; and a mile or so away is all that remains of a border fortress of 700 years ago. But the Dyke is overgrown with trees; only the earthworks known as Liddel Strength are left of the old fortress; and cottagers have made the old tower their home, passing through an imposing gateway into the courtyard.

Close to Liddel Strength is a road from which the Romans had a tempting view of Scotland. A view is all that the church of Kirkandrews has, for it is an uninspired building looking out on to meadows shaded by stalwart oaks and across the Esk to the beautiful woods of Netherby Park.

Four years of war changed more than the views in this neighbourhood for suddenly there arrived here thousands of people working day and night, first to build vast munition works, then to start on the munitions themselves. The Government ruled from Annan to Longtown, running the farms, the inns, and the shops with its officials, and turning this quiet stretch of country to a hive of industry. The mark of those war years was still showing when we passed through.

Between the Esk and the Sark lies Solway Moss. Here is a description of it by William Gilpin, an 18th-century Cumberland writer.

The Great Barrier Bursts Its Bounds

SOLWAY MOSS is a flat area about seven miles in circumference. The substance of it is a gross fluid, composed of mud and the putrid fibres of heath, diluted by internal springs, which arise in every part. The surface is a dry crust, covered with moss and rushes; offering a fair appearance over an unsound bottom—shaking under the least pressure. Cattle by instinct know, and avoid it. Where rushes grow the bottom is soundest. The adventurous passenger, therefore, who sometimes, in dry seasons, traverses this perilous waste to save a few miles, picks his cautious way over the rushy tussocks, as they appear before him. If his foot slip, or if he venture to desert this mark of security, it is possible he may never more be heard of.

Solway Moss is bounded on the south by a cultivated plain which declines gently, through the space of a mile, to the River Esk. This plain is rather lower than the Moss itself, being separated from it by a breastwork formed by digging peat, which makes an irregular, though perpendicular, line of low black boundary.

It was the bursting of the Moss through this peat breastwork, over the plain between it and the Esk, which occasioned that dreadful ruin the effects of which we came hither to explore. The more remarkable circumstances, relating to this calamitous event, as we had them on the best authority, were these.

On the 16th of November 1771, in a dark tempestuous night, the inhabitants of the plain were alarmed with a dreadful crash which they could in no way account for. Many of them were then abroad in the fields watching their cattle lest the Esk, which was rising violently in the storm, would carry them off. None of those miserable people could conceive the noise they had heard to proceed from any cause but the overflowing of the river in some shape, though to them unaccountable. Such indeed as lived nearer the source of the eruption were sensible that the noise came in a different direction, but were equally at a loss for the cause.

In the meantime the enormous mass of fluid substance moved slowly on, spreading itself more and more as it got possession of the plain. Some of the inhabitants, through the terror of the night, could plainly discover it advancing like a moving hill. This was in fact the case, for the gush of mud carried before it through the first two or three hundred yards of its course a part of the breastwork which, though low, was yet several feet in perpendicular height. But it soon deposited this solid mass and became a heavy fluid. One house after another it spread round, filled, and crushed into ruin, just giving time to the terrified inhabitants to escape. Scarce anything was saved except their lives; nothing of their furniture, few of their cattle. Some people were even surprised in their beds and had the additional distress of flying naked from the ruin.

The morning light explained the cause of this amazing scene of horror and showed the calamity in its full extent, and yet among all the conjectures of that dreadful night the mischief which really happened had never been supposed. Who could have imagined that a breastwork which had stood for ages should at length give way, or that those subterranean floods which had been bedded in darkness since the memory of man should ever burst from their black abode?

This dreadful inundation, though the first shock of it was the most tremendous, continued spreading for many weeks till it covered the whole plain, an area of five hundred acres, and, like molten metal poured into a mould, filled all the hollows of it, lying in some parts thirty or forty feet deep, reducing the whole to one level surface. The overplus found its way into the Esk where its quantity was such as to annoy the fish; no salmon, during that season, venturing into the river. We were assured also that many lumps of earth which had floated out to sea were taken up some months later at the Isle of Man.

The Strange Story of Thomas Story

KIRKBAMPTON. It is within three miles of the sea and within six of Scotland, a trim and far-spread village with a little wayside church proud of its fine Norman craftsmanship, and with something twice as old, for in the chancel wall is an inscribed Roman stone.

All about are remains of defensive work which protected the English against the Scots, one acre field with a double ditch and a double rampart. In the churchyard lies a Scottish raider of those days, his gravestone fixed to the south wall, though it was perishing when we called. He is said to have been found asleep in a field by a villager who took up the sword at his side and slew him.

It is the fine Norman doorway that is the proud possession of Kirkbampton, and rare in this countryside. It has columns with carved capitals, a rich and lofty arch, and a tympanum in which a figure with a pastoral staff is wearing away. The finest possession indoors is the massive arch between the white-walled nave and the dim and narrow chancel. The arch rests on scalloped capitals, and is splendid in its simple Norman strength.

There is a fine Norman lancet, one with a modern portrait of Peter, and a 700-year-old trinity of windows with Our Lord and minstrel angels.

A church of fine possessions it is, and yet one thing we remember here above all others, the tragic tale of Thomas Story. He held the living here for 60 years from 1679 to 1739 and he has no memorial, but one thing everybody in Kirkbampton knows is that before he died himself he had *buried every man and woman and child who was living in his parish when he came.*

The Curate's Tragedy

KIRKBRIDE. It lies in the great marshlands at the mouth of the River Wampool, a tiny old church crowning its lonely hill.

We found the rooks holding parliament in the elms which shelter the church the Normans built. They used much material from the

Roman fort once on this site, and though the church has been restored there is much old work in its rough stone walls: a simple Norman doorway, two deep Norman lancets, and a sturdy Norman chancel arch of a very rare kind, for it has an altar recess at each side. The recesses are as old as the arch; their sills were used as altars.

In the east window of the dim chancel are three figures of St Columba, St Patrick, and St Bridget, Bridget being the patron saint; she was the renowned abbess of Kildare, who in her youth wove St Patrick's shroud.

An ancient sculpture of the Entombment hangs on the wall of the chancel arch, and in the sanctuary is a holy-water trough carved with the lamb; it was found in the rector's garden. The font is about 600 years old.

A small brass on the outside wall carved with cherubs tells of a curate's tragedy. He was Lancelot Thompson, who in the 18th century lost his wife and six children in three weeks during an outbreak of smallpox.

The Queen's Ring

KIRKCAMBECK. A very small village and a lonely one, it has a few houses in a hollow, and a hillside mound with a stone arch about as high as a man. Perhaps this arch was part of the old church; we do not know, but we do know that the little 19th-century church has a doorway made of stones from a predecessor 600 years before, and that built into the south wall is an old inscription with a flowered cross between a chalice and a book.

The doorway of the porch gives Kirkcambeck its touch of romance, for over it is a stone carving of a fish, reminding us of the story of St Kentigern to whom the church is dedicated. It is the legend of King Roderick's wife and how she gave her ring to a knight; how the king stole it back and threw it into the River Clyde; and how the queen was condemned to death if she could not produce the ring within three days. She appealed to St Kentigern for help, and after he had prayed a salmon was caught and the ring found inside it.

About a mile from the village is Askerton Castle, thought to have been built in the 16th century, a forbidding place with two massive embattled towers and an array of little windows. There are yews in the garden, and a barn close by is adorned with a quaint weathervane of a man holding a hound in leash.

The Long Green Mounds

KIRKLAND. With a church and a few houses and a small stone bridge over a rushing stream, it lies in distant solitude at the end of two miles of lonely road, the way to the foot of Cross Fell from which there is a magnificent view over six shires.

The church has mountains immediately behind it, and is a very simple place refashioned last century. In its bellcot are two bells rung by chains from bell-ringers standing in the porch. In the nave is a plain oak chest several centuries old; but it is in the chancel that we come upon the chief human delights of Kirkland. Here is a battered stone figure of a 13th-century warrior in a long tunic and with a sword, his hair curling over his ears, and his face seeming to smile though he holds in his hands a broken heart. And here on the floor are brass inscriptions to three charming 17th-century folk, Daniel Fleming, of whom we read that he never failed in courtesy, his wife Isabel, whose epitaph says Let her own works praise her in the gates, and their son, who was just in his ways and faithful to his friend. A most delightful family they are to find in this remote spot among some of England's greatest mountains.

The churchyard has a slender sandstone cross, leaning considerably, with a hole in the head not unlike an eye; and two or three fields away are the three terraces known hereabouts, for no reason we could discover, as the Walls of Mark Anthony, long green mounds thought to have been made long ago for growing cereals. They are perhaps associated with the Roman road called Maiden Way which runs northward from Kirkland.

At Bank Hall, now a farm, are fragments of stables and other buildings still left from the old home of the Crackenthorpes.

Tom Tompion's Nephew

KIRKLINTON. This scattered hamlet near the River Lyne is said to have a bit of Hadrian's Wall in its church. Saxon gravestones are with Norman in the belfry, and the fine Norman chancel arch has been set up again as the tower arch. Four monoliths, two large and two small, are used as shafts to hold up this ancient arch with its two massive rows of ornament. Parts of Kirklinton Hall are 300 years old, but mostly it is 19th century, an imposing house in beautiful grounds, with a splendid avenue of trees down to the river.

Hereabouts was born George Graham, whose astronomical instruments were as wonderfully made as the clocks of his uncle Tom Tompion. Born here in 1673, he was apprenticed at 13 to a London watchmaker. As a young man he was befriended by Tompion, the Father of English Watchmaking, who made him his assistant, and gave him his niece in marriage.

It was not until he launched out for himself that Graham's inventive faculties bore fruit, to make him the foremost man of his age for originality in contriving and skill and accuracy in making clocks, watches, and astronomical instruments. He furnished the apparatus used by Bradley in observing the fixed stars, and the instruments which enabled the French expedition of 1735 to measure an arc of the meridian in the Arctic.

The most complete planetarium then known for demonstrating the movement of the stars (called an orrery after his patron the Earl of Orrery) was his work, but Graham's greatest achievement was a pendulum in which the bob carries a cylinder of mercury, with the effect that when the pendulum is lengthened by heat the quicksilver and its container are expanded and elevated, and the centre of oscillation is thus continued at the same distance from the point of suspension, with the result that the clock continues to keep correct time.

A Quaker, and a member of learned societies, Graham gave his discoveries as freely to the world as he lent money to the needy, without interest. Detesting usury, he refused to bank lest his money should earn interest, but kept his riches in his own safe. He died in 1751, and lies in the same grave with his famous uncle Tompion, in Westminster Abbey.

The Domain of a Great House

KIRKOSWALD. One of the most charming little towns in Cumberland, it is nearly all built of red sandstone and delightfully embowered in trees. Hereabouts are found things left behind by the Romans and the Saxons, and the town has a grim memory of the Scots who raided and burned it after Bannockburn. For the pilgrim today it has three especial attractions, a castle, a church, and a house.

The castle, on high ground, shows finely among the trees and is seen against a background of great mountains. Still protected by a deep and wide moat with water in it, the chief ruins are a wall with vaulted dungeons, and a fine turret 65 feet high, complete except for its battlements. Within is a much-broken spiral stair. Traces of the gatehouse site are still here, and there are considerable remains of the towers 50 feet apart, each with a basement and two floors above. The active life of the castle was about 500 years, for it was founded in the 12th century and dismantled, like so many others, in the 17th. Its famous collection of portraits of our English kings went to Naworth, where they were unhappily destroyed by fire.

The church is extraordinary for having its 19th-century tower 200 yards away, small and low and square. We cannot even see it until we walk a little way up the churchyard, and then it comes into view perched on the hilltop. Below the west window of the church is a stone well whose water comes from a stream flowing under the nave. It is one of the odd features of this exterior; another is the porch, with its projecting gable and its massive, weatherworn beams resting on two great wooden supports on low stone bases. Within is a door with old iron hinges and an old oak bench with poppyheads.

The nave is narrow, separated from the wide aisles by low arcades of three arches. Two arches on each side are Norman, but the western arches are 13th century and rest on great stone heads with savage faces 600 years old. The west window is perhaps 14th century, the built-up south doorway is 13th, and the bowl of the font is Norman. Oldest of all is a fragment built into one of the windowsills, part of a cross-head probably made before the Conqueror was born. Kept here in a small case are fragments of a chalice and a paten found last century in a grave; they must be several centuries old.

The chancel, approached through an unusually high and narrow arch with a big niche one side and a small one the other, contains many inscriptions to the Fetherstonhaughs. Most interesting is one in marble to the devoted Royalist Sir Timothy who was taken prisoner at Wigan Lane and beheaded at Chester in 1651. Another tells of a Timothy 200 years later, who was tragically killed by a falling tree in front of his own house. On the wall is a broken fragment of a 17th-century monument with small kneeling figures of Thomas Bartram and his wife. He is shown in a high collar, and she has a hat like a cottage loaf on a dish. There are also two sons and a daughter. In this church John Fisher, son of a minister who preached at Lorton for 59 years, himself served for 57.

In the churchyard are several medieval gravestones carved with crosses and swords and shears, their inscriptions now hardly legible, and across the road is the charming gateway of the most interesting house in Kirkoswald, called the College since the days before the Reformation.

Through the arches of the gateway are peeps of clipped yew hedges and many tall trees in the garden. The house has the remains of an immensely strong tower, and for more than 300 years it has belonged to the Fetherstonhaughs. Now it is a museum with a great show of old china, glass, pictures, furniture, and other curios of exceptional interest. Here are the long oak table at which the old priests would sit, an old sideboard, a settle, and a fine array of pewter. There is a ring with an enamel miniature of Charles Stuart, and a portrait of him given by Charles the Second in memory of the brave Sir Timothy. It shows the king in a green coat, his hands raised as in astonishment.

Their Cause Prevailed

LAMPLUGH. Two things at Lamplugh will appeal to all who see them, one the group of demon gargoyles looking down from the church, the other a fine Elizabethan gateway with the name and arms of John Lamplugh. It leads to the Hall where the Lamplughs were living 750 years ago, and where some of the farm buildings are made of stones from their fortified tower.

The church has been much renewed, but some of it is 600 years old, and there is a charming little window with two carved faces. One of the old memorials is to Thomas and Francis Lamplugh, the other being to their daughter, who was born in 1693 and died within a few months of her wedding.

The organ was given in gratitude for "the best of wives," and the attractive panelling round the nave is a war memory of three brave sons. Their names are among those on the cross outside, which holds in remembrance all the sons of Lamplugh,

Who, when there was war on Earth
Fought against evil and gave their lives:
But their cause prevailed.

The Noble Monument in the Meadows

LANERCOST. Here in the meadows by the River Irthing stands one of the noblest monuments to the past in all Cumberland, Lanercost Priory, alone with a few houses in a thickly wooded valley where the autumn beeches are glorious. Coming to it from Brampton, we cross the river by a beautiful Tudor bridge of two arches.

The great priory church, 700 years old and more, is the centrepiece of it all, the nave still used for worship and the rest a splendid ruin. With it are other priory buildings of great interest, and here in the meadow is a 12th-century arch from the old gatehouse, interesting as the place where our great Edward the First was three times met by the monks. Once he came here with Queen Eleanor, and at the priory he spent his last winter, terrifying the Scots by his presence, though his day was almost done. Often in the 13th and 14th centuries Lanercost suffered at the hands of raiders from over the border.

The part of the church still used has a splendid west front with a group of three tall lancets above a row of blind arches. At the bottom is a doorway with many mouldings, and at the top in the gable is a niche with a carving of Mary Magdalene and a kneeling monk. Two stone heads on the north wall are said to be portraits of Edward the First and his queen.

The interior of the nave gains its effect from a handsome 13th-century arcade and a singularly beautiful clerestory whose arches are rich with ornament inside and out. A blocked doorway in the aisle makes a frame for the celebrated Lanercost Cross, the shaft of which is here with part of a Latin inscription, saying it was made in 1214, in the 17th year of the Interdict, Innocent the Third holding the Apostolic See, Otho being King of Germany, Philip King of France, John of England, and William of Scotland. The base of the cross is outside in the meadow.

The east end, built after the priory was dismantled, cuts off the nave from the ruins beyond, and has a little 16th-century glass with the arms of the Dacres, to one of whom Henry the Eighth gave the priory. There are some Burne-Jones lancets rich in colour, one showing three figures looking up at an angel; also by Burne-Jones are the medallion portraits of Charles Howard and his wife, with panels below showing the Nativity and the Burial of Our Lord. There is an inscription to George Gilbanks of last century, who preached here 58 years, and a brass tablet to Dr Addison who lies near a yew in the churchyard. The Addison ward in Guy's Hospital is named in honour of this great 18th-century physician, who for 37 years was an unselfish and tireless worker at this famous London hospital.

A door in the aisle brings us into the stately ruins of the transepts, the central tower, and the choir, all roofless, but with their walls almost at full height. The east wall has two sets of three lancets, and high up in it is a Roman altar dedicated to Jupiter, one of the very few in our English churches. Another wall has many Roman stones from Hadrian's Wall built about a thousand years before the Priory.

In the north transept, under an arched recess, is the oldest tomb in Lanercost, that of Sir Roland de Vaux. His name reminds us that it was another de Vaux, Robert, who founded the priory in 1169. In the same transept is a chapel, perfectly vaulted, where we see an impressive 15th-century altar tomb with bold carvings of shields held by angels and curious winged animals. Here lies Lord Humphrey Dacre of Naworth Castle, and his wife who was a kinswoman of Catherine Parr. Near by is an exquisite little terracotta monument by Sir Edgar Boehm, showing Elizabeth Dacre Howard as a smiling baby fast asleep, her right hand holding a rose with a spray of leaves. Among others of the Howards buried at Lanercost are the ninth Earl of Carlisle who died 1911, and his wife, both remembered as workers in the cause of Temperance. The earl, when he came to his title, closed the public houses on his estates in Yorkshire and Cumberland. He is remembered, too, as a skilful painter in water colours, and a great friend of his brother artists; at his home at Castle Howard he had a notable collection of pictures.

On the south side of the choir is an immense tomb filling the space between two pillars of the arcade. It is about 15 feet long and is under a very low arch like a stone bridge. The sides of the tomb are heavily panelled with shields held by winged beasts, angels, and two great fish standing on their tails, all in memory of Lord Thomas Dacre, who commanded the right wing at Flodden Field and more than once helped to defend England from the Scots.

Here on a windowsill when we called was a battered stone figure of another of the Dacres, curious because it has been used as some-one else's memorial. Carved on it is an inscription to John Crow of 1709, who is said to have fallen down from the clerestory.

By a stairway at the west end of the nave we can come to one of the old monastic buildings known as the Dacre Hall, with its old beams in the roof, its remains of a minstrel gallery, and its very large fire-place. A small room close by has a plaster frieze with winged animals holding shields, and a little window looking back into the church.

The windows of the Dacre Hall look down to the cloisters, where there are traces of a fine 13th-century arcade, and where the steps lead down to one of the best sights of all, the undercroft, 102 feet long. It is under what was once the monks' refectory, and has a beautiful vaulted roof resting on pillars which still look new after 700 years. Here is treasured a collection of stones carved by the Normans and the 13th-century men; and here also are fragments of Roman stones and altars, one of the altars with beautiful ornament, and a wild boar, the emblem of the 20th legion.

Among the many old buildings attached to the Priory is Edward's Tower, now the vicarage. It is a 13th-century tower with very thick walls, but greatly altered, and in it we are shown the very place where Edward the First is said to have slept, an oddly-shaped bedroom with very small windows.

They Never Fail

LANGWATHBY. Here is a bridge to lean on for a view of the River Eden, grown broad at this bend, but we must not believe the date 1686 on one of its stones, for the bridge has been made new since then. Among the red houses round the fine big green stands a little red church with a double bellcot, and with stairs in its porch to an upper room, where is an old oak chest.

A window from this vestry looks down into the nave which has roughly shaped beams in its roof and on its west wall pieces of armour which the villagers buckled on in the 16th century. There are two breastplates, a helmet, and other bits from the store which most villages kept ready in those days.

Some 400 years later the villagers again turned soldiers, this time in a world war. Those who never came back are remembered in Byron's proud words, *They never fail who die in a great cause.*

The Giant's Cave

LAZONBY. It stands above a fine curve of the River Eden, with houses looking away to a splendid sandstone bridge of four arches, and with many old possessions. One is a tall Scotch fir over 200 years old; another a weathered stone which was part of the village stocks; and a third an ancient cross crowned by a cube with a little cross tilted back to make a sundial. The shaft is believed to be at least 800 years old.

The 19th-century church is built rather oddly on the side of a great pyramid hill. It has an Elizabethan altar cup, and there is a fragment of a medieval gravestone in the churchyard; but we remember it chiefly for its carving, done by Canon Wilson who was laid here in 1921 after a ministry of 40 years. His loving hands adorned the two screens and the south door and much of the church furniture, and fashioned the little angels on the pulpit. The chancel was panelled and ornamented by him, and more of his carving is cherished in these village homes.

Near Baronwood is the big cave, Giant's Chamber, said to have served as a place of refuge when the Scots came over the border.

Long Meg and Her Daughters

LITTLE SALKELD. Here on a hill is a famous family perhaps twice as old as Christianity, Long Meg and Her Daughters. We may call them Cumberland's Stonehenge, for they make up a stone circle nearly 400 yards round, the biggest in the land after Stonehenge itself.

High above the village we find them, at a magnificent viewpoint where most of the Cumberland mountains are in sight. There are 67 in the family circle, many of the stones being exceptionally large and almost all shapeless. Some are higher than a man, and are 10 or 15 feet round. A few are now level with the ground. Some are rocks of greenstone, others are limestone or granite. Long Meg herself stands alone a few yards away, 18 feet high and 15 feet round, and weighing, we imagine, about 17 tons. She is roughly tapering and slightly round-shouldered, and facing her are four big daughters, making a crude sort of gateway.

It is a place to stand and wonder, a place where history and religion grow dim. Here in the mind's eye we may imagine the ancient folk and their ceremonies, and here we feel as Wordsworth felt when he came and afterwards wrote:

A weight of awe, not easy to be borne,
Fell suddenly upon my spirit, cast
From the dread bosom of the unknown past,
When first I saw that family forlorn.

Little Salkeld has its few houses on a green hillside. It has also a 17th-century Hall much rebuilt in the 18th century, and a very small chapel which was once a barn and still looks like one. It has a tiny wooden porch and a small bell on an iron stand above the roof. More interesting are Lacy's Caves about a mile away by the river Eden, natural cavities artificially enlarged and shaped.

Last Town in England

LONGTOWN. It is the last town in England on the high road from Carlisle to Scotland, a place of exceptionally spacious streets and rather dull old houses. Here a stone bridge of five arches now spans the River Esk, but hereabouts in 1745 the retreating army of the Young Pretender had to wade across, with the water shoulder high. It is said that their pipers began to play as soon as they reached the other side, and that the soldiers set about drying themselves by dancing.

A little way off at Arthuret stands the 17th-century church, a very long building with embattled parapets, and with a massive western tower from whose doorway are spacious views. The interior has beautiful stalls and altar rails, a little old panelling, and a curious font with nine sides; but it is chiefly interesting for its memories of the Grahams, one of whom was rector 47 years. It was by his efforts that the land hereabouts was made a productive area.

There is a wall monument to Sir George Graham of 1657, and another to a more famous figure, Sir James Graham, who was laid to rest here in 1861. Prominent in the politics of his day, he was one of the four who prepared the first Reform Bill. Later becoming a Tory, he served under Sir Robert Peel, and made himself unpopular by ordering that the letters of Mazzini and other political refugees should be opened. He was in office again under Lord Aberdeen and then under Lord Palmerston, but he resigned with Gladstone and others when the conduct of the Crimean War was under criticism.

In the churchyard stands an ancient cross eight feet high, and both here and in the vicarage garden we noticed some old yews. Close by is the earthwork called Arthuret Knowes, a big tree-grown mound with a very long history, for it is said to be the site of the great battle of Ardderyd in 573, about a century and a half after the Romans left our shores and about a generation before Augustine came.

Arthuret was the birthplace of that odd 17th-century figure Archibald Armstrong, known to everyone as Archie. We fear he was chiefly known in Cumberland as a sheep-stealer of Eskdale, but in higher circles he had quite another reputation. He belonged to the household of James the First when he was king only of Scotland, and, coming with him to England, was such a favourite that the king made him Court jester. Under Charles Stuart he held the same post, until, having insulted Archbishop Laud, he was expelled from Court. Back to Arthuret he came in his retirement, and here he lies, but there is no monument to him in this churchyard.

Four miles away at the hamlet of Brackenhill stands an old tower in a setting of fine trees above the River Lyne. It was four years old when Drake finished his game of bowls on Plymouth Hoe.

Wordsworth and Old Yew

LORTON. Its river is the Cocker, flowing from Crummock Water down beautiful Lorton Vale; and its little place in poetry is in Wordsworth, who wrote of the old village yew as

a living thing
Produced too slowly ever to decay;
Of form and aspect too magnificent
To be destroyed.

These words he wrote in 1803, and the great yew for all its broken branches is flourishing still. Beside it, with Cromwell's soldiers looking on, George Fox preached the gospel of Quakerism to a great crowd of people, so many of whom were in the tree itself that he feared they would end the meeting by bringing it down.

The chief beauty of the church is its richly coloured window showing the group of figures round the empty tomb of Jesus. It has little other interest, but what it lacks is found among the graves outside. Here lies Thomas Fisher, who ministered in Lorton for 59 years and saw the first 26 days of the 19th century; his son John was vicar of Kirkoswald for 57 years, so that father and son served the Church for 116 years. Close by lies Daniel Fisher, with a terse little rhyme speaking volumes:

On tombstones praise is vainly spent,
Good works is man's best monument.

The Vale of Lorton is more richly agricultural than the outskirts of the Lake District generally. A good general view of it, up and down, can be seen from the road at Swinside between the Whinlatter Pass and the village of Loweswater.

Old John

LOWESWATER. The lake is a little one, but pretty in the way woodlands come down to its southern edge. The upper part, however, is scarcely typical of Lakeland scenery. Loweswater church is half-way to the next lake, Crummock Water, and the finest thing about it is its setting among the fells.

Its chief human interest lies in its list of parsons, where we find Thomas Cowper coming in 1744 and staying 51 years; and it is almost certain that old John Borranskail, who was laid to rest here in 1674, had been ministering for the great span of 73 years. He would be a boy when the Armada came; he would be preaching here when Queen Elizabeth died, and when Charles died, and Cromwell; and he was preaching long after the second Charles came back.

Twenty Roman Altars

MARYPORT. It was a workaday town when the Romans climbed its steep streets, mounting on both sides of a bold ridge by the sea; they built a station covering four acres here with four gateways and roads radiating to all parts of Cumberland. Today, alas, it is a workaday town no more, for it is in the grip of Depression.

Here it was that there was found last century an unrivalled collection of Roman altars. We have come upon a few here and there in England, but Cumberland has them in dozens. In the great house of Netherhall here, set in lovely gardens at one end of the town with the beautiful park through which the River Ellen runs, it has preserved them as jealously as it preserves its secret room. Nearly 20 Roman altars were found here in pits, where it is thought they may have been put for safety when the camp was deserted for a time, and today the more imposing altars are in the portico of the house, the smaller ones in a summer-house in the garden. One, inscribed to Jupiter, had just been given to Italy when we called, a treasure from almost the farthest north reached by Roman soldiers.

Sheltered by the trees facing the park is a spacious church which was not 50 years old when we called. It has no chancel arch, a rudely carved oak beam dividing the chancel from the nave. The reredos has rich oak canopies, the pulpit is carved in Jacobean style, and there is a lovely wall mosaic of St Martin on horseback giving half of his cloak to the beggar. A fine oriel window looks out of the tower into the nave, a very unexpected peep.

A richly traceried oak screen runs round the peace memorial chapel, where an angel watches over a panel with 68 names that live for evermore. Here it is that we find the best glass in the church, with a scene of the battlefield and a portrait of Major Proud kneeling beside a stretcher with a first-aid case, Our Lord standing by in a red robe with a jewelled crown. In the east window is an unusual Jesse tree, crowned by the Madonna and Child, the branches tracing the descent of Jesus winding between eight scenes of His childhood. Most of the windows round the church fill up the story of His life.

The Poet Wanders Lonely as a Cloud

MATTERDALE. Here we found a sight that thrilled the heart of Wordsworth, and which we should like to feel will be seen here every spring as long as English poetry lasts. For here it was that Wordsworth saw his host of daffodils; here he

Gazed and gazed but little thought
What wealth the show to him had brought.

A thousand times he remembered the sight of these daffodils and he put them in our minds for ever with one of the loveliest verses that have ended an immortal poem:

For oft when on my couch I lie
In vacant or in pensive mood,
They flash upon that inward eye
Which is the bliss of solitude;
And then my heart with pleasure fills,
And dances with the daffodils.

We are here about 1000 feet up, two miles from Ullswater, and the turret of a little church is watching over the road from Keswick to the lake. Simple and dignified, its roots are lost in the centuries. One of the great beams in the low roof is dated several years before the Armada. Very attractive is the old panelled woodwork, including a pulpit with a canopy and a knob for the preacher's gown. The rails round three sides of the altar are 17th century, and above is a charming little coloured window of the Nativity.

The sandstone font stands in an old square singing seat and has had some odd adventures. It was turned out of Greystoke church more than 200 years ago; it was used as a cheese press at a hamlet along the road, and it was put up in this churchyard as a sundial before it found its way into the church.

Riding on down the hill from Dockray we see the mountains rise up in majesty round Ullswater, and we walk across the fields to Aira Force, where a mountain stream pours out in a white torrent and falls foaming for 70 feet between walls of solid rock, marvellously enriched by nature's green. The two little bridges across the water are memorials to faithful servants of the Motherland, one in memory of Sir Cecil Spring-Rice, ambassador at Washington in the difficult years of the Great War, and the other in memory of two of his kin who gave their lives for England.

Aira Force belongs to the nation for ever, together with 750 lovely acres of Gowbarrow Park beside Ullswater. Here stands the 18th-century house called Lyulph's Tower, and it is near here that Wordsworth, wandering lonely as a cloud, saw on the banks of Ullswater

A host of golden daffodils,
Beside the lake, beneath the trees,
Fluttering and dancing in the breeze.

Happily we know exactly where and when Wordsworth had this lovely vision, and also who it was who gave him eyes to see it, and helped him to interpret it. It was his sister Dorothy. On April 15, 1802, the two were staying with Thomas Clarkson at Eusemere, near Pooley Bridge. As we know from Dorothy's entry in her Journal for that day, after their midday meal they set off to walk along the western side of the lake. When they had passed round the foot of the lake they rested awhile in a boathouse. They rested again about two miles further on, in Watermillock Lane. Having passed Gowbarrow Park, and entered the wood beyond, approaching Lyulph's Tower, they saw a few daffodils and fancied the lake had floated the seeds ashore, so close were the flowers to the water.

But, says Dorothy, "As we went along there were more and yet more; and at last under the boughs of the trees we saw that there was a long belt of them along the shore, about the breadth of a country turnpike road. I never saw daffodils so beautiful. They grew among the mossy stones, about and above them; some rested their heads upon these stones, as on a pillow, for weariness; and the rest tossed and reeled and danced, and seemed as if they verily laughed with the wind, they looked so gay, ever glancing, ever changing."

The scenery immediately round Matterdale is commonplace, and only redeemed by the distant views, northward, of the stern, rugged face of Saddleback; but the 500-feet descent southward through woods to Ullswater between Gowbarrow and Glencoin Parks, with Place Fell beyond the lake, High Street and Red Screes still further beyond, and presently the fine uplift of St Sunday Crag, makes an impressive entrance to the upper reach of Ullswater. Many regard this scene as the finest near companionship of gentle inland waters and rugged mountains in Lakeland. This downward approach is only surpassed by the similar combination as seen from Ullswater itself, on the steamer up the lake, which brings into the background Catchedicam, that noble outlier of mighty Helvellyn, and opens out the glens that seam Helvellyn's eastern flank.

Nature's Curious Way

MELMERBY. It is a delightful village at the foot of the mountains between Penrith and Alston. We look up and perhaps see the clouds resting on fells 2000 feet high. We look about us and find a swift mountain torrent, spacious greens, and trees everywhere. An odd feature is the way Melmerby people have planted their trees in little groups of three and four in the gardens and on the greens. Not far away the Roman road called Maiden Way goes over the fells, still traceable and often 18 feet wide. Big fragments of its original stone paving are still visible.

Melmerby Hall of many gables is partly Tudor, and hidden behind its trees is an old church nearly all refashioned last century. The battlemented tower has a curious stepped turret; some of the windows may be 600 years old. On the sanctuary floor are four gravestones, two under the altar. One is a memorial to a Threlkeld from the Hall, and has on it the family shield, a sword, and a flowered cross with what appear to be six big leaves on the stem. The base of the ancient churchyard cross is outside, and a long tunnel of holly and yew leads to the vicarage.

Melmerby is notable for what are called the Helm winds, a curious phenomenon perhaps caused by the cold air above the mountains. When the countryside round about has not a leaf stirring the village may have to battle against half a gale. It can be heard roaring down from the mountains. The cloud which seems to rest on the fells is called the Helm Bar.

A Hallowed Treasure House

MILLOM. A little town with great ironworks at the sandy mouth of the River Duddon, it sees the grandeur of the fells and looks over the water to the hills of Furness. Rising proudly above it as a landmark is the fine steeple of its 19th-century church by the market square; and a mile away, in company with the imposing ruins of an ancient castle, is the finest old church in this corner of Cumberland.

An avenue of limes brings us to the modern church, which is in 13th-century style and has great arches under the tower, a splendid arcade of five bays, a lofty barrel roof, and handsome windows, in two of which we see scenes of the first Easter morning and the Ascension. The oak lectern has an attractive little gallery of six figures in niches along the front: Matthew, Mark, Luke, John, St George, and St Michael with his sword and scales. In the churchyard is a tall cross in memory of the South African heroes, and where the ways meet near the church is a fine figure of St George, in memory of the heroes of the Great War. We saw it with the town gathered round on Armistice Day.

The old church lying so snugly under the castle walls is rich in the work of centuries long gone. Its tall north doorway is Norman, and so are the piers in the nave. The chancel is mainly 15th century, but it has a fine little Norman lancet, a simple piscina perhaps Norman too, a splendid wide arch, and a 14th-century east window with intersecting mullions. The wide south aisle also has some 14th-century windows, especially fine being the great five-light one at the east, the charming oval at the west (nicknamed the Fish Window), and a blocked window seen outside, from which two modern ones are copied. The glass we liked best was that showing Gabriel, Michael and Raphael with their trumpets, and figures of the Madonna and St John.

The organ is in the old gallery of the nave, and seems to lose itself in the ancient timbers of the fine black-and-white roof. Another splendid old roof is over the south aisle. The altar, behind the old rails, stands out from the east wall and is effectively set off against a modern screen with massive twisted pillars, a classical cornice, and a decoration of cherubs' heads. Among the smaller possessions of the church, kept in cases, are two old pitch pipes and two 17th-century pewter flagons.

Special treasures here are the tombs of the Huddlestons, whose arms we see carved on the big 15th-century font. There is a sandstone altar tomb with shields under canopies, believed to be that of

Sir John of 1494; and near by is the beautiful alabaster tomb whose sleeping Tudor figures may perhaps be Sir John's grandson Richard Huddleston and his wife Elizabeth, he a knightly figure with long hair and a collar of stars and roses over his armour, she in a fine gown, but alas without her arms. The tomb is adorned with angels under rich canopies, at their feet tiny kneeling figures. On one of the aisle windows when we called was the lower half of a very worn wooden sculpture, showing armour and traces of a belt. It is thought to represent a knight of the family who lived more than 500 years ago.

In the churchyard we see the Huddleston arms on the shaft of a 15th-century cross now crowned with a sundial. Near the north door is the base of a more ancient cross with traces of figures perhaps fashioned before the Normans came.

We think of the Huddlestons as they sleep in peace in this church, and we remember that it was one of the family, John Huddleston, who administered the last sacrament at the bedside of Charles the Second. We think of them again as we look at Millom Castle, for it was their home until the 18th century. Farm-buildings now stand among its ruined walls, and the gaunt, massive Tudor tower has become a farmhouse; but here still are a fine carved staircase and the old family arms over the fireplace in the courtleet room. In its great days the castle stood in a fine park, and, though never very big, it was very strong; some of the walls still left are seven feet thick. The lords of Millom wielded power over a very wide area, and we are vividly reminded of this in what is known as the Gallows Field not far away, where a 19th-century stone has this inscription:

On this spot stood a gallows, the ancient
Lords of Millom having exercised
Jura Regalia within their Seignory.

It is called the Hangstone, and Jura Regalia means, of course, the power of life and death.

A mile or two away by the sand dunes at Haverigg, close to the southernmost tip of Cumberland, is a simple 19th-century church where we noticed a great bell used as a flower vase.

MORESBY. Its pithead rises high above the 19th-century church, which stands on sea cliffs fortified by the Romans. We could trace the outline of their camp in the turf, and in the church are fragments of their pottery, discovered in the foundations.

The church is a formal little place with many pictures in its windows, and paintings on the pulpit of Christ teaching and Matthew and Paul with their books. On each side of the chancel arch is a bishop's head. A wooden cross from Flanders is in the porch. A holy-water stoup, a stone coffin lid marked with shears and a cross, and a stone head, all came from the old church, whose 13th-century chancel arch stands forlorn in the churchyard.

The old Hall facing the church hides its modern self behind a Jacobean front.

Soaring Carrock Fell

MOSEDALE. It lies on the eastern edge of Lakeland, and its few cottages are dominated by the rugged beauty of Carrock Fell, rising to 2174 feet above them. On the top, in a splendid position for defence, the ancient Britons had a fortified camp.

In our own time Carrock Fell has turned out to be one of the few places in England where the rare substance wolfram is found. From it comes tungsten, highly valuable in the making of steel and the filaments of electric lights.

The Luck of Muncaster

MUNCASTER. It has a noble place in our landscape and a famous place in our history; beauty and grandeur, pathos and tragedy, we think of here. The road over the hill is of great beauty as it skirts the park of Muncaster Castle with its fine gateway, and the beauty grows as we drop down to the valley of the Esk, with the sea in front of us, the river with its charming stone bridge, and the castle proudly set on a green terrace.

The castle is worthy of its lovely setting, standing in gardens surrounded by a park stocked with deer and famous for its rhododendrons. Not far from it are Roman ruins called Walls Castle, which may have been the baths for a Roman fort.

The castle of today goes back 600 years. It is the beautiful home of the long and illustrious line of Penningtons, whose crest of a mountain-cat we come upon in various places. It is a splendid pile of embattled walls and towers, and by the clock tower is still a room called King Henry's bedroom, after the king who slept in it, or lay sleepless in its bed.

He was Henry the Sixth, who was received here by Sir John Pennington and his wife after he had fled from the battle of Hexham;

it is said that the shepherds found him wandering over Muncaster Fell, a pitiful object, broken and defeated, and led him to this hospitable roof where he stayed for nine days.

The famous Luck of Muncaster is still here in memory of the king who gave it to his host with a prayer that the family might prosper so long as the glass remained unbroken. It is a small shallow green bowl decorated with gold and enamel and measuring six inches across. In the king's bedroom has been hanging for generations a picture of the king kneeling before an altar with the bowl in his hand. In the library is an old painting on a wood panel also showing King Henry with the Luck. Another interesting piece of timber in this great house is the panelling in the billiard room; it comes from the Fighting Temeraire, the ship famous on its own account and for Turner's painting of it.

About a mile from the castle on the road to High Eskholme is a white stone monument marking the spot where the unhappy king is believed to have been found by the shepherds.

The memorials to the Penningtons are in the small embattled church just inside the park with fine trees and rhododendrons about it. The oldest monument comes from 1301. A stone to Sir John of 1518 tells us that he stoutly headed his men at Flodden Field, and the memorials bring us up to the first English peer of the family, who fought in the Crimea and died during the Great War more than two generations after. The sword he used in the Crimea is still in the castle, and a cap he wore there has a bullet hole in it.

The church has a white interior, a black-and-white roof, and fine oak benches. Its oldest possessions are the Norman stones in its walls, an ancient doorway filled up, two medieval piscinas, and a 15th-century east window with the Pennington arms carved outside it.

The windows themselves have great companies of angels, a host of 15 appearing to the startled shepherds, another troubling the waters of a pool, another sealing the fate of a king in the mighty camp of Assyria. Particularly interesting is a window in memory of the refashioning of the church last century, for it has one of the few modern Doom pictures we have seen. Above reigns Christ in Glory with saints about him, and below is the Archangel Michael with sword and banner between two groups of people rising from their graves, the saved and the lost.

Behind four chancel windows in which the four Archangels are gorgeously arrayed, a tragic story lies, for the windows were given by Lord Muncaster in memory of four companions who were killed by Greek brigands. It was in 1870 when Lord and Lady Muncaster, travelling in Greece, went with a few friends to Marathon. On the way back to Athens they were surprised by brigands. The ladies of the party were allowed to return, and two days later Lord Muncaster was sent to Athens to convey to the Greek Government the terms of the bandits for the release of the others, threatening that if pursued they would kill their captives.

The British Minister at Athens was willing to pay the ransom but the last word was with the Greek Government, which, unwilling to be dictated to in this way and in spite of having promised not to endanger the lives of the four men still held, sent out troops to intercept the brigands.

From a notebook kept by one of the prisoners it seems that at first the brigands were quite friendly, but when it became clear that troops were trying to trap them, were infuriated, and on April 21 shot two of the men. The other Englishmen were murdered the following day. Opinion in England laid the blame for this tragedy on the Greek Government, particularly for attempting, contrary to its promise, to capture the brigands during negotiations. Most of the gang were later caught and executed.

We found old Saxon or Viking stones in the churchyard, and through the lovely beeches here is a splendid peep of the mountains.

One of the most pathetic pages of our history tells of the story of the wandering king who came to Muncaster.

Uneasy Lay His Head

HENRY THE SIXTH, only son of the Henry of Agincourt and his Catherine of France, was born at Windsor in 1421, crowned King of England at eight years old and enthroned King of France in Paris when he was ten. The Hundred Years War was at its height; Joan of Arc had run her marvellous course, and on his way to Paris the child king was taken to hear parts of her trial, and was in Rouen during her martyrdom.

The age demanded a giant of genius, but Henry, inheriting the weakly constitution of his father, and the unstable mind of his demented French grandfather, was the helpless prey of contending factions renewing at home the warfare on which they had so long prospered in France.

A scholar of sincere piety, he cherished learning and founded three colleges at Eton and Cambridge. He married Margaret of Anjou when he was 24, but his few years of domestic happiness ended in the rebellion of Jack Cade, the rise to power of Richard of York, and a breakdown of health, reducing him to idiocy. His return to sanity after a year led to the expulsion from office of the Protector York, who raised an army which defeated the King's at St Albans in the first battle of the Wars of the Roses. Wounded and captured, Henry was brought to London, where the victor swore allegiance.

In 1460, after defeat at Northampton, Henry was again a prisoner, and compelled to declare York his heir. Thereupon Margaret took arms for her excluded son, and at Wakefield, in the same year defeated and slew his rival. Compelled now to march against his wife, Henry was defeated at the second battle of St Albans, and carried prisoner to her tent. Shortly afterwards Edward rallied, overwhelmed Henry and Margaret at Towton, and was proclaimed king. Henry escaped to Scotland, but was with Margaret and his son in the northern rising of 1464, and shared the defeats at Hedgeley Moor and Hexham.

After Hexham he paused here for shelter, rewarding his host with the famous "Luck of Muncaster." For a year he lurked disguised in the wilds of Lancashire and Yorkshire, then was betrayed at Clitheroe and imprisoned for five years in the Tower. The revolt of Warwick and Margaret led to the flight of Edward and the restoration of Henry, but in five months Edward returned, to fight the battles of Barnet and Tewkesbury, the second ending in the capture of Henry and the death of his son. Henry returned to the Tower where, on the night of his arrival, in May 1471, he was murdered by Richard Crookback on his bloodstained journey to the Throne.

In his three plays on Henry Shakespeare approached as near the truth as posterity may hope to do. The last scene is true to the known character of the king, who, as Richard kills him, dies exclaiming, "O! God forgive my sins and pardon thee."

The Ghostly Horsemen of the Hills

MUNGRISDALE. On three sides it is protected by steep green fells, and on the fourth it looks away from Lakeland to gentle hills and clustering trees. It was on Souter Fell, about 200 years ago, that strange mirages were seen, appearing to the villagers below like horsemen moving briskly in close ranks. More than a score of people saw these airy figures, afterwards attesting their story on oath before a magistrate.

The church was built anew a few years after the spectres were seen, and it has hardly changed since. Very plain and white, it has a view from every window. Some of its possessions from an earlier church are the 15th-century bell, the Black Letter Bible of 1617, and the panelled three-decker pulpit. There is a row of old hat pegs on the wall, a quaint little font like a pillar, and a tablet to Raisley Calvert whose son Raisley was "nursed by Wordsworth."

It is perhaps to the generosity of young Raisley Calvert that we owe the poetry of William Wordsworth.

The Man Who Gave Wordsworth to Poetry

RAISLEY was one of the clever sons of a steward of the Duke of Norfolk who died in 1791. While his brothers lived to achieve fame in art and on the stage, Raisley, a sculptor, fell ill of consumption. William Wordsworth spent much time with him in his sickroom at Penrith and would have discussed the efforts he was making to find an opening on a London newspaper. Raisley passed away at the beginning of 1795 and left his friend a legacy of £900 partly, as Wordsworth told a friend, from a confidence that he had power and attainments which might be of use to mankind.

Wordsworth's fortunes were at their lowest ebb, and he made the fullest use of his legacy. With £100 which he received for the Lyrical Ballads and another £100 which had been left to his sister he contrived to live for eight years with her in a little cottage at Racedown in Dorset. By the end of that time a large sum which had been owing to him from his father's estate reached him and enabled him to continue that serene existence so fruitful of beauty.

In one of his sonnets he immortalised his benefactor.

Calvert! it must not be unheard by them
Who may respect my name that I to thee
Owed many years of early liberty.
This care was thine when sickness did condemn
Thy youth to hopeless wasting, root and stem—
That I, if frugal and severe, might stray
Where'er I liked; and finally array
My temples with the Muse's diadem.
Hence, if in freedom I have loved the truth;
If there be aught of pure, or good, or great,

In my past verse; or shall be, in the lays
Of higher mood, which now I meditate;—
It gladdens me, O worthy, short-lived, Youth!
To think how much of this will be thy praise.

Raisley failed to reach fame as a sculptor but his wisdom and discernment undoubtedly helped to give immortality to his friend and brought comfort to his last moments.

The Home of the Howards

NAWORTH. Here is one of England's proud sights, the home of the Earl of Carlisle and all the Howards before him, and before that of the Dacres, whom we are always meeting in Cumberland. Of all the great castles of the border there is perhaps none more beautifully situated or more striking. Magnificent it stands, below the Carlisle-to-Newcastle road, and above the rocky cliffs of a deep wooded ravine. Green lawns lie about it, including one of the few oval bowling greens we have seen, and among very fine trees in the park are quaint oaks and beeches.

We enter the outer courtyard by a massive gateway, and come to the inner courtyard round which the castle is built. The entrance is a small archway with no ornament save the shields of the Howards, but the old entrance was by a lofty archway high enough for horsemen to ride through without lowering their banners. In it is still a massive lattice gate, and near by are steps down to the dungeons. Above the gateway rises one of the corner towers, a huge pile with a queer stone man looking over the battlements as if to watch for the enemy. The foundations of this tower are thought to be older than the Conquest, and it may well have been the nucleus round which the rest of the fortress grew up from the 14th century onwards.

Up a flight of stone steps and through a massive door we come to the Great Hall, a fine room 100 feet long and famous for its treasures. Its little windows look on to the courtyard; and its fireplace, 15 feet wide, has an arch like a stone bridge. Cherished here are beautiful French tapestries, a Flemish tapestry screen of the 17th century, and four strange beasts, like Alice-in-Wonderland characters. They are heraldic figures in oak, five or six feet high and holding banners, and they represent the Red Bull of Dacre, the Griffin of De Vaux, the Stag of Multon, and the Dolphin of Greystoke.

Several things in this Hall remind us of one of the most famous lords of Naworth, Lord William Howard, the Belted Will in Scott's Lay of the Last Minstrel. Among the suits of armour is one he is said to have worn, and among the pictures are full-length portraits by Janssen of him and his gracious wife Elizabeth Dacre. Here, too, are three little figures said to have been carved for Belted Will, who, according to the story, set them on the battlements to deceive the enemy. Dressed in armour, about half lifesize, maimed and halt and sadly battered, they are yet so droll that he would be dull indeed who does not laugh with them. We remember them as the three jolliest little men in Cumberland.

As interesting as anything the castle has is the old tower, with its thick walls and small spiral staircase, known as Belted Will's Tower. In it is his bedroom, a panelled room looking finely on to the park; and above is the old library with a magnificent oak ceiling, richly moulded and adorned with foliage and shields, reminding us of the ceiling in the Dean's house at Carlisle. The new library has a carpet made in the William Morris factory, and a remarkably fine overmantel showing in gesso work the Battle of Flodden, with Lord William Dacre heading a valiant charge. It is a spirited piece of work designed by Sir Edward Burne-Jones and Sir Edgar Boehm.

There is a fascinating little chapel with a tiny window, a still smaller peephole, a rough wooden chest for an altar, and some valuable fragments of carved alabaster thought to have belonged to the altar screen in the fine church of Lanercost Priory a mile away. All sorts of scenes and figures they show—St Michael and a dragon; John the Baptist; the Madonna amid angels; God as the Ancient of Days, with a crucifix in His hand; the apostles watching the Ascension of the Madonna, with Thomas holding her girdle; and a nun holding a spear while a wretched figure writhes at her feet with a dagger in his heart. Especially fine is a scene of the Betrayal of Our Lord, with the servants of the High Priest crowding round Him, and Judas leaning forward to give the fatal kiss.

One of the walls is enriched with painting of over 400 years ago, in which we see the scourging of Jesus, a pathetic Crucifixion, and a dramatic Resurrection with the soldiers standing in every attitude of horror and amazement.

The famous lord of Naworth was unlike most mighty men of these parts in that he strove to keep the peace and not to break it.

CUMBERLAND

Belted Will

LORD WILLIAM HOWARD, the Belted Will of Scott's Lay of the Last Minstrel, is a historic figure accurately portrayed by the poet, but in reality a little late for the scene in which he is made to figure. He was born at Audley End, Essex, a son of the fourth Duke of Norfolk, who was executed for plotting to marry Mary Queen of Scots, leaving him an orphan at nine.

At 14 he was married to an even younger daughter of Lord Dacre, so that those who knew and loved them in later life said that the pair could not number 25 years between them at their wedding but that when they numbered 140 years they were hearty, well, and merry.

There were many years of trial and tribulation. Elizabeth feared and hated the Howards, and connived at the seizure of young Lady Howard's estates. William's brother was imprisoned when seeking to flee the country as a Roman Catholic, and William was made captive with him. Eventually Lady William was permitted to buy back her own estates for £10,000 and her husband settled down with her at Naworth Castle, to rebuild the old feudal home and live as a model border chieftain, rich in books and manuscripts, though so short of money that for long he dared allow himself only twenty shillings a month pocket money. They had started life together as mere children, but were without regrets in all their domestic relations, for they loved each other and were happy.

In a lawless age Howard was a power enforcing law and order along the border. He kept many retainers, and when he travelled it was with a small army, not to raid or ravage, but to insist on the maintenance of the peace, and to punish wrongdoing.

His procedure did not gain unanimous favour, for to raid and harry, to besiege and plunder, were long-established industries on both sides of the Border. His castle was at once fortress and palace, where armed men guarded the way to the upper chamber in the tower where he delighted to pore over his books and keep his diary and household accounts.

All his treasures and records, the furniture he used, the sword he wielded, and the altar before which he prayed were preserved so completely until fire destroyed them last century that Scott, visiting the scene nearly two centuries after Howard's death, declared he could imagine him ascending the turret stair to greet him.

High Up

NENTHEAD. We try to forget the unloveliness of its tumble-down buildings and rubbish heaps for zinc and copper mines, but we shall long remember the grandeur of its mountain scenery and the impressive list of records which it claims to hold.

Here, with the high road climbing to about 2000 feet, everything seems to be the highest of its kind in England. We find the highest house, the highest vicarage, the highest parish church, and a Methodist chapel claiming to be nearer heaven than any other place of worship in the country.

The church is 19th century, but it has a reading-desk with two poppyheads 600 years old, and there is a little 14th-century work in the altar rails. The organ has been made from a barrel organ, and still has some of the old machinery, with a list of the ten tunes played.

Hereabouts the River Nent rises, and we see it flowing among rocks and trees on its way to Alston. A waterfall is seen from the road, and there is an underground canal not far away.

Young Lochinvar

NETHERBY. With scarcely anything but its imposing Hall, it is yet a place of great interest, for it brings us into touch with literature and history.

Netherby Hall was immortalised by Sir Walter Scott in the ballad sung by Lady Heron in Marmion, telling of young Lochinvar and his love for the fair lady of the Hall—how he carried her off on his horse from a dance, before the very eyes of the "laggard in love and dastard in war" to whom she was unwillingly betrothed.

The great house as we see it is much younger than Flodden Field about which Scott was writing in Marmion. It is chiefly 18th century, but here still is an ancient tower from an earlier house. Close by it is the River Esk, across which Lochinvar swam "where ford there was none." The park is one of the loveliest in Cumberland, magnificent with oaks and yews and beeches, and with woods famous for their rhododendrons. Five nests of herons were here at the time we called.

The Hall has long been the home of the Grahams, and one of them, born here in 1648, brings to Netherby its little touch of history. He was Richard Graham, Viscount Preston, who with Lord Middleton managed the affairs of Parliament for James the Second. The revolution of 1688 found him a keen Protestant, but a loyal Jacobite nevertheless, and under William of Orange he was arrested for his plotting and sent to the Tower. He was sentenced to death for treason, and only released after he had made confessions implicating other Jacobites. He lived to see the first few years of Dutch William's reign, and was laid to rest at Nunnington in Yorkshire.

Valley of Delight

NEWLANDS. It is a delightful valley, next to Borrowdale, with more peace now than it had in Elizabethan times, when the copper and the lead of these hills was being exploited by German miners for the English crown.

The little church is simple and remote, and we found the birds all busy in the eaves. It has been rebuilt since the day in May when Wordsworth saw it among the trees and put it into poetry:

How delicate the leafy veil
Through which yon house of God
Gleams mid the peace of this deep vale,
By few but shepherds trod!

He must have peeped inside, as anybody would, and have seen the attractive panelled pulpit and desk, for they were made in 1610.

Newlands Valley is known chiefly as the return route of the great Borrowdale–Honister–Buttermere drive from Keswick, and for its pleasing pastoral contrast to the stony grimness of the Honister Pass. Yet Newlands is only the other side of the same grim heights, Dale Head, Hindscarth, and Robinson.

The Vale has no village in it. Approached from its lower end, below its little church, it spreads fanlike into four small upland dales, each with its beck. The main beck, Newlands, separated from Derwent water and Borrowdale by the low Cat Bells range, comes down from Dale Head and Hindscarth; the Little Dale Beck comes from between Hindscarth and Robinson; and the Keskadale Beck from Robinson and Buttermere Moss.

These three becks converge in the vicinity of the church, and then go on to Bassenthwaite Lake, after receiving Ridge Beck from the foot of Causey Pike. Above the church highroads cease, except the steep one by Keskadale up to Buttermere House, and down it the coaches still come. So a green, pastoral valley spreads itself higher and higher, breaking up among the mountains that rim it round steeply at the top, and gives colour and gentleness in the midst of sternness and strength.

Rescued From the Marshes

NEWTON ARLOSH. It has an odd little church and a pretty wayside duck pond jutting into the trim churchyard.

One of the fortified churches of the Borderlands, it comes from the days of 600 years ago when Holme Cultram Abbey was the richest religious house in the Lakeland counties. The church was then a low fortresslike tower and a tiny nave with walls five feet thick and narrow windows high up in them. Falling into decay, the church was neglected until its transformation about 100 years ago, when the nave was extended by a wide north aisle without an arcade, the effect being of a wide nave running north and south with the chancel at the northern end.

Joined on to the south-west corner stands the old tower, reached from the nave by a very small doorway and with a stairway leading to two upper rooms, one of which has a fireplace.

It is one of the queerest churches we have seen, with little of interest except for the base of its eagle lectern and the stem of the extraordinary pulpit. They are both made of timber older than any church in England, older than Greece and Rome, for the timber is bog oak rescued from the marshes in which it has been submerged for no man knows how long.

The eagle of the lectern is finely carved, but the pulpit is crudely shaped like a palm tree and is rather a stand than an ordinary rostrum. We found it in a room in the tower when we called, seeming to be in and out of use according to the fancy of the rector. If the stem of the pulpit and the base of the lectern are interesting on their own account, so also is the pedestal of the font, for it is made up of old stones from the abbey. We were told that many of the houses in this countryside have abbey gravestones for their hearthstones.

The Writing in the Roof

NEWTON REIGNY. Its 14th-century church shows its age best within, where the nave has three fine arches on each side, and the chancel is framed by an arch taller and more pointed. One of the arcades ends in a piscina, the other in a delicate little piece of foliage carving.

One of three old beams in the nave brings us a human touch from the past, having an inscription that is easy to see and hard to read. It tells us that the names of the carpenters that have built this roof are John Atkenson and Henere Bymert, and that they did it in 1585. Of the two we like Henere Bymert better. His name looks timid and modest, as though he only put it here to follow John Atkenson. One of the two bells seen in the turret was brought from Shap Abbey when the monasteries were dissolved.

Very attractive on the hill near the village is Catterlen Hall, now a farm. It has a tower of the 15th century, a wing of the 16th, and another of the 17th, with a doorway approached by a flight of steps.

NICHOL FOREST. Once a great forest between England and Scotland, it still has many trees watered by the Liddel and the Kershope; but it lost its old church last century when the pleasant new one was built with an apse and a small slated spire on a wooden belfry. A lonely place it is, but it must have had its charm for Henry Joyce, who spent 53 years as vicar here and now sleeps in the churchyard. He died in 1915.

The Knight and His Dog

OUSBY. Above it towers Thack Moor, rising steeply from a stream flowing swiftly under the trees, and hereabouts on the road to Crewgarth are some slight green mounds marking an earthwork used either as a fortress or as an enclosure for cattle.

The little church is a long way off, a simple nave and chancel still with some of the marks of the 13th-century builders. Chief among these old remains are the piscina and the three sedilia, all with massive gables over trefoil heads. The sedilia are carved with heads of a sad-looking woman and a child, and have been patched up with two fragments of medieval gravestones.

But if there is not very much to see of the 13th-century stonework there is a great treasure here in 13th-century woodwork, one of less than 100 oak figures still left in all England. We found it lying on the sanctuary floor, a magnificent piece of carving which deserves to be mounted on a proper base and given a place of honour in Ousby. It is a lifesize figure of a cross-legged knight who was probably a crusader, very well preserved after 700 years though one arm has gone and the hand of the other is broken off. He wears a tunic over his armour, with a short dagger hanging from his belt, and his very shapely feet are resting on his faithful dog.

One of the old rectors here soon after the Restoration was Thomas Robinson, who shepherded this flock for 47 years, and found time to write books on the natural history of Cumberland and Westmorland.

The Roman Chancel Arch

OVER DENTON. Guarded by a roofless tower above a ravine, this bleak village on the borders of Northumberland has one of the most remarkable little shrines in the country. It is about 16 yards long, and the tower is about 600 years old.

It takes us back to the very roots of our history, for it was built by Saxons who took much of their masonry from the Roman Wall nearby. It has a small Saxon window with a wooden lintel and a narrow doorway without a porch. On the wall is an ancient consecration cross still visible after the passage of many centuries. The old font, too, is very primitive, for it is made of porous stone so that it need not be emptied.

But it is the chancel arch that thrills us, for it is one of the oldest arches standing in any church, having been first built by the Romans at Birdoswald. Left standing by the Romans when they went back to Rome, it stood for centuries until the Saxons, when building this church, thought it would be useful. They took it down, carried it across the fields, and set it up again, as the Saxons had done at Corbridge, across the border. These two are the only Roman arches we know in any of our churches.

In the churchyard, with its fine view of the bare hills, lies Margaret Teesdale of 1777, with a quaint epitaph on her gravestone. Born at Mumps Hall a mile away, and living to be 98, she is interesting to all who love Scott's books, for she is thought to be Tib Mumps, the landlady in Guy Mannering.

Cumbria's Old Capital

PENRITH. It has been the capital of Cumbria, it has suffered from the Scottish raiders and seen the Jacobite rebels, it has kept a rather pathetic fragment of a castle, and has some charming peeps of the old world for those who walk to see them.

Everyone sees the tower that has been on Beacon Hill for over two centuries, but not so obvious are the inn (full of old-world things) where Richard of Gloucester may have stayed before he was king, the little gabled front of an Elizabethan house and the new front of an Elizabethan grammar school, both overlooking the churchyard, and the very attractive school of 1670 in Middlegate.

It was to another little school at Penrith that William and Dorothy Wordsworth came in their early childhood, and here William met the Mary Hutchinson who became his wife. In the churchyard we see the grave of Mary's parents, and here in an unknown grave sleeps the mother of Wordsworth himself. She was a mother who lived only long enough to watch over her child in his youngest years, for she passed away when William was eight. She herself was but 31 when she faded away, but the poet never forgot her loving care and refers in the Prelude to

My honoured mother, she who was the heart
And hinge of all our learnings and our loves.

Again, in writing of his earliest years in that long poem, he writes of her with intense feeling:

Blest the babe,
Nursed in his mother's arms, who sinks to sleep,
Rocked on his mother's breast; who with his soul
Drinks in the feelings of his mother's eye!
For him in one dear presence there exists
A virtue which irradiates and exalts
Objects through widest intercourse of sense.

The poet goes on to describe the serene devotion with which she educated her young children. We know that he himself caused her some anxiety by his stiff, moody, and violent temper, so that she prophesied that he would be remarkable for good or for ill.

She was Anne, daughter of William Cookson, a mercer of Penrith. She was laid to rest here in 1778.

One of the sights of Penrith has been in this churchyard for 1000 years. It is the group nicknamed the Giant's Grave, and it consists of two worn crosses and four of the ancient stones known as hogbacks. Probably these six memorials were put up originally to kings or princes of Cumbria in the greatest days of the town, and no doubt they were first grouped as we see them when the Normans built a church here. The crosses are now only stumps about twice the height of a man, their carving much weathered. The hogbacks were put up as little houses of the dead, their tops being carved to look like the tiles on a roof. One of the four shows traces of a carved twisting serpent; another has its coiling patterns still clear. Equally old is a cross standing by itself, called the Giant's Thumb.

The body of the church is 18th century. The lowest parts of the tower are 13th, and the top was probably built two centuries later by Warwick the Kingmaker, who was lord of the manor of Penrith. His sign was the ragged staff, and of the eight he put on the tower as pinnacles only one is left. The interior has all the dignity of its day. The pillars surporting the panelled gallery are remarkable because each is a single stone ten feet high and four feet round, from a Westmorland quarry worked by the Romans. The chancel walls are decorated with very dark paintings done about a century ago by Jacob Thompson who was born at Penrith and became known in London as a landscape-painter. One picture is the Agony in the Garden, the other is the Shepherds seeing the Angels, with a dog also looking up.

Many treasures older than the present building are in it. There are two old fonts and stone figures of a 17th-century lawyer and his wife; in the vestry wall there is a striking row of fine Tudor memorials carved with shields and letters, one being the stone of a border hero whose name was used to frighten the children; and there are three little portraits in old glass that take us straight into history. One is a king wearing his crown, in a window which has also an angel with a rope and some jumbled fragments. The other two are Richard Duke of York, with his yellow hair and beard, and his wife Cicily Neville, with jewels in her hair; and a remarkable pair they were. He was the Yorkist heir slain at Wakefield, after which his head was crowned in mockery and impaled on the walls of York. She was the 23rd child of Ralph Neville, Shakespeare's Earl of Westmorland. Two of their children became kings of England; a third married Henry the Seventh, making this old couple the ancestors of every British sovereign. Two of their grandchildren were the little princes murdered in the Tower.

The two brass candelabra, each for 24 candles, were given to the people of Penrith by the Duke of Portland as a memento of their loyalty in the 1745 rebellion.

An old stone in the wall recalls the terrible ravage of the plague at the end of Elizabeth's reign, when 2260 people died in and about Penrith. Still standing in a field beside the Kendal road is the square plague-stone, like a great font, in which the townsfolk washed their money and to which the countryfolk brought their goods in exchange.

More historic than beautiful are the ruins of the castle, once a big square fortress of war and now approached through a gateway of peace set up in memory of 200 men and a woman who died for us. The chief part of the walls still standing were built in the 14th century by William Strickland, a benefactor of Penrith who became Bishop of Carlisle. One pathetic wall is here of the red tower raised by Ralph Neville, and a few low walls and foundations are part of the additions made by Richard of Gloucester, who, we are told, set himself up here in great pomp.

The Fugitive from Marston Moor

PLUMBLAND. From its church between the hamlets of Arkleby Green and Parsonby is a grand view of Cumberland's mountains and those of Scotland beyond the sea; and under the ancient yew in the churchyard is a stone which has been here 1000 years.

It is one of those known as hogbacks from their shape, a style of gravestone the Norsemen brought from Scandinavia, only found in England in the north. This one was carved with knotwork some time in the 10th century, shortly before the kings of Denmark became the kings of England. It has cracked, and at one end is some later carving as if for a corbel.

Then came the Normans, and this church, though it was made new last century, has kept a chancel arch of their time with rich chevron mouldings and three shafts clustered each side; and a narrow Norman doorway under the tower, which has in its walls a fragment with a crude chevron which may have been carved in Saxon England. The trefoiled piscina with beautiful mouldings is 13th century.

The church is dedicated to Cuthbert, the hermit prior of Farne Island, and he is here in the windows with Bede and John the Baptist, while George of England and St Martin, carrying the fleur-de-lys of France, are here in memory of men who fought in Flanders. Below them are little scenes of the fight with the dragon and the cutting of the cloak outside the castle gates. A modern knight with shield and sword also has his portrait in the windows. He is Edward Stanley Curwen of Workington Hall, who died in 1878. A brass engraved with figures of Mercury and St Andrew is to a rector who died when all the world was at war.

In a field by the church is a little stone building which once housed the pigeons of a medieval manor house.

By two cottages a mile away is the shapely old mulberry tree up which Thomas Dykes, an ardent Royalist, hid after the battle of Marston Moor, his wife and daughter bringing him food from Ward Hall, the home no longer here. The old tree hid him safely, but later he was captured, and died a prisoner in Cockermouth Castle.

On Ward Hill are the remains of a camp from the warlike days before history. In later days watch was kept here and a beacon lighted in time of danger.

It is believed that Plumbland was the birthplace in 1655 of William Nicholson, the antiquarian bishop who aroused much controversy in his day, but whom we remember with gratitude for his zeal in preserving manuscripts and records.

The Twentieth-Century Church

PLUMPTON WALL. Its roads have resounded with the tramp of Roman legions; today its old smithy sees and hears the almost ceaseless traffic on the Great North Road.

Here was the station which the Romans called Voreda and the people now call Castlesteads. We can trace the outline of the ramparts with the stones of one of the gates still in place, and we found cattle grazing where great buildings stood. Not far away is a stone-lined Roman wall. Just before Trafalgar a gold fibula decorated with bears and griffins was found here, and just before Waterloo were found five Roman altars carved with figures of gods.

Life was going on here in the second century, and these ramparts are from those days. The little church with an embattled tower is perhaps the first Cumberland church of the 20th century, a neat and trim place with no east window, the nave and chancel divided by an iron screen and covered with a wagon roof carved with roses, red and gold ones over the sanctuary. A church of much distinction, it was designed by Sir Robert Lorimer, architect of Scotland's National Peace Memorial. The oak reredos, the sedilia, the pulpit, and the lectern, have all fine carving of linenfold and vines. On the reredos is a pelican sitting in a basket feeding her young. On the lectern are six little birds pecking at grapes, and on the pulpit is a child angel. An oak cupboard with a striking mass of linenfold is the work of Kendal School of Art.

We come to the church through a lychgate with stout oak timbers, in memory of four men who did not come back.

The Proud Stanleys of the North

PONSONBY. Its ancient church and its 18th-century Hall seem almost to be part of Calderbridge, for the rest of tiny Ponsonby is a mile away on the opposite hill.

Girt with fine trees, the Hall has a portico with columns, 12 feet high, each cut from a single block of stone. It has been the home of the Stanleys who came here in the 14th century, that proud family whom we come upon so often in Lancashire. It was a Stanley who picked up the crown at Bosworth Field and set it on the head of Henry the Seventh, and another who became immortal in our literature when Scott wrote the famous lines:

" On, Stanley, on! "
Were the last words of Marmion.

In the church are memorials to several of them from the Ponsonby branch, including Edward Stanley of 1863 who sat in parliament 20 years and could count back 24 generations to his ancestor Henry Stanleigh.

Yet this church, with its little dry moat crossed by a bridge, and with all its lovely setting in the park of the great house, has a longer memory of Ponsonby than even the Stanleys, a memory of its first building 700 years ago. Still here are the walls of the 13th-century builders, their chancel arch, one of their lancet windows, and part of a piscina like a fluted capital. The tower with its vaulted roof and the spire are modern, and so are some of the best features of the neat interior—richly panelled pulpit and chancel seats, and the pleasing glass which lends colour to it all. The east window has the Crucifixion, with figures also of Peter and Paul and John and Barnabas. Another window shows Christ as King, with a scene of the Nativity; and two lancets in the tower have figures of Faith and Hope.

The oldest memorials must be the two ancient coffin stones in the chancel, one with a sword by its cross and the other with shears; but there is a frame of ornamented stonework 700 years old round the monument to Thomas Curwen of 1653, which has a quaint touch we much enjoyed. Carved in relief at the sides of the crumbling epitaph are two very odd old men with beards, wearing shorts and buttoned coats and strange little bowler hats stuck on the very top of their heads. One man is digging and the other is meditating, but we feel sure the sculptor himself never handled a spade with such a grip, and we know that among these hills he never kept a hat on his head as he has placed these hats here.

The churchyard has part of its ancient cross still left, and here on John Fletcher's tomb we read that the last day will discover what manner of man he was, that he had a short married life and a long widowhood, and that notwithstanding the narrowness of his circumstances he gave his only son two years of University life and lived to see him chaplain of an Oxford college.

Beauty From a Hilltop

RAUGHTON HEAD. Its white houses cluster on the hilltop and look over the lovely valley of the Caldew. Below them is the church three times refashioned in the last three centuries, with a low tower like a fortress, not yet a centenarian. The oak panels in the pulpit are Jacobean, the oak chancel screen is modern. In the windows are scenes of Calvary and Gethsemane with the Good Shepherd and Paul preaching.

A small marble relief of a student is a memorial to Robert Monkhouse who died in 1822; it is one of the earliest works of his pupil, the Cumberland sculptor Musgrave Watson, of whom we read at Dalston. In the churchyard in a grave with an upright stone near the chancel lies Susanna Blamire, who was born on what is now a farm near Dalston but what was then Cardew Hall. She lived and died in Cumberland and wrote charming poems of country life.

From the church door we look down on the park round Rose Castle, home of the Bishops of Carlisle for 700 years, and half a mile away, near a stone bridge in a pretty setting over the river, we have a splendid view of the house made new but with medieval walls and towers, and with terraced gardens which give life and colour to its rather sombre lines.

An Outpost of the Caesars

RAVENGLASS. It has lost its old fame as the foremost port in north-west Britain, but its wide street still straggles along the estuary where the Irt and the Mite and the Esk all fall into the sea. Sheltered by fine hills and the glorious woodlands of Muncaster Castle, it is perhaps the oldest sea port in Cumberland, and is said to have been built from Roman materials. The imagination can picture a Roman fleet at anchor in its harbour, where great sandy stretches are left bare by every tide. Here among the sandhills the seagulls love to nest.

But it is not all imagination in Ravenglass, for this place is the guardian of a crumbling fragment of the Roman Empire, something from its great days when England was under the Caesars. It stands by a fine avenue near the foot of the hill and is called Walls Castle, one of the best preserved Roman buildings in this half of the country. Most probably a villa, though it may be a bath connected with Muncaster, it has walls of red freestone a yard thick, and in places the ivied ruins are as much as 12 feet high. Roman cement is still clinging to the inside of the walls, and the great strength of it all is enough to support huge blocks of overhanging masonry. One of the rooms is 13 feet by 16, another incomplete one is bigger, and there are parts of three more. In one of the walls is a domed niche; and it is not surprising to find that many relics of the Romans and the Saxons have been discovered hereabouts.

The Romans laid down roads to Ravenglass, one of them being guarded by Hard Knott Castle. Today the pilgrim can come in a very different fashion, travelling in a toy-like train on a famous little railway through the glories of Eskdale.

RENWICK. Small and bleak, it clings to the side of Thackmoor, while giving its name to another Fell down which torrents tumble into the fir trees. Its tiny church, with nave and chancel under one roof, was made new last century, but kept its two-decker pulpit, and a bell which has fallen silent after 500 years. On a green mound a mile or so away are fragments of stone walls in places ten feet high, all that is left of Haresceugh Castle after 600 years.

He Lies in His Tree

ROCKCLIFFE. Quaint and charming and miles from anywhere, it has spacious views of the wooded country near the meeting of the Eden and Esk, only a mile or two from the estuary of the Solway. Across the river we look towards Burgh-on-Sands where Edward the First finished his course, and northwards we see the Scottish border where lived the men who feared him.

Only a little walk from the Eden is the church among these houses, with a tall spire widely seen in this level part of the county. Refashioned after the lightning damaged it a generation or two ago, it has only one thing to see inside, an inscription to a sailor who in 35 years service captured 31 enemy ships and received a special gold medal from George the Third. But in this churchyard several things are worth finding—two old gravestones with flowered crosses; a very crude cross with a thick shaft and five bosses, said to have been shaped with a pick about 900 years ago; and the gravestone of a vicar here for 56 years of the 18th century, with this charming epitaph:

I, living, planted trees; of one is made
This chest wherein my body now is laid.

A Cumbrian Saint of Long Ago

ST BEES. Deep in a valley near the sea it lies, a grey village of much antiquity and charm. Its church is the oldest and finest in West Cumberland; its school is ancient, and so is its bridge; but oldest of all is its delightful story of St Bega (or St Bee) and how she got her nunnery.

The church has grown from the church of a rich priory which began about 1125 as an offshoot of St Mary's great abbey in York. The priory was built where the nunnery has stood (from the 7th century until the Danes destroyed it in the 10th), and this church is carrying on its ancient tradition. But the most interesting possession of St Bees is a relic of the nunnery itself, a remarkable stone believed to date from the eighth century.

We see it in the wall between the churchyard and the vicarage, where it forms the lintel of an alcove. It is carved with an ugly dragon turning to snarl at a tiny armed figure attacking it from behind. One end of the stone is decorated with plaitwork, and with the knotwork at the other end is a very curious carving which looks like a boar's head. Standing in the alcove is another relic, a stout stone cross on which the bearers of a coffin would rest their load.

The cross-shaped church with its fine central tower has been altered in modern times, but the greater part was built only a few decades after the priory. It has a magnificent Norman doorway without an equal for many miles. The arch has four rich chevron mouldings, beak-heads of men and serpents, and a ram; and carved on one of the capitals is a figure swinging like a monkey from the branches. Three trefoils on stalks make an unusual decoration at the top of the dripstone, and are perhaps meant to represent the Trinity. The oak door is modern, and has decorated hinges.

Ennerdale The Smuggler's Retreat

Borrowdale Scafell from Rosthwaite

Penrith The Market Place

Whitbeck The Farms and the Fells

Borrowdale By the River at Grange

Silloth The Docks

Workington A Blast Furnace

A Springtime Pastoral near Windermere

The Market Place of Appleby

Appleby The Castle Keep

Kendal Where Romney Lived

Orton A Charming Byway

Brougham The Ruined Castle

Brougham The Old Hall

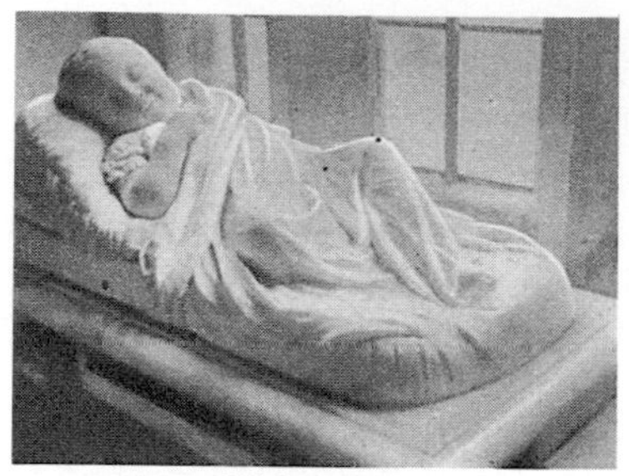

Witherslack
Monument to a 19th-century baby

Kendal
Zacchary Hubbersty's Memorial

Choir Stalls

Panel of Triptych

The Resurrection

Visit of the Wise Men

Carved Woodwork in St Wilfred's Chapel, Brougham

The interior is lofty and spacious, and the nave has a fine modern roof above its arcades of six bays. There are two rose windows and many lancets, but most beautiful of all are eight lancets in the chancel, all richly moulded inside and out, the three at the east being divided by niches. We say in the chancel, but we should say in the original chancel, for the greater part of it is shut off by a windowless wall carved with tracery. The splendid chancel arch is filled with a metal screen more novel than beautiful, made up of fanciful tracery with a huge cross, no doubt weighing some tons.

Among the stones kept here as relics are a stoup, a piscina, and a mortar, all of the 12th century. Others are probably parts of still older cross-shafts with primitive carving, and one is the upper part of a 10th-century shaft decorated on each side with chain and scroll. There are coffin stones 800 years old, carved with crosses and swords and shears: a very fine one engraved with an archer drawing his bow, an elaborate 13th-century stone, and another charmingly engraved with the portrait of 14th-century Johanna Lucy in a graceful gown her hair in plaited coils.

A Queen Anne wall monument shows a woman weeping over a tomb; and there is a bust of William Ainger, vicar here for 24 years last century; but the most moving of the modern monuments is to a child of four on a tomb under a rich recess, a pathetic little figure as she lies asleep, a spray of lilies in her hand.

The church has one of the most perfect old registers in the county, the entries beginning in fine writing in 1538. It has, also in the vestry, a very interesting music cupboard with carved portraits of men famous in the English musical world. We see the great Samuel Wesley, the celebrated organists Henry Smart and William Best, and Henry Willis whose firm built the splendid organ here.

In the churchyard is an ancient cross carved with a serpent, and near by are two more of the old monuments in which St Bees is so rich, battered figures of knights, of the 13th and 14th centuries. A detached building south of the chancel treasures two very old memorial stones, one with the remains of an inscription to Walter de Rualton who died in 1281, and the other finely engraved with the portrait of Prior Thomas de Cotyngham of 1300, shown as a monk.

In company with the church is the school, attractively built round three sides of a quadrangle. One wing is the original 16th-century building, and over the doorway is a stone with the arms of its founder, Archbishop Grindal, who gave the church one of its three Elizabethan chalices. The stone has been brought from the village bridge built in his time.

A mile or two away St Bees Head sweeps out into the sea, its red rocks guarded by a lighthouse 99 feet high.

The sight of this land must have been welcome to the fleeing princess whose name it now bears.

Snow on Midsummer Day

SHE was an Irish princess who lived in the 7th century. As a child she made up her mind to serve God and not to marry, and as a pledge of her determination she kept a bracelet said to have been given to her by an angel. But she was the most beautiful woman in the country, and her father betrothed her to a Norwegian prince. Bega (as she was often called) was guarded so that she should not run away, but on the eve of the wedding everyone joined in merrymaking and she was able to escape, crossing the sea to Northumbria.

Legend tells us that she was well received by a great lady there, who asked her husband to give her land for a nunnery. He jokingly said he would give as much land as was covered by snow on Midsummer day, and on that morning there was snow for three miles round. Snow has been known on Cumberland mountains on Midsummer day, and possibly the story grew up as an explanation of the irregular shape of the parish. Bega built her nunnery, serving food to the workers with her own hands. As abbess she cared for the sick and poor of the district and became greatly loved.

Those who declare that there was no Saint Bega assert that the origin of her story is to be found in a ring kept at St Bees until the 13th century, venerated as the bracelet given to Bega by the angel. Actually this was a Norse ring from a pagan temple, taken into the Christian church and referred to as Sancta Bega, Latin for Holy and Anglo-Saxon for Ring; a misunderstanding of these words would account for belief in a saint named Bega. But it is likely that Bega was a real abbess, for the people of north-east England long looked upon her as the protector of the oppressed and the poor.

The Rider in the Romantic Vale

ST JOHN'S-IN-THE-VALE. High up on the side of this lovely green valley near Keswick is the remote little church, a charming place of rest for any pilgrim walking in Lakeland. It shows us its old pewter vessels in a case and its sundial of 300 years ago; and its attractive woodwork includes an old canopied pulpit.

In the churchyard lies John Richardson, whose life was given to poetry and the service of this little place. Following his father's trade as a mason, he became a builder, and rebuilt the church and parsonage and the school, in which he laboured as master for a generation. His writings in dialect brought him a great local reputation.

The Vale of St John is one of the most charming and romantic little valleys in Lakeland. Its beck brings down the spare waters of Thirlmere into the River Greta below Threlkeld. The narrow vale is sunk between Naddle Fell on the western side and the peaks and rocks of the northern end of Helvellyn on the eastern side. Helvellyn ends with White Pike. Opposite the church on the Naddle side of the vale Wanthwaite Crags sink precipitously from Helvellyn, and farther up the vale Great Dodd and Watson's Dodd drop steeply to it as it climbs toward Thirlmere. Then, almost at the top of the narrowed vale, appears something like a huge castle commanding the defile—really a natural rock at the foot of Watson's Dodd, though the illusion of a castle is so strong that Scott used it as his fairy castle in his poetic romance the Bridal of Triermain.

This is how he saw it:

Paled in by many a lofty hill,
The narrow dale lay smooth and still,
And, down its verdant bosom led,
A winding brooklet found its bed.
But, midmost of the vale, a mound
Arose with airy turrets crowned,
Buttress, and rampire's circling bound,
And mighty keep and tower.
Beneath the castle's gloomy pride
In ample round did Arthur ride
Three times; nor living thing he spied,
Nor heard a living sound,
Save that, awakening from her dream
The owlet now began to scream,
In concert with the rushing stream,
That washed the battled mound.

Above this scene, and making part of it if we follow up the stream, is the wooded Great Howe and the lofty Raven Crag, and we are on the main road between Grasmere and Keswick at Smeathwaite

Bridge. It seemed strange to us that so few should take the longer way to Keswick down this romantic vale.

The Broken Altar and Fallen Castle

SCALEBY. Hidden away amid much loveliness, it is a peaceful place abounding in trees. Here are oaks and beeches guarding a little company of houses and farms, and a simple church, rather gaunt, treasuring a great rarity such as we have come upon only a few times in our ten thousand visits. It is a broken Roman altar about a yard high, a most interesting relic, with two battered figures of robed men whose heads are gone. In their hands they have what looked to us like crosses.

Some of the church is old, though much restored, and among its possessions are a Queen Anne font and two old bells still ringing in the tower.

But after the Roman altar it is the castle we come to see in Scaleby, a massive ruined shell with a much newer house half in it and half out. In all Cumberland we remember nothing more derelict and melancholy than this old place, darkened by giant trees and with its moat still full of water. Traces of the drawbridge over the outer moat are visible yet.

A broken gateway brings us to a kind of outer courtyard, but the castle's oldest part is its original tower, with a tiny inner courtyard. The tower is 14th century on the west side, and the hall on the east is 15th. The gatehouse has two towers, square and octagonal, and over the arch are the arms of the Gilpins whose home this was. One of them planted the roadside oaks between which we come to the castle. Another, William Gilpin, born here in 1724, wrote the story of his family and their ancient home; he is also remembered as the biographer of Wycliffe, Latimer, and Cranmer.

The castle was twice besieged in the Civil War, and its walls still bear on them the marks of fire.

SCOTBY. We liked its green and its trees, its white houses with rustic porches, and the tower curiously placed at the south-east of the 19th-century church; but best of all we liked the two haymakers we found in a house a mile away, called Rosehill. Made lifesize in lead, we were told that they were Dutch and had belonged to Nell Gwynn. A stone adze used before the Romans came, and some Anglo-Saxon pennies, are Scotby's contributions to our museums.

Windows by the Sea

SEASCALE. It is a lovable little seaside place for many things—for its fine open stretches of sand and for the beauty of the hills and mountains which rise magnificently in the east. Monarch of all the fine array is the wild twin-peaked mountain mass which climbs 12 miles away to the highest point in England, Scafell Pike, 3210 feet above the sea.

The spacious church stands proudly at a high corner of the village, near a cross carved with vines and knotwork in memory of the men who did not come back. Hardly older than the 20th century, the nave has five round bays built in Norman fashion, but for the chief delights of the church we turn to its craftsmanship in oak and glass.

It is everywhere about us, for the sanctuaries are finely panelled, the reredos is bordered with grape and vine, the priests' seats have figures of John the Baptist and Isaiah under rich canopies, and the marble font is crowned by a fine little cover. The windows make a striking gallery of sacred and historic figures. The east window is a fine blending of blues and reds, and is full of story. In the tracery are scenes of the Creation, and below is the Madonna in blue (the Child with a daffodil), Christ holding a ship in which a bishop sits, the Shepherds and Saints adoring, and fine figures of the Four Evangelists. At the foot are the Twelve Apostles in a row. Another window has the Women at the Tomb, another Our Lord with the children and healing the sick, and another bright scenes of the Transfiguration and the Entry into Jerusalem. At the west end are notable figures in the early story of Christianity in the North: St Cuthbert in a jewelled breastplate, and St Hilda as a nun, both with their churches in the background; Queen Ethelberga in crimson; and Bede as a monk, writing. A dainty window by the font, with two angels and a dove, was given by the children.

An old farmhouse a little way off was built as the manor house in the 17th century, and there is also in the neighbourhood, about a mile away, one great stone standing near the golf links to tell of a lost temple, the only stone remaining of a prehistoric Circle of the Stone Age, the others having sunk into the ground.

Two Poets and a Sculptor

SEBERGHAM. It is charmingly set among the hills at the northern end of the fells which rise majestically a few miles away. Its houses cling to the steep banks of a lovely glen where the River Caldew flows under an old stone bridge.

Two boys of this small place have found their way on to our national roll of fame; Josiah Relph, poet and curate and schoolmaster, and Thomas Denton, parson and poet. Another name well known here is that of Musgrave Lewthwaite Watson. His father, Thomas, who is buried in the churchyard, insisted on his taking up law, but immediately on his father's death in 1823 young Musgrave escaped to Rome to follow his own chosen profession of sculptor. While there he carved the memorial to his father which is in the church; it is a marble plaque showing the graceful heads and outstretched arms of three women. The sculptor's story belongs to Dalston, where he was born.

The church which this classical sculpture adorns was made new towards the end of last century, but it has kept four lancet windows 700 years old. The tiny tower has an outside flight of steps to the belfry, and a fine little oval window inside looking down on the nave or up to its hammerbeam roof. One of the nave lancets has a fine picture of the Good Samaritan, and on the wall near it is a charming mosaic of Our Lord with the little ones.

There is nothing left now of the days when the church began here; it may have had its origin in the 12th century when the hermit William of Wastell lived in a cell in the fields on a lonely hill. On the walls is a tablet to the poet curate Josiah Relph, who, although he died at 31, made a great name in the village by his energies in educating the children, and left behind a volume of dialect verses. He it was who made Thomas Denton a curate and a poet.

Whittle-Gate

SETMURTHY. One of its temples goes back beyond history, the stone circle on Elva Hill where about a dozen great stones are still visible, though sunk deeply in the ground. Not so impressive as the one at Keswick, this ancient circle has the same width of 100 feet and something of the same fine situation.

The other temple of this scattered place is the church, with a quaint little font of 1661 and a memorial brass to one woman and two men who died for us in the War.

One of the 19th-century parsons of Setmurthy was Charles Southey, the poet's son. In the 18th century this was one of the churches served not by a priest but by a reader, whose miserable pittance hardly allowed him to live. He was helped, however, by the custom which allowed him what was called whittle-gate, the privilege of going from house to house and staying a certain time in each. His whittle was the knife with which he shared in the food provided by each family.

SILLOTH. Since the coming of the railway in 1857 it has grown from an untidy village to a neat little port with wide tree-lined streets and a green park going down to the sea. A mile up the coast is a wooden lighthouse, and beyond the Solway Firth rise the hills of Scotland. Of stone, granite, and brick, the tall church of last century is in the style of 700 years ago, with two arcades of brick arches on stone pillars, and a chancel apse panelled in oak with a reredos of fine tracery. In a window Peter holds two keys, one gold, one silver.

The Font of Gratitude

SKELTON. A big village of grey-and-white with a church in its own little corner among the trees. As we approach it a fine peace memorial lychgate almost hides the sturdy 15th-century tower.

Little else of the church is old, and the interior is only attractive in one or two of its small things. The pulpit is carved in classical style, and the handsome font was given last century by two parents who lost their first little one and were full of thankfulness for the second. There is a quaint tablet to a couple in Queen Anne's time, telling how their little family was scattered far and wide. A more tragic memorial is that of an officer who lost his life in the submarine disaster which darkened the early weeks of 1932.

Half a mile from Skelton is Hardrigg Hall, one of the old fortified houses now a farm. Its strength lay in a tower now ruined; there are broken walls and arches still to be seen.

A Merry Company

SKIRWITH. Four roads with mossy walls meet at this charming village among the oaks, which a rushing stream from the Cumberland Fells divides into two halves linked by a stone bridge.

High above the stream is a group of old homes and a little 19th-century church of red stone with a gallery of faces outside its walls, a good-humoured company of men and women, old and young. A quaint and striking landmark is the small stone spire, with eight gable windows rising from the tower. The church is just as pleasing inside, though the only things of note are the oak screen to the south chapel, a little 17th-century panelling on the chapel wall, and a gilded candelabra with flowers and sprays of leaves.

The big house in the park is of no great age and only its name of Skirwith Abbey connects the site with one of the houses of the Knights Templars.

Carlisle's Next-Door Neighbour

STANWIX. Only a bridge over the Eden separates it from Carlisle, a handsome bridge designed by Robert Smirke.

Where the Romans built a camp a modern church stands today, with a gravestone which may be Norman in its north transept, and Christ with angels and archangels in the seven windows of its apse. In the churchyard we found the battered stone figure of a medieval priest, and a stone engraving of a priest with hands raised as if to ward off a blow. We were told that both were shortly to be taken into the shelter of the church.

Two castles here have come down in the world, both now farms. Drawdykes Castle has on its parapet three curiously carved heads, and in one of its walls something far older, a Roman tablet showing lions holding a mask, and in the pediment a woman's head. We imagine it came from their camp by the church. Linstock Castle is two miles away, with a medieval tower and walls six feet thick.

The Lonely Shrine

STAPLETON. There are few close neighbours in this scattered village by the little River Lyne. Even the 19th-century church is alone in a lonely field, with the gravestone of an Elizabethan, Robert Forrester, lying down beside it.

In a hollow among the trees two miles away stands Shank Castle with its fortified wall four storeys high and five feet thick at the base, an imposing shell of medieval strength which is now a farmhouse.

The Story that Moved Wordsworth

THRELKELD. The long irregular line of Blencathra towers magnificently above it, facing across the valley to a slope on which our British ancestors lived in a prehistoric village.

Threlkeld was once famous for its wrestlers, and then for its huntsmen, 45 of whom are named and remembered on a monument in the churchyard. Among them is John Crozier, master of the pack for 64 of his 80 years.

The simple church is 18th century, and its interest lies in its possessions. There are two bells at least 500 years old, a well-worn Black Letter Bible of 1613, and a handsome modern font made of Threlkeld granite by a Threlkeld man. The church records go back to Queen Elizabeth's time, and tell of the quaint local custom by which a person making a promise of marriage promised also to pay five shillings to the poor if he or she broke the contract.

The old farm called Threlkeld Hall and the mountain slopes near by have between them a memory taking us back to the Wars of the Roses. The original Threlkeld Hall was a home of Sir Lancelot Threlkeld, who used to say that of his three great houses one was for pleasure, another for profit and warmth in the winter, and this one to provide him with tenants to go to the wars. He married Lady Clifford, whose cruel first husband had been slain at Towton and whose young son Henry Clifford was in danger of his life from the Yorkists. Here the boy came for hiding and protection, and here as a shepherd on the fells part of his boyhood was spent.

The imagination of Wordsworth was touched by this story of the shepherd lord who went back to the home of his ancestors when the Red Rose triumphed, and in the poem which describes it all, the Song at the Feast of Brougham Castle, there are four beautiful lines telling of the boy's simple upbringing on these hills.

Love had he found in huts where poor men lie;
His daily teachers had been woods and rills,
The silence that is in the starry sky,
The sleep that is among the lonely hills.

The Bridge Blown Down by the Wind

THURSBY. It had a shrine before Christianity came, for foundations belonging to a pagan temple have been dug up half a mile from the church.

Today this little place, gathered so pleasantly round a green, has its shrine set on a hill looking down on the roofs clustered at its foot. It has nothing very old in it, for it is 19th century, but it has an imposing tower, and a brass lectern and a tall oak pulpit have come to it from Carlisle Cathedral. In a glass case is a deep pewter alms-dish, and a tulip-shaped pewter flagon of the 18th century. The best window has a fine modern figure of St Andrew.

It was a boy of this village, Sir Thomas Bouch, who built the Tay Bridge, scene of the most appalling disaster in British railway history.

After experience on various railways in the north of England, Thomas Bouch, who helped to give London and other cities their tramway systems, went to Scotland, where he built the first train ferries across the Forth and the Tay. His great opportunity came with the Tay Bridge, two miles long, comprising 85 spans of lattice girders.

The bridge was opened in May 1878, and in 18 months a train, with 70 passengers, was crossing the bridge in a gale of 150 miles an hour when an overwhelming blast carried away 400 yards of the structure and flung the train into the river. Not one soul escaped, and some of the bodies were found four miles away.

Greater engineers than Bouch had foreseen some such calamity; Sir John Fowler, creator of the Forth Bridge, pointed out that if the engineer had given to his supports the "straddle" that Holbein gave Henry the Eighth the bridge might have stood the wind. But all was guesswork when Bouch began.

A Government report declared that the bridge was badly designed, badly constructed, and badly maintained, and that defects in the structure must sooner or later have brought it down. Broken by the calamity, the unfortunate engineer sank under his burden of sorrow, dying at Moffat in Dumfriesshire in October 1880.

A Superb Viewpoint

TORPENHOW. Its grey houses line a long street from which we see the Solway and Scotland beyond. At one end is the church, attractive enough from outside but a pure delight within. What is new in this ancient building is fitting, and what is old has been splendidly restored.

All about us is the hand of the Normans. In the porch we are greeted by their fine doorway; in the nave we see their rugged arches; and in the chancel we see them using a carved Roman stone in a deep window a few inches wide. More impressive still is the chancel arch, one of its capitals a portrait gallery of odd faces, the other showing a group of four little men linking arms and legs. There is a Norman font carved with arches, and an unusual piscina.

The east window is 13th century; so is the transept in which the worn figure of a woman is lying. The lintel of the west window is somebody's coffin stone of 600 years ago, carved with cross and sword.

One of the newest possessions of the church is the panelled roof of the nave. It is 17th century, said to be made of fir; its painted cherubs watch us as we walk about.

The Roman stone in the chancel window and others in the walls are thought to come from Caermote Hill, a mile or two from the village. On it was an ancient fort, and its position made it a superb place for military purposes. It is equally superb as a viewpoint, its grand outlook including the Solway Firth, the Scottish mountains, the Pennine range, and the gathering peaks of Lakeland.

Traveller's Joy

ULPHA. We must be grateful to it for ever, for Wordsworth loved it, and its beauty stirred his heart. It comes into his sonnets of the Duddon, which he began to write just after Trafalgar and was still writing after Waterloo.

Between the fine Duddon Bridge and Ulpha village are three miles of an entrancing valley where the river divides Furness from Cumberland. Three miles of thrilling delight it is as we come up the steep and tortuous road threading in and out of the rocks high up on the Furness side; we look down on a scene of exquisite beauty where hills clothed in trees and bracken rise from the crystal stream. A glory of gold and green in autumn, it is in spring and summer too a scene of delight which Wordsworth himself could hardly paint.

It is an ancient and pretty stone bridge which brings us over the river, and the houses of Ulpha deck the valley. In a charming spot on the spur of a hill the little church stands as Wordsworth knew it; it was as welcome to the traveller, he said, as a star shining through a black cloud:

Or as a fruitful palm-tree towering high
O'er the parched waste beside an Arab's tent;
Or the Indian tree whose branches, downward bent,
Take root again, a boundless canopy.

The lychgate brings us to the lovely old church in which the light is pouring through windows which need no other pictures than the hills around. Its spick and span white walls have fragments of 18th-century decoration, with the arms of Queen Anne, and there are old timbers in the black-and-white roof. The font bowl and the piscina are old, but Ulpha church is loved for its simplicity and there is little more. It was strange to find two pairs of handcuffs in the vestry, relics of the days when the sexton was the village policeman.

How sweet were leisure, said Wordsworth, could it yield no more than in this wave-washed churchyard to recline. He must have sat and looked across at the romantic ruins of Frith Hall silhouetted against the sky, once a wayside inn where coaches changed horses on the way to Whitehaven. Within a mile of it are the ruins of the tower of Ulpha Old Hall, which has among its stories that of a lady who was drowned in the ravine below while fleeing from a wolf.

Much farther back goes the story of the hills, for there are ancient British settlements, and on the top of the huge mass of solid stone known as the Wallowbarrow Crag, is a tiny Druid circle. The crag belongs to us all, for the National Trust has it in its keeping, 75 acres by the river, lovely always, but a favourite place when spring flowers are blooming. Then we should come with Wordsworth and read here his Duddon Sonnets.

Wordsworth's Sonnets on the Duddon

THE 34 Sonnets Wordsworth wrote on the little River Duddon have an interesting place in the story of his genius. He knew and loved the river from early boyhood as a frequent visitor to Broughton-in-Furness, near where the Duddon enters Duddon Sands. He traced it so far into the hills with grown-up fishermen that he had to be carried home pick-a-back, tired out. He was 36, a poet of ever-increasing renown, when he wrote his first sonnet on the stream, at a place where it cleaves a passage through the wilderness attended only by its own voice, the clouds, and the fowls of the air.

That sonnet was laid aside to wait until, 14 years after it was written, they were all gathered together in a series of 34, and the first being now numbered as 14. Wordsworth was now 50, and in these sonnets we see the last glow of his genius. He wrote on for a quarter of a century, but the gleam was dimmed.

Rising close by the summit of Wrynose Pass where Cumberland, Lancashire, and Westmorland meet, the Duddon river fed by many becks from the two first counties (which it divides) reaches the sea on Duddon Sands, 14 miles away, without having on its banks a single village with grouped houses. There are only broad-spread towns with a scattering of houses here and there. Thus Ulpha extends from the sea to the Wrynose Pass on the Cumberland side of the stream, and on the Lancashire side are Dunnerdale and Seathwaite. It is a lonely river.

In his sonnets the poet sketches a series of typical scenes. At first he admits that Desolation is the Duddon's patron saint. Then he traces the changes in the surroundings of a journey from the river's source to the sea as it becomes less stern; the appearance of the first cottage "rude and grey," where trees become a shelter, and ruddy children the stream's associates. He tries to imagine the kind of men who first came to these solitudes. Stepping stones across the stream and the play of human feeling associated with them provide two sonnets. The Duddon has several examples of stepping-stones. A gorge in which the river almost disappears causes a display of conjectural fancy. The antiquities of the vale are brought in, such as a Roman Camp. The tributary stream from Seathwaite introduces the poet's ideal rural pastor, Robert Walker, who is also in the Excursion. On reaching the broader expanse of Dunnerdale there is a pensive description of the church at Ulpha, and finally the Duddon is traced to its smooth and unambitious mingling with the sea, overlooked by blue-topped hills from afar, and the poet ends:

And may thy Poet, cloud-born Stream, be free
(The sweets of earth contentedly resigned,
And each tumultuous working left behind
At seemly distance) to advance like thee;
Prepared in peace of heart, in calm of mind
And soul, to mingle with Eternity.

But no, it is not quite the end. The poet has an after-thought in which he sounds a deeper note, profound and impressive and known to all who love their Wordsworth:

I thought of Thee, my partner and my Guide,
As being past away—vain sympathies!
For, backward, Duddon, as I cast my eyes,
I see what was, and is, and will abide:
Still glides the Stream, and shall for ever glide,
The Form remains, the Function never dies;
While we, the brave, the mighty, and the wise,
We Men, who in our morn of youth defied

The elements, must vanish: be it so!
Enough if something from our hands have power
To live, and act, and serve the future hour;
And if, as toward the silent tomb we go,
Through love, through hope, and faith's transcendant dower,
We feel that we are greater than we know.

It is a sublime ending to one of the most pleasing and personal of Wordsworth's Nature poems.

Great Heights from the Little Churchyard

WABERTHWAITE. A lonely little place near the coast, we come to it either across an old ford at low tide or by the more venturesome way down a steep lane. Here the River Esk flows round the finely wooded hill of Muncaster Castle, with its beacon tower 250 feet up; and here, on the edge of a sandy creek, crouches one of Cumberland's ancient white-walled churches.

Low and simple, it has only five windows to light it, some of them 15th century. The east window is enriched with a picture of the Good Shepherd. The 300-year-old pulpit has carved panels and borders; and hidden in one of the old box pews is a Norman font two feet high, looking rather like the base of a pillar. The bell turret was rebuilt in Queen Anne's reign, but its two bells were ringing long before, when our English Church still belonged to Rome.

Waberthwaite has its share of the very old carved stones not uncommon in Cumberland, portions of crosses set up generations before the Conqueror landed. One in the vestry is part of a cross-shaft thought to be from the ninth century; and another in the churchyard is a splendid tenth-century shaft over six feet high, enriched with elaborate scrollwork. For many years it formed the lintel of the doorway, but is now back again in its old socket.

Every traveller must remember the fine view from this lonely churchyard of the Lake mountains dominated by Scafell.

WALTON. Very small but very attractive, it has a fine view of the Irthing valley, a few white cottages round a three-cornered green, and a little sandstone church looking on. The church is modern, and boasts one of the heaviest bells for miles around; it has also an unusual reredos in the form of a big mosaic panel with vines and acanthus leaves on a background of blue.

On the way to Brampton we pass Castlesteads, a great house

almost on the site of a Roman camp. The three acres of the camp have become its beautiful garden, a much-loved place where Roman figures and altars have been dug up and set among flowers and trees.

Little Warwick

WARWICK. It is Cumberland's little namesake of one of our most famous towns, with the green mounds of an ancient earthwork at Warwick Knowe, and a splendid 19th-century bridge of three arches.

Only a few yards from the bridge, yet so hidden away as to be easily missed, is a remarkable little church with the work of Norman builders who may have come over with the Conqueror. It is just a nave and a chancel, much restored, but it treasures still a striking Norman apse and a splendid Norman arch.

The apse is curious outside for having no less than 12 buttresses, each about 16 inches wide and 16 inches apart. They are quite plain like stone pillars, resting on a kind of ledge and supporting a plain parapet. The chancel interior has the unpardonable fault of a country church, darkness, being lighted only by small windows, three of them in the immensely thick wall of the apse. One, however, is most attractive in its dark setting, a window over the altar showing the King of Kings.

The nave opens into a modern vestibule, and here we pass under the lovely Norman arch. It has two deep mouldings, and fine shafts with simple but very massive capitals.

Warwick has a busy village neighbour, Warwick Bridge, where, as well as the factories for woollens and tweeds, we noticed a big white inn and a little white house, one of the few thatched homes hereabouts. There is a pleasing little Roman Catholic church, and, much more prominent, an impressive nunnery among the beeches. It was built last century in Tudor style, with many gables, embattled turrets, and a great array of tall chimneys in groups.

The Shadow of the Highest Hill on the Deepest Lake

WASDALE. It has some of Lakeland's loveliest places in its keeping, England's highest mountain throwing its shadow on her deepest lake.

It lies in a spacious hollow of the hills, with the silence broken only by the music of streams rushing under narrow bridges, a charming setting for the maypole on the village green and the little white church.

The oak panelling of this small sanctuary, with rich borders of flowers, fruit, and cherubs, has the proud distinction of having been in York Minster; it was there when the minster was fired by a madman. The chalice of beaten silver is Elizabethan, and the tiny font's cover and the almsbox on a cherub's head are both old. There are 14 little cherubs round the roofs.

It was surprising to find in the vicar's garden a Chile pine 40 feet high, but a lane threading through the hills brings us to one of the finest collections of pines and fir trees in England, in the grounds of Wasdale Hall, a house full of fine oak carving, almost buried in trees at the end of Wastwater Lake.

Here it is that we find in close company our deepest lake and our highest peak, for looking high at the eastern end of Wastwater is the great mass of Scafell. The lake at its foot is 200 feet above the sea and 260 feet deep in the middle, over three miles long, and half a mile wide. Thrilling and awe-inspiring is the journey along its rock-strewn shore, winding in and out like a serpent and up and down like a switchback, while gaunt bare mountains rise sharply all round. It is always a widely magnificent scene with magical colour as the seasons come and go.

Locked in the heart of the mountains at the end of the lake is the remote little village of Wasdale Head, with narrow walled lanes, grey stone houses with 50 people in them, and streams cascading down the hills. It is famous as the centre for the highest climbs in Lakeland and many well-known men have sat in the kitchen of its white-walled inn listening to tales of Cumbrian life.

Here amid Nature's stupendous pageantry is one of the smallest churches in the land, 40 feet long and 17 wide, with only three windows and a roof which on one side is less than six feet high. It stands in a field hidden by a screen of yews, 32 fine ones; they clothe the church as in a mantle, shading it from the fury of the storms, while another old yew stands sentinel at the door.

A plain little church it is, having neat oak seats with bobbin ends, some old beams in the roof, an old piscina in the chancel, and a crude silver chalice older than the Armada. There must have been a few old men about when we called who could just remember the days when this place was derelict without either fence or doors, a thorn bush keeping out the sheep. In those days the church was bedded with bracken like a stable, and there were only two pews and a few other seats made from sheep-forms on trestles. In the churchyard are the graves of some of those who perished in climbing the rocky heights that dominate the scene.

Darby and Joan of Long Ago

WATERMILLOCK. It is on the noble slopes above Ullswater, and it has lost the little church it once had on the water's edge; but up the hill, with the lovely lake just out of sight, is an impressive new church with several things to show.

One attractive window shows the scene of Paul's conversion; in another he is preaching at Athens, and the window is in memory of a man who preached here 56 years. The font keeps in remembrance five little ones "called away in the springtime of their lives."

A brass inscription tells of an old couple in Tudor England who lived together 60 years and were buried together one New Year's Day; and there is a tablet to Gerald Spring-Rice, who went from his home here to die for us in France. Another tablet like it is in memory of Sir Cecil Spring-Rice, our ambassador in America during the Great War, who died at Ottawa in 1918 while waiting for the ship that was to bring him home.

Giant Barwis

WESTWARD. Its farms are scattered on the little hills or hiding in trees with the church and the school in a deep valley of the Wiza Beck. From the road above the village we have the majestic mass of Criffell towering beyond Solway Firth, and a sight of Carlisle and Dumfries. Sharing in this view of mountain grandeur is the plain little church which has lost all trace of the Norman's work and has little that is old.

The oldest things we found were two brass plates to the Barwis family, one to Richard of 1648, whose plate is engraved with a shield and two sitting figures blowing trumpets. The motto has the words Truth and Fame, and of Richard's fame there is no doubt, for he was known as Great Barwis, and many tales are told of his strength. It is said that he could walk round his court at Islekirk Hall carrying his wife at arm's length in one hand and a huge stone in the other.

Fame in Marble

WETHERAL. Proud of its fame as one of the prettiest villages in Cumberland, it stands on a high cliff above the river Eden, many of its dignified houses grouped round a green and a very tall old cross. In one of the garden walls are five great millstones.

The big Priory gatehouse which is set near some old trees within a hundred yards of the cliff edge, looking toward Corby Castle, gives Wetheral a great distinction. Built in three storeys of red sandstone, with embattled walls and a vaulted archway, it is a reminder of the Priory founded here in 1100.

Halfway down the sharp slope to the river stands the church which houses treasures of the past, the oldest being a piece of a Saxon cross. On a table tomb lie the worn alabaster figures of Sir Richard Salkeld and his wife; they must have been superb when they were made, about 1500. Sir Richard, who was Captain and Keeper of Carlisle castle, lies in finely chased armour, with a helmet for a pillow and a collar of roses linked by a delicate chain. At his belt are a sword, dagger, and an eagle-headed knife. Lady Salkeld wears a long gown with a dainty collar.

The pride of the village is in two magnificent marble monuments kept behind locked gates in the chapel of the Howards of Corby Castle. One is to Adela Howard, who kneels on a cushion, a cloak over her lovely head; the other, in memory of Marie Archer, wife of Henry Howard, is an exquisite group to which Wordsworth wrote the sonnet beginning

Stretched on the dying mother's lap, lies dead
Her new born babe.

The sculptor, the fashionable and miserly Joseph Nollekens, has shown Marie lying barefooted in a long gown, the dead child on her lap, her head falling back on the arm of a beautiful woman who is pointing heavenward.

We leave the churchyard, with its fine old yew, and go down the steep lane, past the charming little white houses of the lower village to where the Eden flows between steep, wooded banks. At the water's edge is a delightful path leading to three caves known as St Constantine's Cell, which lie 40 feet above the river, a figure of the saint, nearly 100 years old, facing the cell. The worn inscriptions on the rocks near by are supposed to be Roman.

Battlefield and Arrow Field

WHICHAM. Its homes cluster beneath Black Combe's towering mass at the entrance to the charming Whicham Valley. Sheltered by trees is a trim little church with a doorway made by the Normans, stout walls of the 13th century, a massive font centuries old, two bells which were ringing 500 years ago, and a flagon and a paten from Stuart England. Six massive beams support a modern black-and-white roof, and there is fine oak carving in the new stalls, the pulpit, and the eagle lectern.

Two fields recall by their names the far-off days. Near Whicham Hall, now a farm, is Scots Croft, supposed to be the site of a battle between the English and the Scots; and on the way to the sea is Arrow Field, humped with an ancient tumulus.

The Lady of Annaside

WHITBECK. It is grey with farms and cottages like the rock of the mountain side to which they cling. A little beck splashes and roars over the rocks as it rushes to the sea; another falls in lovely cascades in a deep cleft of Black Combe, from whose towering height of nearly 2000 feet we have one of the most marvellous panoramas in England. We are told that 14 counties of England and Scotland can be seen, with Talke-o'-the-Hill in Staffordshire a hundred miles away.

The Lady of Annaside has slept in this place for 600 years and more. They laid her here when the old church was new, and through much of its long story her graceful stone figure weathered the storms across the churchyard. The 13th-century church has been made new, and the Lady of Annaside is now indoors by the font, an attractive figure in a flowing gown with a wimple and a veil. She is thought to be one of the Huddlestons from the hamlet of that name two miles away. This fine old lady of about 1300, the grey stone chancel arch, and the font with a shallow bowl formed by the hollowing-out of the capitals of its clustered pillars, are all that is left of the 13th century. But here also is a pewter flagon, and a leather case hoary with age in which the chalice was kept.

The Romans made a road close by, the Druids left their stones about, and about a mile away at Monk Foss is the Cockpit which may once have been the fishpond of the monks; it is at a farm sheltered by trees, where a thread-like stream leaps down the mountain side.

In a Hollow by the Sea

WHITEHAVEN. Snugly it lies in a great hollow by the sea, the third town in Cumberland, with a good harbour and a life won from coal and iron. Here was laid out one of the earliest railways, an affair of wooden rails and horse trucks; here, during his many years as a doctor in the 18th century, William Brownrigg made important discoveries in the chemistry of coal gas; and into this harbour in 1788 sailed Paul Jones in his American privateer The Ranger, damaging the shipping but failing to capture the town.

It is astonishing to read of the story of Whitehaven in the 17th century, for from a village of nine thatched cottages in 1633 it rose to a town of 2222 people in 1693. For much of its growth it had to thank the Lowther family, especially Sir John and his son Sir James, who fostered it as a port and encouraged the development of its coal industry. It was Sir John Lowther who in 1644 began the building of the Castle, now a hospital in a finely wooded park beloved by the people as a pleasure ground.

Whitehaven has two churches from the 18th century. One is Holy Trinity, a very plain building with great balconies and a pulpit about 12 feet high. It has a tablet to Thomas Dalton who ministerd 57 years; a monument to Sir James Lowther of 1755 carved with a sarcophagus, four children, and an altar of five; and a marble memorial showing James Spedding of 1788 with his long pigtail and cravat. The other church is St James, with a beautiful altar piece as its best possession, a painting of the Transfiguration by Correggio's pupil Procaccini. The plaster decoration of the ceiling shows a scene of the Ascension, angels and a dove in the clouds, and a rural picture with a woman and a sheep and a church. In the windows are pictures of the Good Shepherd, the Good Samaritan in memory of a doctor, Christ at the house of Lazarus, and Christ offering a crown to a knight in memory of one who was vicar 24 years; but the glass we liked best was to a New Zealander who fell in the war, a picture of an angel offering a crown to a knight in a red mantle.

The mother church of the town is, we imagine, St Nicholas, standing finely in a big rock garden in the heart of the busy street. It is a 17th-century church rebuilt in the 19th century by a daughter in memory of her parents. The sturdy tower has three fine arches inside, and under it we saw a length of clay piping so ancient that we wondered if it were Roman. The interior has a lofty wagon roof and is lit by a clerestory having ten windows on each side. In the chancel there are two scenes of the Last Supper, in the east window and in the dim oil painting which serves as the reredos; but the finest possession of the church is a very beautiful modern screen with lovely fan-vaulting, a cornice of grape and vine, and tracery tipped with roses.

Here, preserved in a glass case, are old manuscripts and cuttings, and a finely kept account book, where we chanced to read that on July 18 in 1693 the sum of £6 16s was paid to the Bishop of Chester's secretary at the consecration of the church. It was "for gunpowder at His Lordship's departure," from which we may conclude that in those days bishops went off with a bang! We read also that labourers were then earning about 7d and 8d a day.

It is a Whitehaven woman who figures in one of the greatest of all the romances of English literature.

The Marvellous Experiences of Two Immortal Children

WHEN Sir Walter Scott, turning from poetry and novels, sat down to write the life and edit the 19 volumes of works of Jonathan Swift he found that the author of Gulliver had left a scrap of autobiography.

In it he told how, when he was a puny, sickly year-old child in a poverty-stricken Dublin home, his nurse, a Whitehaven girl, being called to the deathbed of a relative from whom she expected a legacy, could not find it in her heart to part from this child whom she loved, but stole him and carried him off to Whitehaven with her.

Arrived at Whitehaven, she wrote to Mrs Swift confessing what she had done, and Mrs Swift, fearing to expose her delicate child to a second crossing of a perilous sea, bade the girl keep him until he was better able to face the hazard. For three years the little boy who in later days was to shake the world with his writings, dwelt in Whitehaven, the adored pensioner of the girl who had stolen him. He grew strong and healthy, learned with phenomenal precocity, and within a year of being restored by his nurse to his mother he could read any chapter in the Bible.

Such was the story Scott found awaiting him, a thrilling send-off for his biography. Scott died, and Lockhart in due course began his greater biography of this still far greater man. After he had progressed far he opened by chance an old bureau at Abbotsford, found that Scott, like Swift, had left unsuspected autobiographical diaries, and, still greater surprise, a tale of his own childhood out-Swifting Swift's.

The event had occurred in Sir Walter's life at the same period as that in which Swift had been imperilled. When just over a year, Scott was seized by the terrible malady, which, discovered more than a century later to have been infantile paralysis, was then unknown and incurable. In three days it left him lame for life in his right leg.

Country air appearing to be the only hope for him, he was sent, in charge of his nurse, from Edinburgh to Sandy Knowe. The girl longing passionately to return to her sweetheart in Edinburgh, but compelled to remain forlorn at Sandy Knowe, her love for her charge turned to violent hatred. She carried him to the Craigs, intending to dispose of him and to bury his body in the moss.

Fortunately she communicated her thoughts to old Alison Wilson, the Scott's housekeeper, and was instantly dismissed; and so Scott lived to read Swift's extraordinary adventure and to cap it with one of his own.

Seven Centuries of Market Life

WIGTON. A little workaday town on the fringe of the great fells, it has seven centuries of market life behind it, and memories of several men who were known in the wider world. Here was born the Cumberland poet Ewan Clark, and the historical painter Robert Smirke whose architect son designed the British Museum. Here also in the churchyard lies John Rooke, the farmer who studied political economy and became an apostle of free trade.

In the marketplace stands an elaborate 19th-century fountain set up in memory of his wife by George Moore, with bronze panels on which are scenes of healing, charity, music, and women with heads bowed round a deathbed; but finer as a memorial is one in Wigton cemetery over the grave of William Banks, a well-known figure in county affairs last century. He was a judge, and here in his honour is a fine statue of Justice as a winged angel with sword and scales.

The church is a plain building refashioned in the 18th century, but it stands on a more ancient site. The interior made us think of a concert hall, its unusual decoration being a study in grey relieved here and there with gold. Even the pews are grey in this neat and rather cold colour scheme. The glass includes pictures of the Good Samaritan, the Wise Men, Charity, the Light of the World, and the Women at the Tomb; but best of all are Christ appearing to Mary in the Garden and a beautiful Annunciation with Mary in blue beside a pool. The oak lectern is an eagle on a richly carved pedestal, and the oak pulpit stands 11 feet high, like a great tulip on its stem. There is fine work in the litany stool, which has Mary and John under rich canopies, and a kneeling angel at each side.

From its predecessor the church has a brass plate to Colonel Thomas Barwise of the Civil War time, and in the churchyard is a raised stone with lettering said to have been cut by the 17th vicar whose memorial it is. It says:

Thomas Warcop prepared this stone
To remind him of his eternal home.

Second Town in Cumberland

WORKINGTON. Next to Carlisle in its importance as a town, a place of narrow grey streets at the mouth of the Derwent, it is busy with its markets, with iron, and with coal mined under the sea. But it has a memory, too, the memory of a tragic queen who comes to mind as we catch a glimpse of Workington Hall among the trees on a hill overlooking the river. It is the home of perhaps the oldest family in the county, the Curwens, and it was the courtly Sir Henry Curwen who in 1568 entertained Mary Queen of Scots. She was on her way to Cockermouth and Carlisle, and it was here, at the beginning of her long imprisonment, that she wrote her well-known letter of appeal to Queen Elizabeth. What is called the Queen's Room is still preserved, and a contemporary portrait of her hangs in the picture gallery; but the house was nearly all rebuilt last century. As a family home it has 700 years of history behind it, and over the entrance is a shield with the Curwen arms of 1665.

We are reminded of the Curwens again in St Michael's church not far from the dockyards, where two of them lie on a fine 15th-century tomb rich with canopies and shields. They are Sir Christopher Curwen and his Elizabeth, both holding hearts, he in plate armour and she in a square headdress and a mantle held by a rose clasp. He rests his head on a helmet with a crest of a unicorn's head, and hers rests on cushions held by angels. Two dogs hold the hem of her gown.

St Michael's is a refashioned building with a massive tower and lofty arcades, but it has a list of rectors going back to 1150, and one or two things the first rector on the list may have seen. There is a simple Norman arch in the tower, a Norman capital, and a Norman font bowl no longer used. There are fragments of ancient crosses with interlaced work, and several medieval coffin stones. The richly traceried pulpit stands high on marble columns, and among the many coloured windows are attractive pictures of the Annunciation, Christ in the workshop and with the woman at the well, the Ascension, and the women at the Tomb. The east window is bright with a crowded scene of Calvary, and has the Nativity below.

Two other churches in Workington are remarkable for the settings of their altars. The lofty Roman Catholic church has three altars with the reredos finely carved in stone, angels and saints, scenes of the Nativity, and the Crucifixion, under lovely canopies. We see the Crucifixion again over the doorway, above a sculpture of the crowning of the Madonna; and on the walls of the north chapel are some fine fragments of ancient sculptured alabaster found at Jerveaux Abbey in Yorkshire: the Crucifixion, the Resurrection, the Descent of the Holy Spirit, and figures of the Madonna and St George.

St John's church, with its imposing front of four great columns supporting a pediment, was built in 1823 and has a tower with a dome. The interior is mostly prim and formal, but over the altar is an extraordinary coloured canopy, perhaps 20 ft. high, with a flat top supported on four massive columns of gleaming gold. Hanging at the back is an elaborate star-like medallion with a figure of St John; and altogether, with the rich red drapery of the altar and the wall, the effect is striking.

The fine pulpit is twice as high as a man, and has cherubs on its panels. The font has a remarkable cover with a spire-like top in blue and gold, resting on eight columns. The ceiling of the church is elaborately moulded and has 12 painted shields, and high up in a window on the east wall are the Four Evangelists and the Master.

For a brief interval between her years as a Queen and her years as a prisoner Workington knew Mary Queen of Scots and was charmed by her.

Mary Stuart Comes this Way

ONE day in the May of 1568 an open fishing boat crossed the Solway Firth and landed at Workington some 30 refugees from Scotland, chief of whom was Mary Queen of Scots, a suppliant for the favour of her cousin, Queen Elizabeth.

Mary was 25, and in the heyday of her loveliness, mistress of modern languages, a poet and writer of admirable prose, a musician whose very speech was melody. Into ten years had been crowded triumph and tragedy enough for many lives: married at 16, Queen of

France at 17, and a widow in a year, at 23 she had married Darnley, and two years afterwards was privy to his murder by Bothwell, whom, to the horror of the world, she married within two months of the crime. The country had risen against her and shattered and scattered her forces; and here she came flying to throw herself on the mercy of Elizabeth.

She was received by Sir Henry and Lady Curwen with chivalrous courtesy, and welcomed to Workington Hall. All were dazzled by her beauty, and as we follow where she walked we see her through Wordsworth's eyes:

Dear to the Loves, and to the Graces vowed,
The Queen drew back the wimple that she wore . . .
She smiled; but Time, the old Saturnian Seer,
Sighed on the wing as her foot pressed the strand. . . .

While resting under the kindly care of the Curwens, Mary wrote her famous letter of appeal to Elizabeth which, having given her own version of the events leading to her flight from Scotland, went on:

I entreat you to send for me as soon as possible, for I am in a pitiable condition, not only for a queen, but even for a gentlewoman, having nothing in the world but the clothes in which I escaped, riding sixty miles the first day, and not daring to travel afterwards except by night, as I hope to be able to show you, if it please you to have compassion on my great misfortunes, and permit me to come and bewail them to you.

Not to weary you, I will now pray God to give you health and a long and happy life, and to myself patience, and that consolation I await from you, to whom I present my humble commendations.

From Workington, this 17th of May. Your very faithful and affectionate good sister and cousin and escaped prisoner, Marie R.

Mary left here after writing her letter, and rode to Cockermouth, and from there to Carlisle, where she had apartments in the castle. She was already sowing seeds of mischief by writing to her uncle, the Cardinal of Lorraine, imploring him to send an army from France, at the same time giving him a memorable description of her plight:

I have endured injuries, calumnies, imprisonment, famine, cold, heat, flight, not knowing whither, 92 miles across the country without stopping or alighting, and I have had to sleep on the ground, and drink sour milk, and eat oatmeal without bread, and have been three nights like the owls, without a female in this country, where, to crown all, I am little else than a prisoner.

Prisoner she became indeed, and so remained for the last 19 years of her life, at Bolton, Tutbury, Wingfield, Coventry, Chatsworth, Sheffield, Buxton, Chartley, and finally Fotheringay. There, in February 1587, having been found guilty of the part in Babington's plot to assassinate the Queen, she laid her head on the block and met her death with dignity and resignation that made her death appear a martyrdom to her devoted partisans.

The Great Achievement of Sarah Losh

WREAY. We may wish she had a more romantic name, but we can hardly wish for her a more conspicuous monument. Here in the second century were the Romans; from here in the 19th century Miss Losh sent the local mason out to Rome to prepare himself for setting up among these stately elms, by this odd-shaped green, a church in the style of a Roman basilica.

Her father, John Losh, had grown rich from the chemical works he established with his brother and the Earl of Dundonald, and had been a great traveller before he retired and settled down at Woodside. He had two daughters, who went to school together in London and at Bath, travelled together in Italy and France, and together chose to remain unmarried. Sarah was the belle of the Assize balls in Carlisle, an accomplished linguist, a great tree planter, and was interested in science and art. She loved her sister Catherine, and after Catherine's death in 1835 Sarah remained alone at Woodside, living in seclusion in a barely furnished room, overcome with grief. She was a familiar figure round about her home, visiting her neighbours in her black bonnet and long black cloak, befriending them in every way and helping on good causes; and in memory of Catherine she began setting up drinking troughs for horses, restoring wells, and beautifying churches.

But the chief monument to Catherine she set up in their own neighbourhood, building an infant school at Wreay, the school on the green, a schoolmaster's cottage like those she had seen at Pompeii, a cemetery chapel like the ancient oratory at St Piran in Cornwall, and finally the remarkable church at Wreay which stands by the green.

Miss Losh was her own architect; the local mason was her master builder; his son William Hinsdon did most of the carving; and these three have left their mark greatly on this village among the little hills. The school and the cottages, the church and the vicarage, are scattered round the green. In all the carving the favourite emblems are the arrow and the cone, both thought to be associated with a major killed by an arrow in India, William Thain, who was a schoolboy here.

Their church was not yet a centenarian when we called, for it was built in the early years of the Victorian Era, a striking place packed with symbolism, with fine craftsmanship, and with curious and unusual things. Under the roof of the nave outside is a strange company of gargoyles among which we noticed snakes, tortoises, and alligators, and round the west doorway and the three windows above it are water lilies, birds, beetles, butterflies, caterpillars, and carved fossils—an extremely rare thing to come upon. Above all these are 18 tiny windows round the gable, and in the doorway below is a fine oak door (its lock shaped like two cones) in a frame carved with figs and leaves among which are two butterflies.

There are 84 windows in the church, 29 of them high up in the wall of the apse, and at the east end of the chancel light pours through seven globes of golden glass fitted into seven small holes; they look like stars. A round arch brings us into the chancel, with a head on each side presented by the enthusiastic mason, the only human forms in all this mass of carving. There is an arcade of 13 stone seats round the wall, divided by single stone pillars with capitals all richly carved and all different. The capital at one end has an eagle and a serpent, and at the other end is a bat and a pelican catching a newt. The wall forming the backs of these seats is painted with Our Lord and the Twelve Apostles. The marble altar in the middle of the apse rests on two fine bronze eagles, and on it are two alabaster candlesticks carved like lotus flowers by Miss Losh.

The alabaster font is elaborately carved (perhaps too elaborately); it has flowers, wheat, grapes, figs, a dove, a butterfly, and a dragonfly; and inside the bowl, acting oddly as a cover, is a mirror looking like a pool on which water lilies float, sculptured lilies standing on the glass.

We must all appreciate the ingenuity and the loving labour put into this remarkable place, as well as the fine craftsmanship. In some of the windows of the nave are fragments of old glass picked up in the ruins of an Archbishop's palace in Paris, or collected as odds and ends from various places, and many of the small windows are unique in our experience for having thin alabaster instead of glass, the light coming through flowers and leaves cut out like fret-work. The chancel has 13 of these, making a fine little gallery of fossil pictures showing some of the first forms of life.

Here also we are in the presence of something which is older than any church standing on the earth. It must be thrilling for the preacher here to remember that he is in a pulpit made from a tree that was growing before the world had heard of Bethlehem. The pulpit was fashioned from the hollow trunk of a single piece of bog oak, rescued from a submerged forest in such fine condition that it was possible to transform it into this beautiful rostrum and to shape it after its natural form and decorate it with fossils. A small branch at one side is carved with leaves to make a candle-holder.

The pulpit is part of the fine woodwork which enriches the whole church, much of it coming from Woodside near by, the home of Miss Losh. The finely carved timbers of the roof were made from Woodside trees, and the bog oak of the pulpit, the lectern, and the reading desk was dug up at Woodside by men excavating to join two lakes. On the lectern is a magnificent eagle carved in chestnut, and on the reading desk is a beautifully poised chestnut pelican. Seven angels standing between palm trees are set in a row above the chancel arch, and on the wall on each side of the arch are fine wood figures of Gabriel and Michael.

The beautiful bracket close by is carved with two lions and two birds, a cock, and an owl; and the carvings have a story, for much of the work was done by John Scott, a cripple at Dalston a few miles away. We are told that he charged five pounds each for the eagle and the pelican, and eighteenpence for bringing them to the church on a farm cart.

Truly Wreay may be proud of its three artists, the lady of Woodside, the local mason, and John Scott the cripple. One little tale we heard of the mason. It was characteristic of Sarah Losh, who did all this work for love, that she should wish no name to appear anywhere on the church; it was to be a work of faith and love with no self-praise in it, and not a single name or mark of recognition was to appear. So the church stood all through the Victorian Era and into our own century, and then one day it was necessary to remove the font, and as the bowl was lifted from the shaft a well-kept secret was revealed. It was the man and not the woman who could not keep a secret, for on the bottom of the bowl, where he thought it never would be seen, the proud mason had slyly carved his name.

One or two things not made by local hands there are—two chairs from abroad with ancient panels of scenes from Bethlehem, and a holy water vessel about 700 years old embossed with figures, so precious that it is locked in the safe. Locked in the safe also are the gold necklaces of Sarah Losh and her sister, given for fastening the lamps to the metal stands in the sanctuary, which are copies of those found at Pompeii.

Outside it all, in a corner of the churchyard are the fine memorials of the Losh family, some of them flat stones carved with fine crosses, some rough-hewn and carved with fossil forms, and one a truly splendid copy of the seventh-century cross at Bewcastle.

Near the cross stands the stone-walled mausoleum of the Losh family, with portrait medallions of the father and mother on the walls. Through a little panel window in the door we may peep and see a white marble figure sitting as if she were thinking about it all. It is Sarah Losh's sister Catherine, and below is this inscription: "Catherine Isabella, sweet, lovely, sisterly sister: always wilt thou be most dear to me; dear, too, now is thy pale lifeless image." When the time came for Sarah to follow her (18 years later, in 1853) she was buried with her sister, one stone covering their graves.

We found the children playing on the green and went into their school and found it full of interest. Only one or two houses has the village itself, but it has this fine green and this fine school, and little scholars come for miles and bring their meals. Well they are rewarded, for in the school we found a multitude of interests, and were much struck by the little shop where the children buy and sell to learn arithmetic.

We may hope they remember something of the tale of Sarah Losh and all the village owes to her, and we may think they do, for rarely have we found a place where school and church and all concerned have a warmer atmosphere of common friendliness.

The Inn That Was Drowned

WYTHBURN. Lying at the edge of Thirlmere and in the shadow of Helvellyn, it has scarcely anything but its church, an attractive little building in which we walk uphill toward the altar. The chancel is an apse with three little pictures in glass of David and Jesus and Peter, and has been built since the days when the extreme simplicity of Wythburn church was being sung by the poets of Lakeland. It appealed to Wordsworth as

a modest House of prayer
As lowly as the lowliest dwelling;

and to Hartley Coleridge, who wrote these lines about it:

Humble it is, and meek, and very low,
And speaks its purpose by a single bell;
But God Himself, and He alone, can know
If spiry temples please Him half so well.

The Cherry Tree Inn, where Wordsworth laid a gay scene of feasting and dancing in his poem The Waggoner, was lost for ever at the end of last century, when Thirlmere became not only a lake but a reservoir. Its level was raised 50 feet by a great dam, its area was more than doubled, and from it the water now runs about 100 miles to supply the needs of Manchester. Some of the lake's charm has gone with these changes, but there is every sign that Nature is gradually making the new outline of Thirlmere her own.

A little south of Wythburn the high road climbs up and crosses over into Westmorland. Beside it at the top of the pass is the great heap of stones called Dunmail Raise, with its own little tradition of something that happened on this boundary 1000 years ago. Here, it is thought, the battle took place in which the Saxon king Edmund defeated Dunmail, the last king of Cumbria, whose territory was then handed over to King Malcolm of Scotland.

Along the old road over the pass William Ball drove every Sunday from Rydal to the little Friends Meeting House at Colthouse. One of his horses fell dead in harness, and in harness he was buried where a stone in the wall of the old road, near the top of the Raise, bears the inscription Mr Ball wrote in memory of his faithful friend, whose "only fault was dying."

From the point of view of scenery the approach to Wythburn from Keswick is preferably on the western side of Thirlmere. The straight main road on the eastern side hugs closely the foot of Helvellyn, and is tame. The western side of the lake, underneath Armboth Fell, has woods and fine crags close at hand, and the lake as foreground to Helvellyn. Before Thirlmere was made a reservoir for Manchester the lake lapped gently up to the road under Helvellyn and invited the footsore pedestrian to paddle. Manchester has greatly increased the expanse of the lake and has had wise consideration for its amenities. Thirlmere is the second highest of the large lakes, Hawes Water being first, and Ullswater third.

Wythburn is the place where a highroad is nearest to Helvellyn's summit, and a pony track makes the connection. A direct ascent can be made up Whelpside Gill behind the church. On this side, however, Helvellyn is dull, and the climber's reward does not come till the top is reached and the romantic side of the mountain is revealed.

The Jewelled Sword

WYTHOP. Lonely and remote, it is scattered widely among the hills and vales. Its Hall was once a fortified mansion and is now a farm; its humble Tudor chapel has almost gone; but its 19th-century church is finely placed on the fell side and has a good view of Bassenthwaite Lake.

At Routenbeck House here was born Dr John Hudson, an eminent Oxford scholar who became Keeper of the Bodleian Library, giving many books to it.

A great treasure found near Wythop Mill, once proudly worn by an ancient Briton, is now in the British Museum; it is a sword with an iron blade in a bronze sheath, with red and green jewels on the hilt.

WESTMORLAND

The Central Town of Westmorland

AMBLESIDE. On the main highway through the Lakes, it is Westmorland's most central town, as Grasmere is its central village. It stands at the foot of Wansfell Pike, where the Stock Gill and the Kirkstone Pass, coming down from the lofty Red Screes, enter the green valley of the Rothay, a mile above the head of Windermere.

Its situation, as seen when we come to it up the lake, is very beautiful. Though the town nestles somewhat closely under the hills, views of great and varied beauty expand from trifling ascents on any side.

Shut in by Wansfell on the east, it is faced on the north by ridges which lead up to the summits of the Fairfield range, and hold the upland valleys of Rydal and Scandale. Loughrigg Fell blocks the head of the lake with the Rothay, a river of many memories, passing its foot on its way from the Vale of Grasmere, and the Brathay from the Langdales on the other side. A very short walk along the lower slope of Wansfell to Jenkin Crag opens out the western view of the Langdales, with the chief summits of the highest mountain mass in England in the distance. Loughrigg, a small plateau with rocky points of view rising from it, just across the flat of the Rothay valley, has easy paths to where lake and valleys and sternly solemn hills are spread around in haunting beauty.

Ambleside has few memories of a distant past. The old cross stands in the marketplace. Only one building in the town catches the eye of the passer-by. It is a tiny place built on a round arch that spans a rushing stream. It has two rooms, one above the other, linked by a stone staircase built outside. Charming it must have looked nearly 300 years ago when it was the summerhouse of Ambleside Hall and apple trees grew beside it. Older people still call it the applehouse, though the orchard is no longer there. The house is safe as the property of the National Trust.

Of Ambleside Hall itself only the barn and one wing remain. It is now a cottage, and has an old oak staircase and a delightful balustrade. From this house, standing where the road begins its steep ascent of the Kirkstone Pass to Patterdale, we may see a pretty scene on a certain July evening. Down the village street come 200 school children, dressed in their best and laden with flowers and rushes. They are on the way to church for the rush-bearing ceremony, a relic of the time when churches had clay floors and once a year fresh rushes were brought and laid down by the young people of the place.

It is to St Mary's, the 19th-century church designed by Sir Gilbert Scott, that the procession goes. The church has a memorial window to Wordsworth subscribed for by English and American admirers, others to his sister and his wife, and one to Matthew Arnold. It also has a handsome Bible presented by Wordsworth's widow, a thrilling book to see, for often the poet must have sat in his armchair reading it. There is a Bible of 1611, and a 17th-century cup.

St Anne's church, made new 42 years before St Mary's, has a little font which is said to have been a stoup in Furness Abbey. Near by the old church, where the stocks used to be, hurries the Stock Gill, full of energy, to join the Rothay, after having tumbled 120 feet down the rocks above, as Stock Gill Force.

Ambleside was not the home of any of the Lake poets. They lived at Grasmere, Rydal, and Keswick. But it became through them a centre of intellectual interest. Dr Arnold built himself a holiday home here after he became Master of Rugby School, and here he brought up his clever family. Mr W. E. Forster, who introduced popular education into Parliament and broke himself in trying to govern Ireland, married a daughter of Dr Arnold and lived at the foot of Loughrigg Fell. Harriet Martineau came in 1846 and built The Knoll, and here she lived for 30 years and wrote with burning zeal on the social topics of her day. Here came many famous men and women, Charlotte Brontë, Emerson, and George Eliot, all liking to talk with this strongminded woman.

In Miss Martineau's time the garden, now trim with flower beds, was a miniature forest. Her sundial, inscribed "Come, Light, Visit Me," can have seen little of the sun until 40 trees were hewn down around it 20 years ago.

It had been long known that a considerable Roman fort had stood at the head of Lake Windermere. Camden discussed it three centuries ago. But in 1900 evidences of a significant Roman road leading to the fort were found, and by 1920 the site known as Borrans Field had been thoroughly excavated, and it now figures as the twice-made Roman fort of Galava. It seems to have been first made by Agricola about 79 A.D. Apparently it was liable to flooding, and it has been discovered that it was raised by adding a thick bed of clay. About the year 122 Hadrian's engineers raised another fort on the old site, to guard the Roman road from Manchester.

Today what can be seen there is some piles of stones on a grassy platform, 150 by 100 yards. Still we can trace two of the gates, and the stout walls of the praetorium, the commandant's headquarters and the foundations of the granaries are also to be seen, an important department in a Roman camp, where the army expected wheat bread as its staple food. The sill of the south gate is in a wonderful condition. It is a stone nearly 11 feet by 5, about a foot thick, and in its ends are the holes the Romans cut to receive the pivots of the double gates.

Once the hobnailed sandals of Roman soldiers made a great clatter on the flagstones of the fort; today all is still; Borrans Field is the most peaceful spot in Ambleside, now, we rejoice to say, under the preserving care of the National Trust.

Harriet Martineau was 44 when she built her house at Ambleside, the house in which she died 30 years later.

Old Lady of Ambleside

HER early days had been far from happy, but by this time she had, through her writing, found fame and friends and relief from the financial worry she had known all her life. Lack of money was not, however, the first incentive to her writing, for her first article was the outcome of a strong conviction that women equally with men could be leaders and teachers. Yet she had to conform to public opinion and sign the article with a man's name or it would never have been printed.

She was one of eight children, brought up at Norwich in an austere Unitarian home. Her father, a manufacturer, died when she was 24, leaving the family worse off than ever. She earned a little by writing rather ponderous religious essays and moral stories, and then her health broke down. She had been a sickly child, was permanently deaf and deprived of any sense of taste and smell; now she became seriously ill, but was better in time to meet the complete failure of the family's small investments.

She came up to London and tramped through the city till she found a publisher willing to bring out two educational stories at half-profits; and a most lucrative bargain it proved for him, for a first edition of 15,000 was exhausted in ten days. Story followed story; social problem after social problem she wrapped round with its plot and fictional characters. Everyone with a good cause wanted her to make a tale of it. Lord Brougham asked her to write a tale dealing with pauperism, and this (called The Parish) was one of her best. She was London's latest literary lion. She visited America and wrote against slavery. She never spared herself, though her health was never good. Three Prime Ministers offered her a civil pension, and each she refused in order to maintain her independence.

She came to live in Ambleside, to be visited by many whose names are milestones of that period, including the Wordsworths. She lectured to local workmen and ran a model farm. She had the journalist's gift of turning every experience into copy. Her writings grew in depth and breadth. She concerned herself with the origins of religions and brought out a book called Eastern Life, completing with its royalties the purchase of her Ambleside home. Here she wrote her History of the Thirty Years of Peace from 1816 to 1846, and here she translated and condensed Comte's Philosophy so excellently that Comte recommended her version rather than the original to his disciples. Many of her friends were offended by her bold and broad views, but she was sincerity itself, and what she thought she wrote.

In 1855 she completed her autobiography; yet she lived another 20 years, an invalid but never a helpless one. Her kindly ways and strong good sense made her a dear neighbour, and children loved her. When she died at the Knoll in 1876 she left a memory of a delicate yet progressive old lady in a lace cap, with hands as busy as her tireless brain.

Church and Castle

APPLEBY. Westmorland's most historic town, it is tucked away in the green valley of the River Eden, with bare fells far above, and the lonely miles of Stainmoor near by. Only a small place, it goes back to the days before the Conqueror. It claims to be England's smallest county town and her smallest assize town, and the Corporation is one of our oldest. Its population was 12,000 in 1388; to-day it is 1600.

The Romans marched this way to the great wall, Saxons and Normans built churches here, a king captured the castle and a little lady defended it. It is round the castle walls that the old town gathers itself, its most important street running between two black-and-white pillars with sundials on them; they are at each end of the street, one with an inscription saying to its people: "Retain your loyalty, preserve your rights," the other marking the site of the old market cross.

The sycamore under which John Wesley preached is still here; and, though the 16th-century grammar school has been made new, it has a fine library of old books, and many honourable names. One of its scholars was the father of Addison, and two others have the immortal name of Washington—Lawrence and Augustine, brothers of the famous President. Lawrence was at Appleby school the year George Washington was born; and he and his brother must have been looked upon as great travellers, for in those days it was a wonderful thing to cross the Atlantic. George outlived both his Lakeland scholar brothers, and it was one of them who bequeathed to him his famous home, Mount Vernon.

John Robinson, who was baptised at the font of St Lawrence's church here in 1727, was at this school about the same time, and would know the Washingtons. He became M.P. for Westmorland and built himself a white house in Appleby, where he lived in magnificent style. His house is still here, but he spent his last days at Isleworth, where he planted millions of acorns. He is remembered for the chance he once gave Sheridan of making a clever answer in Parliament. "Name, name!" the House shouted, to which Sheridan replied, with his eyes fixed on Robinson, and well remembering that names must not be used in Parliament, "Yes, I could name him as soon as I could say Jack Robinson," a telling use of the familiar phrase.

The old bull ring still stands in Boroughgate, and by the road uphill to the castle are green lawns shaded with limes. Here is a charming group of cottages round a quadrangle, low red houses with a chapel in a cobbled square. They make a pretty picture through an arched entrance, and are a gracious memorial to a famous woman of Appleby, Lady Anne, one of the most remarkable of the Cliffords. It was she who saved Appleby's old churches and built these almhouses.

St Michael's has traces of a structure about a thousand years old, for here is one of the stones known as a hogback with a band of interlacing strands which may once have been over the grave of a Saxon. Now it is the lintel of a blocked doorway, which, with the north and west walls of the nave, and a window in the tower, are 12th century. There are medieval coffin stones, and a lady of about 1400 lies in her cloak with hanging sleeves and flat headdress, the arms of Vipont on her cushion. One of two medieval bells may be 13th century. Here sleeps Sir Richard Pearson, who was born at Appleby in 1731 and lost one of the most terrible sea fights ever fought in English waters. It was while protecting a fleet of merchant ships that he fell in with the pirate Paul Jones off Flamborough Head. The other ships ran into Scarborough, but Captain Pearson stayed to fight the pirate and, though he lost the fight after a desperate conflict, he was knighted for his bravery.

St Lawrence's church keeps company with fine trees and pleasing cloisters. Its tower is Norman and 15th century with a 600-year-old arch, and the medieval porch has a 17th-century roof. Twice burned by the Scots and twice rebuilt, it has fragments of Norman work, notably the carving over the doorway and a window in the baptistry; and in spite of much misfortune much of the nave has been here over 700 years. Its dignity is unspoiled.

Among its great possessions are three chained books, a Bible and a Prayer Book of the 17th century, and some old pewter. Very fine is a handsome oak screen which is probably 15th century, and the Appleby Castle pew with its rich carving. A pew reserved for the corporation has wrought iron stands for the sword and mace, painted bright red, both beautiful examples of 18th-century metal work. The organ is said to have been in Carlisle Cathedral, and to have been played there from Queen Elizabeth's day for about a hundred years.

On a tapering stone is the head and shoulders of a figure above a lovely cross, perhaps a lady who lived 600 years ago. Of much interest are two memorials of Lady Anne Clifford and her mother Margaret Russell. Margaret Countess of Cumberland lies on a tomb wearing a widow's hood and metal coronet. A black-and-white marble monument is the memorial of the famous Lady Anne, a lady bountiful of the 17th century who built castles and churches and loved to go about doing good. There is something pathetic about her, for the family of which she was so proud died with her, and with her passing ended the most stirring chapter in the story of Westmorland.

She loved Appleby Castle and spared no expense in looking after it. It has huge moats and ramparts that may have been here before the Conqueror, and were perhaps part of a British fortress; its stone towers were built in the 12th century, strong defences on a bold headland above the river. Here are two wards and a keep known as Caesar's Tower, with a 15th-century gateway and a round tower near it older still. The keep still has its ancient well. The chapel built by Thomas Clifford in the 15th century is bravely weathering the storms.

The gateway brings us on to the lovely lawns about the keep. It was up this hill and round these walls that the wild Saxons came shouting. They were here many times, and in 1388 they captured the castle and destroyed the town, a blow from which the castle never recovered. There was much fighting here in Charles Stuart's time; and the indomitable Lady Anne, losing patience with her husband (whom she called a disloyal simpleton), fortified the castle and held it three years. Cromwell left her in peace, having a secret admiration for his fair enemy, and with his great love of fairness he allowed her to repair the damage. It has been added to since her day, but the castle has not lost the dignity its early builders gave it.

It has still some treasures of those days. It has a splendid portrait of the famous George Clifford, showing him as the bold earl who sailed the Spanish Main, and carried the news to Elizabeth that the Great Armada was destroyed. Here is Francis Clifford of 1589, Robert of 1591, and John Clifford, 'the Butcher,' who was killed at Towton, father of the Shepherd Lord who comes into Wordsworth. Lady Anne's necklace, probably the oldest pearl necklace in England, is also here, but even more interesting is the huge triptych covering a wall of the hall, showing her as a girl in the left panel, as an old lady in the right panel, and in the centre with her husband and two children, her books and various family portraits. This picture has been fully described by Dr George Williamson in his exhaustive Life of Lady Anne Clifford.

The Famous Lady Anne

THE stout Lord Cliffords, descended from the Dukes of Normandy, ended in Lady Anne, a woman not unworthy of the place of her house in history. She was born at Skipton Castle in 1590, the only surviving child of the third Earl of Cumberland, the chivalrous but eccentric sea wanderer who, besides fighting bravely against the Armada, fitted out eleven expeditions at his own cost to fight our enemies and to trade in latitudes forbidden by Spain and Holland.

Carefully educated, with the poet Daniel for tutor, Anne was married at 19 to the third Earl of Dorset, a talented, licentious spendthrift. She became the mother of five children, but was left a widow at 34. Six years later she married Philip Sidney's nephew, the fourth Earl of Pembroke.

She wrote that the marble pillars of Wilton, the seat of the Herberts, were "often times but the gay arbours of anguish" to her, and that she had lived retired and alone with her books. A lawsuit lasting 38 years, between the men and women of the Clifford family, was ended by the death of the men, and Anne, now widowed again, was left with vast wealth and estates.

Allied to inexhaustible generosity, there mingled in her strong and sincere nature two passions, one for building, the other for the vindication of her legal rights. She once embarked on a law case against a tenant who had neglected or refused to pay her his feudal due of a hen once a year. Having won her action she invited the loser to dinner and shared the hen with him.

Her second husband, as an ardent royalist, had been intensely disliked by the Parliament, and Anne incurred something of the odium attaching to his name. She owned the castles of Appleby, Skipton, Brougham, Brough, Pendragon, and Barden Tower; and she restored or rebuilt them all. This looked like a defiance of the Commonwealth, and Cromwell informed her that he would knock her castles about her ears. But she went placidly on and completed her work.

She lavished equal care on the churches of Appleby, Skipton, and Bongate, and on the chapels of Brougham, Ninekirks, Mallerstang, and Bardon; she founded the almshouses here; raised the memorial in Westminster Abbey to Edmund Spenser, her mother's favourite poet, a monument to her old tutor, Daniel, and set a cross on the Appleby–Brougham road to mark the spot where she last parted from her mother.

A scholar who, in the words of Donne, "could discourse of all things from predestination to slea-silk," she was a munificent patron of learning. Her home was a school for the young and a retreat for the aged. She stayed at each of her castles in turn, queen at once of learning and of hospitality. However lavish her table, she was a model of abstemiousness, and never took wine or physic. So successful was her way of life that she lived nearly 87 years, an epitome of the best qualities of the illustrious line that ended in the grave with her when she died in 1676.

The Lonely Towers

ARNSIDE. It is the only place where Westmorland comes down to the sea, by the calm waters of Morecambe Bay and not far from Arnside Knot, a hill crowned with noble larches. Its houses look over the estuary of the River Kent where the railway runs over fifty arches to the Lakeland hills.

By an apple orchard stands the church, little more than half a century old, but round about are traces of six or seven towers, places of refuge and defence in the days of the Scottish invasions. One is Hazelslack Tower enshrined in trees, a lonely place a mile away. Roughly built about 500 years ago, it has walls three feet thick and traces of great fireplaces. We can still go up its winding stair for the magnificent view from the top; we found three trees and a gooseberry bush growing in the crumbling stone.

A desolate place is Arnside Tower, where a watch was kept over Morecambe Bay and the meadows by the river. A fortified house of the 15th century, it is about 50 feet long and 30 wide, with a noble turret and a spiral staircase. One of its walls fell in a storm last century and no one thought it worth while to remove the stones, so that it stands a rather pitiful and forbidding ruin, with four elder trees to keep it company.

Old Farms and Ancient Mills

ASKHAM. It has farmhouses that have hardly changed in 300 years, and ancient mills that are a joy to see. Not far off are stone circles, and a great boulder known as Copt Stone said to mark where a British Chief has been sleeping over 20 centuries. One of the few tithe barns in Westmorland is close by, and from the moors above are splendid views of woods and valleys.

The village has 18th-century cottages, a fine green, a white inn, a seat under a venerable oak, and a 19th-century church on the site of a very old one. The font, which has the date 1661 on its square bowl, has a curious pedestal like a milestone. There is a 17th-century altar table, and a medieval corbel in a chapel, carved with a head. Its windows frame charming pictures of the park round Askham Hall, a noble old house by the river. Some of its stones are probably 13th century. Its tower is 34 feet wide and over twice as long. It was all much rebuilt in the 16th century, but has kept its embattled parapet and turrets, and the lower walls are six feet thick. The old Hall has a spacious courtyard and an imposing gateway, and very delightful are the little windows. The entrance hall has a massive oak staircase made new in Charles the Second's day. One of the old buildings is a dairy which was once a chapel, and has a piscina in the wall.

Village Boys Who Became Bishops

BAMPTON. Among its old houses is Bampton Hall, which has seen many changes, Knipe Hall of the 16th century, and the Elizabethan Thornthwaite Hall. Not far off is the grave of an ancient Briton, and a cross in the cemetery is said to have been an old boundary stone on Knipe Moor, about 600 years old.

Made new two centuries ago, Bampton's church is one of the rare ones with timber arcades; a table in the vestry and the pulpit are 18th century, and the altar rails and a chest are a little older. The font may be Norman.

Two bishops are remembered in this small place, both educated at the grammar school. One was the notorious Hugh Curwen, a Bampton boy who became chaplain to Henry the Eighth, and preached a sermon before the king which sent John Frith of Westerham to a martyr's death. As Archbishop of Dublin he pretended to be a fervent Roman Catholic; in Elizabeth's time he became a Protestant and ordered the cross he had set up to be taken down.

The other bishop remembered at Bampton was Edmund Gibson, who was baptised in the old church in 1669. His mother and father sleep here and have a marble monument, and hanging on the wall is his portrait. He was Bishop of London, and in preaching and writing he vigorously attacked the loose living of the times, not being afraid to tell the king what he thought of his court masques.

BARBON. It looks up to many hills and hears the Barbon Beck coming down from the Pennines to meet the Lune, hurrying under a charming packhorse bridge. There are traces of a Roman road close by, and on a small green hill not far from Whelprigg Hall is a stone with a cross perhaps a thousand years old.

Barbon has a simple 19th-century church on an older site, keeping three 17th-century relics, a chest, a carved chair, and a cupboard. A fragment of a medieval capital was found in a barn. The churchyard was full of flowers when we called, the gardens were delightful, and a lane by a wood was carpeted with bluebells.

WESTMORLAND

A Poor Boy Comes Back

BARTON. This delightful village by Ullswater has some magnificent houses. By the road to Yanwath is Kirkbarrow Hall, a fine Tudor house with a tiny room over the porch and three grand old doors which still have the marks of the adze, the old wooden pegs, and heavy iron hinges. Barton Hall is famous for its oak panelling and delightful windows, an Elizabethan drawing-room with a splendid plaster ceiling, and carvings of oak leaves, roses, thistles, and vines.

Yanwath Hall is a gracious place with the charm of 300 years in its walls and rooms. It has a fine courtyard, two huge buttresses, lovely windows, and a handsome doorway. The battlemented 14th-century tower, with its turrets, is a noble structure over 50 feet high with foundations six feet thick, and a base with a vaulted roof. In what is now a farmhouse are magnificent oak beams. One of the rooms known as the Lord's Chamber has the arms of Queen Elizabeth in plaster over the fireplace, and a delightful oriel; and a smaller room, said to have sheltered Mary Queen of Scots, has a stone fireplace with a low oak kerb at which the queen may have warmed her feet.

With some of the loveliest scenery of the lakes roundabout, the church has a low Norman central tower, with two Norman arches under which broader ones were built in the 14th century. A 17th-century porch leads inside, where a north arcade of about 1300 and a 13th-century south arcade open to the aisles. The east window, like most of the chancel, is 600 years old, as are a stoup and a piscina. A stone reredos in a chapel, with carvings of trees, flowers, and birds, was the work of a craftsman in the 16th century.

The 14th-century font has a beautiful 15th-century cover with a top delicately carved to look like a pineapple; and the finely carved altar rails and a chair were here in Charles Stuart's day. There are many old gravestones in the chancel, one with a cross, sword, and shield of the 14th century. The stabling north of the tower was used for its original purpose within living memory.

In the chancel is a brass inscription to the wife of Lancelot Dawes, who lived through the Civil War, and of whom we are told that the sun itself blushed at her appearance, and that in this wonderful lady did so many graces dwell that "God plucked my rose that he might take a smell."

Seventy years before this extravagant inscription was placed in the church to express a husband's sorrow, a poor lad of the village was leaving for Oxford to continue his education there as best he could.

He was 17. Queen's College took him in as a servitor, and after eleven years he was back at Barton with a fine reputation, the best degrees, a college fellowship, and an offer of the living of his native village. He stayed there all his life, 45 more years. More honours came to him. He became a Doctor of Divinity and had a stall in Carlisle Cathedral. He was one of the preachers at Paul's Cross. He was energetic in the work of preserving churches under his care. They show you his house, though he died nearly 300 years ago. They show you also the fine house of his son, who became lord of the manor, and put up the inscription so sorrowfully lamenting his wife.

The Fairy Steps and the Golden Hoard

BEETHAM. It lost some of its possessions in the 17th century and found a heap of money in the 19th. Not far from the estuary of the River Kent, and once important with much trade, it fell asleep in some Long Ago. It looks away to Arnside, has a beautiful bridge of three arches over the little River Bela, and is proud of its Fairy Steps, curiously shaped rocks in a lovely pinewood. There is a heronry guarded by great oaks in the park, and not far off is Dallam Tower, built 200 years ago from the ruins of an older one.

Beetham Hall was a noble place in the 14th century. Fragments of an outer wall 70 yards long and about 15 feet high surround it, and it has a barn with traceried windows, a huge kitchen, a tower with an ancient fireplace and a chapel. Much of the hall was built in the 15th century, but a simple wing with a quaint 17th-century porch is Jacobean. In a field close by is a huge rock about which no man knows.

Among charming cottages in the parish of Haverbrack, near a mill, a tiny waterfall, and a bridge, is Beetham church, its tower perhaps 12th century except for the 16th-century belfry. The south arcade was built in the last days of the 15th century, as is the clerestory. The roofs (except for that of the south aisle) are over 400 years old. There are two medieval piscinas, an Elizabethan altar table, a 17th-century chest, a small library of books given to the church in 1705, an old sundial on the chapel doorway, and a scratch dial on a buttress. On a tomb in the chancel, carved with shields and quatrefoils, lie two figures, a man in armour and a woman in a cloak, perhaps

Thomas Beetham and his wife of over 500 years ago. They were much battered in the Civil War. Then also was lost the rarest treasure of the church, the work of master craftsmen in its windows. It was lost in an hour, smashed by a fanatic. Fragments survive, among them a quaint picture of Henry the Fourth looking very timid in an ermine robe of gold embroidery. Others show bishops, a Crucifixion, a Madonna and Child; and among the heraldry are the arms of the Earls of Derby, who received Beetham Hall as a reward for their services to the Tudor dynasty at Bosworth Field.

A curious surprise we found here, for the bowl of the font is enclosed by the lower stage of its richly carved cover, as it has been since Charles Stuart's days. A golden surprise somebody had here also long ago, for hidden under a pillar in the nave was a hoard of money, a store of over a hundred coins of the time of Edward the Confessor and the Conqueror. They may have been left when the church was built, hidden for a while by someone who meant to come back in a day or two but did not come back, so that his hoard of coins lay here undisturbed for many centuries.

Over a mile away stands Hazelslack Tower. Once part of a larger building, it comes from late in the 14th century, and fell into ruin three centuries later.

The Mysterious Stone

BOLTON. It has Bewley Castle in a lovely dell a little way from the village, the ruin of an ancient fortress in which the Bishops of Carlisle took refuge from the Scots. The walls are five feet thick, and there are broken arches with grandeur still left in them, vaulted cellars, and part of a 14th-century chapel.

The church, with a 17th-century bell turret, is one of the noblest small buildings for a long way round, with two Norman doorways and two sundials, an ancient one scratched on a buttress and an 18th-century dial on a stone which may be a thousand years old. We come in by a Norman doorway with an arch carved with petalled rosettes and a rude picture of a little man with a hammer and an axe on one of its capitals. By this doorway is the figure of a lady of the 14th century, once on a tomb indoors but now built into the wall outside, greeting all who come. The other Norman doorway is built up and has a window inset. In the wall above it is a charming sculpture of a scene which might fit a child's Noah's Ark; it is a picture from a tournament 800 years ago and shows two knights riding horses rather like polar bears. One warrior has an oval shield and holds his lance at the throat of the second, whose lance carries a banner. This quaint carving, wonderfully preserved, must be counted one of the most remarkable exhibits in our national gallery of medieval sculpture. It has a worn inscription which no one can interpret.

The striking spectacle indoors is the unusual chancel screen of open tracery, with quatrefoils and geometrical patterns. A stout oak chest with three massive locks may be 16th century, and a poor-box is 300 years old. Oak beams in a roof are said to have sailed the seas in the bottom of a ship.

Roman Camp and Norman Stronghold

BROUGH. On the great road from York to Carlisle, it was once an outpost of the Roman Empire, and it has a castle built by the Normans. It is finely cared for by the Office of Works.

Hereabouts the Pennines go up 2000 feet above the sea, and among the mountains is the Roman road to Bowes, a desolate highway over Stainmoor said to have been the worst coaching road in England. Caesar's legions marched this way; the warring Scots knew how bleak it was.

The ruins of a Roman camp and a Norman castle are by the river Swindale, flowing from the Pennines to the Eden. Over 150 yards long and 130 yards wide, the camp was a splendid base for the Norman castle of Robert Vipont, the first thing we see in Brough, a noble pile with little grace but immense strength. Though much restored by Lady Anne Clifford, it is now a majestic ruin. With foundations resting on fragments of the Roman Empire, it has parts of a massive wall protecting a great keep about 60 feet high. Its doorway comes from Stuart times, but the walls were here before Magna Carta. The three storeys of the keep have a stair in the turret going up to a parapet from which are magnificent views of the Eden valley, and of Brough church enshrined in trees. Some of the windows and fireplaces are Norman, others are Tudor. The great hall is 14th century and the gatehouse has Norman stones. Very imposing is Clifford's Tower, partly destroyed in 1763, and in one of the cellars is a museum with treasures of Norman and Roman times.

Most of the church is 14th and 16th century, but the south doorway with its beakheads and chevrons is Norman. The tower is over 400 years old, and the nave arcade of seven bays comes from the three medieval centuries. The oak roof of the nave may be 16th century, and that of the aisle a little younger. There is an altar stone with two crosses, and medieval coffin lids in the porch; a medieval gable cross is in the vestry, and in the churchyard are remains of a cross from about the same time. The stone pulpit may be older than its 17th-century date. A chair, a desk in the tower, and a door in the second storey of the tower are 17th century.

Among the fragments of old glass are figures of John the Baptist, a bishop with attendant priests, and a Crucifixion scene. Other fragments, in the vicarage, include a woman wearing her crown, a bishop, and angels.

Among an unusually large group of brass inscriptions of the 18th century is a tribute to a vicar who had "a manly form and a seraphic mind," and a poem crammed with more virtues than we should have thought possible in 20 lines in praise of a certain Isabella. Older still is a verse on a 17th-century gravestone here which has now probably faded away; we are told of Thomas Gabelis, who died in 1694, that he

Was fresh and understanding too
At 86 as those who woo,
When Death with crooked scythe and glass
Set out the bounds he should not pass.

But young indeed are all these inscriptions compared with two stones found in this place. One is still in the porch and has part of a Roman inscription, perhaps a memorial to a soldier; the other is so important that it has found its way to the Fitzwilliam Museum in Cambridge. It has a simple border of palm leaves and a Greek poem of five lines in memory of Hermes of Commagene in Syria, who died in an expedition against the Cimmerians when he was a boy. The expedition in which he lost his young life was probably that of Septimus Severus against the tribes north of Hadrian's Wall in the year 209. It stirs us to think that in our English soil sleeps this Syrian boy whose stone is written in the language of Euripides.

The Home of the Fighting Cliffords

BROUGHAM. It has an impressive ruin which sets us thinking of the ages of history that have rolled over its walls; and it has a fine Hall still full of treasure and still one of our stately homes.

Romans, Saxons, Normans, have all known Brougham. The

Romans had a camp close by, the Saxons built a church, the Normans occupied the castle and left their mark on the little church of St Ninian by the river. It has over the altar the initials of Lady Anne Clifford, the most remarkable of the Cliffords of Brougham Castle; she made the church new in 1660, from when come the screen with a modern cornice, the pulpit with sounding-board, the altar rails, the canopied pews, and oak seats with carved arm-rests. The font and the offertory boxes from those days are still in use. There is a massive medieval chest with iron bands; a 13th-century coffin lid is in the nave, and two others are in the churchyard. Here sleep Broughams of many generations, Henry with his wife on a Tudor brass; Thomas of Jacobean days on another brass with his wife facing him.

In the chancel are two gravestones having a thrilling story, for under them were laid two famous warriors of very long ago. One was Udard de Brougham, a crusader and a rebel in the days of our Norman kings, whose sword is still in Brougham Hall, taken from the coffin in which it lay with him about 700 years. The other is thought to have been a giant of those days, over six feet high, Gilbert Brougham. Their skeletons were found below the chancel in the middle of the 19th century. Udard was perfect, his legs crossed and his iron spur still round his left heel, his arms down beside his body, his teeth white and clean. With him was a fragment of enamelled glass something like half an egg, supposed to be Phoenician; it may have been a charm brought by the crusader from the Holy Land.

It was the discovery of Udard's skeleton during repairs in the Brougham vault which led to a search bringing to light eight other skeletons, the giant's among them. In the giant's grave were found two fragments of a stirrup, reminding us of the days when Gilbert Brougham rode his horse in Normandy in the wars of King John. By the body lay a skeleton with a remarkable ornament of Saxon work, a metal circlet beautifully engraved with angels. It was probably an armlet or a rim of a drinking cup; certainly it is evidence of the dignity with which they laid these men to rest so long ago. They were reburied and lie still beneath the chancel, some of the relics preserved among the treasures of the great house.

On the border of the parish is a plain little building rich with treasure; it is the chapel of St Wilfrid, made new by Lady Anne Clifford. Its treasure is in its medieval woodwork, a truly remarkable collection, some of which has been attributed to Albert Durer. The piece so wonderful as to merit this possibility is the triptych on the reredos, a remarkable carving done about the year 1500, with a centre panel of the Crucifixion and a group below it. The sculptured scenes are set in borders of extraordinarily fine work, and there is a deep canopy above it. On the other panels Our Lord is seen as a child in the temple, and again bearing the Cross, and there are further scenes of the Baptism, the Entombment, and the Descent from the Cross.

Apparently by the same master craftsman is a locker with a vivid carving of the Resurrection on the door showing Christ rising from the Tomb while its guardians sleep. The hinges and the lock of the door are magnificent. There is wonderful panelling on the walls, with scenes of the early life of Christ, Cain and Abel, David and Goliath, and old carving has also been fitted into the organ case, with panels of the Entry into Jerusalem, the Madonna and Child, and the Crucifixion. One of the most remarkable wall panels shows the Wise Men bringing their gifts, a primitive but fascinating scene. The pulpit has also medieval carving worked into it, the screen has rich round posts supporting arches and its beautiful cornice, and the stalls are superb. In all Westmorland there is nothing more surprising than the superb treasure lying within the plain walls of this simple, low, long building, all unguessed at by those who pass by.

Brougham Hall, half castle and half country house, was made new about a hundred years ago, though it keeps much that is Tudor and has an impressive old gateway. Its windows look out across miles of Westmorland that have belonged to famous families for 800 years. It has a great hall 40 feet long, 20 feet wide, and 20 feet up to its gilded roof; in it are kept an ancient ivory horn, a small sanctus bell which rang in Saxon England, and the sword which Udard Brougham flashed in eastern sunlight and desired to be buried with him, as it was until it saw the sun again in 1846.

The chapel of the Hall has a font at which the children were baptised before the Reformation, but the great treasure of this place, with its fine panelled roof, is in its splendid oak enrichments. There are canopied stalls, poppyhead pews, an elaborately carved pulpit, and an elegant screen, all brought from the Continent by Lord Chancellor Brougham. The 15th-century altar piece is a rare triptych with sculptured and gilded Crucifixion scenes.

But for most of us the memory we bring away is of the impressive mass of the castle ruin standing finely on the river bank, its foundations deep in a Roman camp. The great gateway leads us into a spacious courtyard defended by a portcullis. Most of the walls have been here about 600 years. The keep, rising above the ruin, is as old as Magna Carta and has walls 11 feet thick, the whole structure being about 40 feet square. It has a dungeon below the guardroom, and two old wells, in one of which fragments of a broken water jar have been found. There are the remains of a chapel with two graceful windows and stone seats for priests, and on the third floor is a 13th-century oratory with a piscina in the wall.

This stern old place was long the home of the fighting Cliffords, whose name rang through England in the Middle Ages. One was at Crecy and Poitiers and was among the founders of the Order of the Garter. One was the first to tell Queen Elizabeth that the Great Armada was destroyed. One was Lady Anne Clifford, who lies in Appleby Church, but perhaps the one we remember best was the Shepherd Lord. His father had killed an earl and the boy was sent away to hide from his enemies in the middle of the 15th century.

A thousand yards from the castle stands the Countess's Pillar, 14 feet high, adorned with arms and sundials. It was erected in 1656 to commemorate the last parting between Lady Anne and her mother.

This is the romantic story of the Good Lord Clifford who lives in legend and in history, and is immortal in Wordsworth.

The Shepherd Comes into His Own Again

ROUND a table sat a group of men, some of them grey old lawyers, some sunburned soldiers in the prime of life. Before them stood a pretty young woman, like a deer at bay. They were plying her with questions and threats, trying to drag from her the hiding-place of her children.

The young woman was Lady Clifford. Her husband had just been killed, as his father had been killed, fighting for the Red Rose of Lancaster. At Towton Lord Clifford lost his life, and the Yorkist Edward the Fourth gained his crown.

The new king set about the work of vengeance. How shall my heirs be safe upon the throne, he said, if the heirs of my enemies live? Lord Clifford was dead, but he left two sons, and both must die.

So rough men came to rob the nursery. It was empty. Then Lady

Clifford was summoned to deliver up her sons or reveal their hiding-place, and she declared she did not know what her servant had done with them.

At length the Yorkists came to believe that she spoke the truth. Much they hoped that the servant had robbed and murdered his charges. Nothing was to be gained by killing the widow, so they let her go, bestowing the Clifford estates on others.

Eight years went by. Then the Court was suddenly startled by a rumour that Lord Clifford's heir was alive, hiding in Yorkshire.

Now there lived at Court a dame who had been a friend of the boy's mother. Politics might prevent their companionship, but it could not sever their hearts, so the Yorkist woman sent a message of warning to the Lancastrian woman. Soon afterwards spies, soldiers, and sheriffs began to search the moors and dales of Yorkshire, but no trace of a Clifford was found.

Fifteen years later came the Battle of Bosworth. York was defeated, and Henry of the Red Rose became Henry the Seventh of England. Then many exiles came home, and many banished men threw off their disguises. Lady Clifford announced that her elder son lived. The House of Lords summoned Henry to appear and take back his titles and estates.

Rarely had that ancient chamber seen a more romantic sight. There were assembled all the great ones of England, dressed in fur-trimmed garments of velvet or gay-coloured cloth, with rings, and jewel-hilted daggers. They bore themselves like men who were used to power. Many of them were scholars. None of them had ever wielded a heavier weapon than a pen or a sword.

Then up the floor of the House came walking the new member. He was a field labourer. He trudged like a ploughman, and his great hands were horny with toil. This was Henry Clifford, come to claim the Barony of Westmorland and the Castle of Skipton. He could not read or write.

When he was seven years old he had been taken away from his home and left in a miserable cottage. He had to wear rags, go barefoot, and sleep on straw. But the woman who lived in the cottage had once been his nurse, and she was very kind to him. Her shepherd husband treated the boy as if he were his own son. Henry forgot the life of his babyhood. He worked with the peasant and learned from him how to tell the time by sun and stars, how to care for sheep, and how to master his temper. He learned nothing else; that was knowledge enough for a shepherd boy.

One night a grand-looking man had ridden up to the cottage and had said to the shepherd: "The hunt is up. You must find a fresh lair." The next day the cottage was empty. Some time after a shepherd and his wife and son took a farm near the Scottish border. There for 15 years Henry Clifford rose with the lark and toiled in the fields till nightfall.

Once a wonderful thing happened. Two men and a beautiful grey-haired woman had ridden up to the farm, their fine garments soiled from a long journey. The lady had gazed at him, kissed him, wept over him, and then been dragged away by the men, who seemed terrified. The young labourer had been too awestruck to speak.

Now he was suddenly one of the lords of England, and stood among his peers. But the Shepherd Lord, as he was called, behaved with wisdom and dignity. He went to live near Bolton Abbey, where there were some famous learned monks, and became their pupil, learning to read when he was 30. Soon he was almost as much ahead of most 15th-century noblemen as he had been behind them. His favourite study was astronomy; the old shepherd had taught him to love the stars.

He was so loyal a servant to the King, so good a master to his tenants, and so true a friend to all, that he was called "the best of his race." In time he acquired courtly graces: his virtues he had learned from a shepherd. The King was glad that Lord Clifford's son should be the companion of his own son. He seemed to have a genius for generalship, and won fame by skill and valour on Flodden Field.

The little boy condemned to die at seven lived to be 70; the lad who had obeyed a shepherd lived to command knights and yeomen.

Wordsworth loved this story and founded one of his poems on it. Beautiful are the verses of his Song at the Feast of Brougham Castle on the coming into his own of Lord Clifford, the Shepherd.

Love had he found in huts where poor men lie;
His daily teachers had been woods and rills,
The silence that is in the starry sky,
The sleep that is among the lonely hills.

In him the savage virtue of the Race,
Revenge, and all ferocious thoughts were dead:
Nor did he change; but kept in lofty place
The wisdom which adversity had bred.

Glad were the vales, and every cottage hearth;
The Shepherd Lord was honoured more and more;
And, ages after he was laid in earth,
The Good Lord Clifford was the name he bore.

Tweedledum and Tweedledee of the Stars

BURNESIDE. It has four old halls and a church made new last century, village craftsmen having carved the reredos with flowers. The church has fine oak roofs, a richly carved doorway, 12 clerestory windows, and a rather queer spire.

The old Hall of the 14th century has become a rambling farmhouse as charming as anything we could wish to see. There is still a wall about 70 feet long, a gatehouse, a spacious courtyard, and a ruined tower. The farmhouse also preserves a banqueting hall 25 feet long with a massive oak screen and an elaborate cornice all nearly 400 years old, and the chapel and the porter's lodge are still standing.

Here still stands also the very charming Tolson Hall built by a rich tobacco merchant of Charles Stuart's day, Thomas Tolson. It has an imposing entrance like the gate of Lancaster Castle, and has 17th-century glass showing the sort of clay pipes Sir Walter Raleigh would know. A quaint inscription thanks God for giving Thomas Tolson the means to build this house. It was one of William Pitt's admirers at Tolson Hall who raised an obelisk in his memory on a hill above the village.

The other fine houses are Godmond Hall, a venerable house about three centuries old, and Strickland Ketel, the home of Sir George Wharton. Here dwelt for a time this man of strife, royalist and astrologer.

Wharton, a blacksmith's son whose father left him fifty pounds a year, managed to reach Oxford University, where he devoted himself to mathematics and astrology. On the outbreak of the Civil War he sold all he had and raised and lost a regiment for the King, with whom he returned to Oxford.

He brought out an astrological almanac every year, so that the Royalists had an interpreter of the stars at their headquarters while the Cromwellians had theirs in William Lilly. A great quarrel grew up between them about the stars and their interpretations, and many broadsides were published. The dispute was marked by great ferocity, and became a pitched battle between the Tweedledum and Tweedledee of the stars, but it had a curious and rather charming ending. Beaten out of Oxford, beggared and a wanderer, Wharton settled in London, was imprisoned, escaped, and lived by writing lampoons on Parliament. He was again arrested, and this time his friend Elias Ashmole learned that the intention was to hang the astrologer-critic.

The faithful Ashmole turned about for help and sought Wharton's bitterest enemy, the outraged Lilly. To Lilly's credit he acted magnanimously, moved a patron to plead, and saved the fiery Royalist. Ashmole then took Wharton out of harm's way, housing him and his family until the Restoration.

All was now plain sailing for Wharton. He was given an appointment at the Tower. There he continued his almanacs till he was tired, collected the verse with which he had enlivened them, and died in peace, being buried within the famous walls.

Cromwell's Horseman

BURTON. An oldfashioned place on the Lancashire border, it has a spacious square, charming cottages, and 18th-century houses, one with fine fireplaces and ceilings by Robert Adam, the most famous architect of his day. In the square is the 18th-century market cross with the leg-irons which served as stocks.

The church, made partly new, has its medieval porch, and a mainly Norman tower with its original arch, and a 14th-century west window. The south arcade is 14th century, and the north is over 400 years old. The clerestory of nave and chancel is modern, but 16th-century timbering remains in the roofs. One chair is 17th century, and another carved and panelled is a little younger. The fine oak pulpit of Shakespeare's day has a new cornice and base.

Its oldest possessions are three fine fragments of a stone cross carved before the Conqueror's Domesday Book was made; one showing two figures under an arch, and a larger figure holding a cross below.

A lonely hawthorn at the roadside is said to mark the grave of one of Cromwell's horsemen who was found dead here, the village folk burying him where they found him, and planting this hawthorn.

Charlotte Brontë's Sad Year

CASTERTON. It comes into one of the most famous books in the world, and, beautiful as it is, it was remembered with bitterness by Charlotte Brontë, who spent twelve unhappy months at

Cowan Bridge close by, where her school can still be seen. She was only nine when she left, but she never forgot how wretched she had been, and she tells us of it all in Jane Eyre.

Much forgotten history was made round about this place near the River Lune, a mile or so from Kirkby Lonsdale. The Romans had a camp here, and a silver ornament 20 centuries old has been found.

The Old Hall has long been famous for its splendid 17th-century oak, and its wonderful fireplaces and cabinets. One of its possessions when we called was a marvellous tapestry showing a beautiful garden, the work of clever needlewomen of three centuries ago.

On a little hill above the Hall stands the 19th-century church, its chief possession being a series of paintings on the walls by Henry Holiday and James Clark. Holiday was a great friend of Holman Hunt and Burne-Jones, one of the last survivors of that great group of artists, and these pictures illustrate the stories of the Bible.

Hereabouts is the Standing Cross, on the track of an old road called Roman Road; and a stone circle of 20 stones, 18 of varying heights up to 20 inches, and two only just above the turf.

From Leafy Vallombrosa

CLIBURN. It has fragments of the Roman Empire under its feet, a little river hurrying by, an Elizabethan Hall and a church the Normans built, now made partly new.

We come into the church through a doorway on which the Norman sculptors used their chisels boldly and set two queer figures in the lintel; the last of them built the chancel arch, and their mark is on the font. A Norman window and a 13th-century lancet are in the chancel.

And yet how young the Norman seems in this small place! Its walls have a fragment of a cross that was here when the Conqueror came; but even Saxon is young at Cliburn, for in the porch are two inscribed Roman stones found during restoration.

On the English altar here is something very beautiful, a gift from an admiral of the American Navy who went out from the Elizabethan Hall. He was Admiral Cleburne, and he found this beautiful thing in Italy and brought it home for his native village. It is a cross made of olive wood and ebony inlaid with gold, and was made by a craftsman of the days of Francis of Assisi. For 700 years it was treasured in the abbey of Vallombrosa and, being homeless when the monastery was closed last century, the admiral found a home for it in this village of Lakeland.

So we have here a little gem from the lovely neighbourhood of Florence which most of us know from Milton's Paradise Lost:

he so endured till on the beach
Of that inflamed sea he stood and called
His legions—angel forms who lay entranced,
Thick as autumnal leaves that strow the brooks
In Vallombrosa.

The Last Battle on English Soil

CLIFTON. It comes into history as the place where a prince slept in a cottage and as the scene of the last battle fought on English soil. Its son Christopher Airay is remembered as one of the first Englishmen to write on logic. He has been sleeping in Milford church in Hampshire since 1670.

Like many old houses in Westmorland, Clifton Manor was the home of one family for centuries. Built as a tower of defence, it has an embattled roof and a winding stairway in a turret, but it has fallen on hard times and is now a farm building, with one watch-tower left on its embattled top. In a wall of the modern farmhouse is a Roman stone with two carved figures and an inscription.

Nothing is left of the church which was here perhaps a thousand years ago, said to be one of the resting-places on St Cuthbert's last ride; but there are remains of a Norman structure in the south doorway; and 13th-century lancets and a doorway are in the chancel. The 600-year-old north doorway is now blocked. A piscina and two brackets and a coffin lid with a cross and sword are all medieval. The altar table and a few panels in the chancel are 17th century. A figure of the Madonna in a window is 500 years old. A small window has a charming picture of Eleanor d'Engayne, mistress of Clifton Hall in the 14th century; she is in a white and gold cloak over a blue gown, and her face is full of care. Her husband's shield in gold and crimson is on the wall.

The pulpit, old and new, is the church's best possession. It has two attractive carvings showing the Shepherds, and the Three Wise Men bringing their gifts to the manger, while very understanding oxen look on in wonder. It is thought to be the work of a French craftsman, and was given to Clifton by Lord Chancellor Brougham.

Three things in the village remind us of its place in history. One is an old tree known as the Rebel Oak; another is the churchyard in which 11 soldiers were buried after fighting on Clifton Moor; the third is a tiny pink cottage where the Young Pretender is said to have slept, if sleep ever came to him when he was retreating from Scotland. What is said to have been the last battle fought in England was fought on Clifton Moor in December 1745, an inglorious encounter which Scott describes in Waverley.

The burial of the 11 dragoons is recorded in the register, and it is on record elsewhere that before they were buried the clerk's wife stripped their holland shirts from them, and "that woman never did a day's good after."

Poor King in the Yorkshire Hills

CRACKENTHORPE. It has in it the memory of its ancient church and a sad memory of a king. Its chief possession is a Hall near the River Eden with massive foundations going back 700 years, though most of what we see is 17th century. An oak staircase and much woodwork is of this time. It was the home of the Machells for 500 years and came back to them after a century's lapse, the last son of the house laying down his life at the Battle of the Somme. Hereabouts is a corner called Roger Head, in memory of Roger Machell who was drowned off the coast of Cyprus while crusading with Richard Coeur-de-lion. On the gables of the Hall is the crest of the Machells, and built into the wall are Roman stones said to have been used as altars.

Here long, long ago a Machell welcomed a fugitive king, the poor mad Henry the Sixth, a hunted wanderer after the Battle of Hexham. For a year he wandered about the hills of Yorkshire and Westmorland, and more than once he hid at Crackenthorpe Hall. There is a room in which he is said to have slept, and a garden in the grounds is still called the King's Garden. The story is told that the king put on the gardener's clothes and worked in the flower-beds here, so deceiving the troops who were hunting him, and winning a little longer freedom.

From the beautiful grounds of the hall we see Appleby Castle through the trees, and on a clear day we have a peep of Helvellyn.

In the River Eden is Peg's Stone, of which every boy and girl in Crackenthorpe will tell you the tale. Peg Sleddall made so much trouble when she lived that to prevent her being troublesome dead they took her coffin and buried her in the river under this stone.

Little Gem in a Green Fold

CROSBY GARRETT. A little gem in a green fold of the hills, its ancient church keeps watch above. Over its 15th-century chancel arch are remains of a narrow arch which was here perhaps before the coming of the Normans, who built the north arcade with its massive pillars and capitals carved with leaves and heads. The chancel has a 13th-century piscina and a doorway a century younger; the nave roof is over 300 years old, and a carved chair is 17th century. One of two old bells here may be 13th century.

Addison's Father

CROSBY RAVENSWORTH. Here lived the ancient Britons; their stone circles are on the moors. Here came the Romans, building a road from Borrowbridge to Kirkby Thore; traces of it can still be seen. Here the Normans laid the foundations of the church, and here was born a man who was to grow up to be a dean and to have a son to crown his name with immortality.

The church by the little River Lyvennet has been called a miniature cathedral, so charming is it everywhere. The changes of the ages have not robbed it of its loveliness; the old and the new keep their dignity. Its 15th-century tower with a modern top is seen from far off and draws many a traveller to this village among the fells and camps and graves of people long forgotten.

There are charming houses: Flass House in lovely grounds, Meaburn Hall with 16th-century woodwork, Crosby Hall made new in the 16th century but still on its old foundations.

On the moor at Black Dub is a monument eight feet high where Charles the Second and his soldiers refreshed themselves by a stream; they were near the birthplace of the king's chaplain, Launcelot Addison, who became Dean of Lichfield and gave England that Joseph Addison whose essays are one of the precious possessions of our Literature. A stone at Maulds Meaburn marks where the old home of the Addisons stood.

Sir Launcelot Threlkeld of Crosby Hall who died in 1512 lies in the church, the altar tomb in the 14th-century chapel is believed to be his. Through a 13th-century doorway with lovely mouldings we come to nave arcades as old, with nail-head on the capitals of the south side.

Above them is a modern clerestory. Three arches of the central crossing are about 1200 and the other is new. On one of the walls is a 19th-century fresco of Christ blessing the children. The church has two old fonts, a 17th-century one in use and a 13th-century one in the vestry, with its antiquity hidden by a coat of paint which an old sexton thought would improve it. It has an interest of a kind unusual to fonts for on it is carved the Greek inscription, appearing in several churches, which reads the same both ways, and means Wash not only my face but my sins.

We noticed in the churchyard a gravestone a little unusual with the badge of the Cyclist's Touring Club on it; it is in memory of Henry Morris, who did so much for cyclists. Here also are remains of a medieval cross and several ancient coffin lids.

The Best Seats

CROSTHWAITE. It is like fairyland in spring, when its orchards are wonderful with damson blossoms. Not far from Windermere and in a charming valley, it is a lovely place with trees and old houses and a glorious view. Close by is Gilpin Dale, as fair as anything in Westmorland; and sheltered by Whitbarrow Scar is Cowmire Hall, a 17th-century farmhouse. It has a quaint canopied doorway, round chimneys of a kind we see in hardly any other county, and little windows looking across the valley to Cartmel Fell.

The small church has a font given by the builders and workmen who made the church new last century, and an old bowl lies in the churchyard. There is an oak screen with stained glass in the panels; and a silver chalice made before Elizabeth was crowned. One of the odd things on the walls is a plan showing where the people sat in Henry the Eighth's day; we noticed that the men had all the best seats. We noticed also a note of the gift of a man who died 200 years ago and left 2*s*. 6*d*. a year to be paid to a villager for whipping dogs out of the church. He left to two friends his best and second-best coats.

Penrith's Table Round

EAMONT BRIDGE. A little of it is in Cumberland and more is in Westmorland, where the first house over the border tells us in Latin that a brave man is at home wherever he treads. The house was put up a few years after the Commonwealth, and several of its neighbours are cottages with 18th-century dates. Here certainly all Englishmen must be at home, for it is England charming.

The clear waters of the Eamont make the county boundary, and the bridge itself is a fine piece of medieval building saved and widened for our Motor Age. Its three arches have a total span of about 120 feet and were built 500 years ago, part of their cost being met by the sale of Papal Indulgences.

Beside the road is a stone cross sculptured with the portraits of two men (out of four from here) who fell in South Africa. It stands in a corner of one of the two village earthworks which have set a hard puzzle to antiquarians. This one is the Round Table, a round flat space surrounded by what looks like a dried moat. Its age may be anything, and its use can only be guessed. Perhaps it was rightly described by Scott as a tilting ground:

Penrith's Table Round,
For feats of chivalry renowned.

The other earthwork is Mayburgh, looking, as we see it across the field, like a little hill with an opening. Going up to it we find a huge embankment of earth and stones, about 380 feet across, with a solitary monolith ten feet high in the middle. Tradition takes it back to the Druids, but next to nothing seems to be certain about it.

At the end of the village are the gateways of two stately homes of England, one leading to Brougham Hall near by, the other to Lowther Castle three miles away. There is no church; perhaps it is a compensation that the earthworks are easy to see, both good ones.

George Fox Declares the Truth

FIRBANK. It lies among the grandeur of the Pennines, a tiny village on the Yorkshire border, with purple moors, high mountains, green valleys with shining streams round about it, and, far above the little 18th-century church, a rock known as Fox's Pulpit. By it rise five tall larches, like faithful sentries.

It was up here that George Fox preached to a thousand people one summer's day about 300 years ago. His simple message went straight to the hearts of the dalesfolk who heard him, and many young men became his disciples, afterwards preaching up and down England and making Friends everywhere.

The jagged rock on which he preached is near the site of old Firbank chapel where five weather-beaten tombstones remain. Fox gives us this interesting picture in his diary of this famous Sunday here:

I went to a brook and got me a little water, and so I came and sat me down atop of a rock and the people gathered about me with several teachers; and it was judged there were a thousand people, among whom I declared God's everlasting truth about three hours.

Here Wordsworth Sleeps

GRASMERE. Like an epitome of all that is best in Lakeland, summarised in its central lake and village, it lies

Within its mountain urn
Smiling so tranquilly and set so deep.

Looked at as we descend to it from the Loughrigg footpath or Red Bank, a shining mirror with a central island, fringed with wood and a green floor of level vale around, steep hills rising from the rim of the flat expanse till they are crested with rugged rocks, beauty nestling in the arms of strength, what could be more perfect?

It is enchanted ground as the eye alone sees it, but a deeper enrichment comes to the mind that understands, to those who know that here lived one who more than any other poet felt the gracious power of Nature in such scenes as these, and taught us how to respond to it.

Grasmere is twice blessed, for it has a natural wonder of its own and the glory that he gave it. It is the interpretation of his life and poetry. The heart of Lake Country, it has associations with all the poets and writers of this rare corner of our Motherland. Coleridge knew it, Ruskin loved it, De Quincey and Southey wrote of it, but it is the spirit of Wordsworth that enriches it. To come to the Lakes knowing nothing of Wordsworth is to miss half their charm, for he and they are one, and at Grasmere he sleeps.

Wordsworth touched everything here. He strode like a fellman over the mountains, wrote of the Langdales, and found Michael's sheepfold near Greenhead. Often he would gather broom from the hillsides and row with it to the only island in the lake, making a bed of the broom so that he could rest and see the loveliness he praised in one of his sonnets:

A voice is near;
Great Pan himself low-whispering through the reeds,
Be thankful thou, for if unholy deeds
Ravage the world, tranquillity is here.

In the woods near the lake he found the first celandine; and somewhere here he saw the glory of the daffodils. He saw the bare rocks called the Lion and the Lamb, thinking of them as an astrologer at his desk and an old woman:

Dread pair that, spite of wind and weather,
Sit still upon the crag together.

He was 29 when he came to Grasmere with his sister Dorothy. He had already become famous by his Tintern Abbey, but it was while he lived at Dove Cottage that his genius came to full strength. Few great men have lived in a smaller house. Tucked away in the trees near the old road to Ambleside, and protected by great hills, it is one of a small group known as Townend. Here in 1802 he brought his Mary Hutchinson, and we may wonder how he managed to crowd his sister and Mary's sister and De Quincey and Coleridge into this tiny place. For many years the home of De Quincey after the Wordsworths left, the rooms are furnished almost as when the poet was here. All may see them. Many sit where he sat in his garden or in the little guest room where Charles Lamb and he would talk for hours. The parlour has a stone floor and much old woodwork, and on the same floor is Dorothy's bedroom. This is his staircase, up and down which tripped the light feet of his wife in the early days of their happy life together. It brings us to the sitting-room over the parlour, with three chairs covered by Dora Wordsworth, Edith Southey, and Sara Coleridge; and a shelf with the first editions of Wordsworth's books. His bedroom, with the bed he died on, is next to it. Close by is the guest room, and a smaller room papered with the newspapers Dorothy pasted on the walls. Two other rooms have been added on this floor, but they are interesting for their relics of the poet, and have his grandfather's sword.

Simplicity is the keynote of it all. His mind full of ennobling thoughts, his spirit free as the air on the hills, he was content with simple fare and rough comfort. From this house he set off on his walks over the fells and by the lakes; and under this roof many of his poems and sonnets were written—the Ode to Duty, the Excursion, the Prelude, the Intimations of Immortality. His children laughed with him in the little room looking on the garden, where John and Dora learned to walk. As lovely now as when he knew it, the garden is a plot of ground for ever England, for here he penned his Farewell to Grasmere on that day when he set out for Calais, returning through Yorkshire to marry Mary Hutchinson and bring her here:

The Natural Glory of Grasmere

Grasmere Church, where Wordsworth Sleeps

The Place that Wordsworth Loved

The Fields below the Pikes

The Lonely Blea Tarn

Langdale in its Splendour

Winding Road to Windermere

Troutbeck Village and the Snow-capped Mountains

In the Kirkstone Pass

Nab Cottage, home of Hartley Coleridge and de Quincey

Dove Cottage, the Grasmere home of Wordsworth

Rydal Mount, where Wordsworth lived

Homes of the Lakeland Poets

Barton Yanwath Hall

Helsington Sizergh Castle

Bolton The Chancel and its Curious Screen

Morland
Carved Coffin Lid

Windermere
Wooden Statue of St Martin

Bolton
Norman Tournament Scene

Bolton
Medieval Figure

Troutbeck The Church below the Hills

Kirkby Lonsdale The Peace Memorial by the Old Church

Kendal The Ancient Church

Lord Wharton and his wives at Kirkby Stephen

Satan on a Carved Stone at Kirkby Stephen

Sir Richard Musgrave on his Tomb at Kirkby Stephen

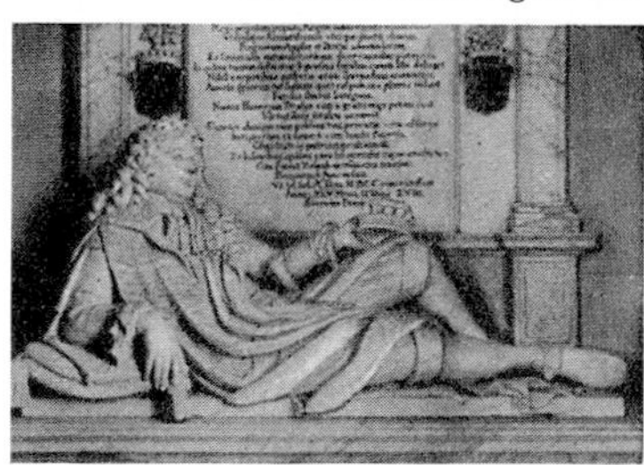

John, Viscount Lonsdale, at Lowther

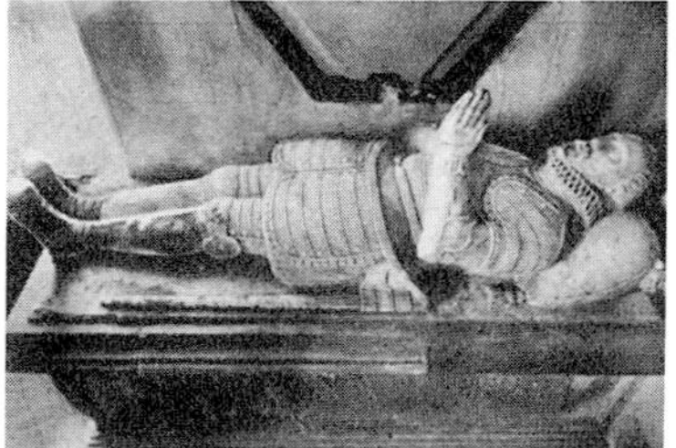

Sir Richard Lowther at Lowther

Sculptures of Old Westmorland

Raven's Crag Near Ambleside

Ambleside Stepping Stones across the Stream

Levens Hall

The Garden at Levens Hall

One of Lakeland's Great Houses

The Great House in the Park

The Ancient Avenue of Yews

Lowther, Pride of Westmorland

The Ruins of Kendal Castle

Kendal and its Bridge over the River Kent

Beetham Church

Shap Abbey

Kirkby Stephen The Winding High Street

Askham The Village Green

Patterdale and the Head of Ullswater

On the Bridge at Ambleside

The Church at Patterdale

Kirkby Lonsdale The Bridge over the Lune

Ulpha Old Bridge over the Duddon

Warcop Bridge across the Eden

The Bridge across Mosedale Beck in Wasdale

The Lovely Duddon Valley of Wordsworth's Sonnets

The lovely cottage in the guardian nook
Hath stirred me deeply, with its own dear brook,
Its own small pasture, almost its own sky!

Among these apple trees, by these old steps and rocks, he meditated at five o'clock in the morning. Here he wrote his poem to a skylark, and in this garden-orchard he sat listening to his Green Linnet and wrote these lines:

In this sequestered nook how sweet
To sit upon my orchard seat!
And birds and flowers once more to greet,
My last year's friends together.

In 1808 Wordsworth left Dove Cottage for Allan Bank, and in 1813 he went to Rydal Mount, but Grasmere is the place where we come nearest him. Dove Cottage for long housed many of his letters and manuscripts, and some of these and many relics of other poets have now found a more spacious home in an old barn across the lane; the barn belonged to the cottage of Molly Fisher, the servant of the Wordsworths. The new museum owes much to Mr Gordon Wordsworth, the poet's grandson, who devoted some years to sorting the manuscripts here, which include The Prelude, Dorothy's journals, and Coleridge's Dejection and Christabel. Gathered together in these two rooms are a hundred things that Wordsworth lovers will be touched to see, books he handled and things he used.

Not far from Dove Cottage is the roughly-built church, massive, dark, and low, begun in Norman times, made new 600 years ago, and changed again in the 17th century. It has a sturdy 14th-century tower and a porch 400 years old, and though it is not beautiful its strength and simplicity give it charm. Keeping company with the old bridge over the Rothay, it has changed little since Wordsworth sat in its pews, and his description of it is still true:

Not raised in nice proportions was the pile,
But large and massy, for duration built;
With pillars crowded, and the roof upheld
By naked rafters intricately crossed,
Like leafless underboughs, mid some thick grove,
All withered by the depth of shade above.

Its unusual feature is the two-storeyed continuous north arcade, the lower coming from the 16th century and the upper from the 17th. The font has a medieval bowl on a stem. There is a 14th-century piscina, a poor-box of 1648, two chairs and a chest over 200 years old, and fragments of old glass. A stone in the tower has two sides carved with foliage, one with a monster, and one with a man holding a sword; it is nearly 800 years old. The carvings of fruit on the pulpit were the work of a verger who was also a gardener. The lovely old custom of rushbearing is still kept up here, as in the days when churches had clay floors and were strewn with rushes once a year. Every year the children come with flowers in procession to the church leaving their garlands behind. In this old place is a medallion of Wordsworth with an inscription by John Keble, and in the churchyard is a memorial to Arthur Hugh Clough, who lies far away in Florence. In the churchyard lies one of our famous Arctic explorers, Sir John Richardson.

But it is a little corner of this churchyard, by one or two simple stones, that will always draw the multitude that comes this way. So close to the river that we can hear the water rippling by the wall is the place where Wordsworth sleeps, with poor Hartley Coleridge close by him. Here lies his dust, returned to earth of which it was a part. Let William Watson describe it:

The old rude church, with bare bold tower, is here;
Beneath its shadow high-born Rotha flows;
Rotha remembering well who slumbers near,
And with cool murmur lulling his repose.

It is a simple place, fit for his great simplicity. As Bishop Wordsworth wrote, "he desired no splendid tomb in a public mausoleum; he reposes beneath the green turf, among the dalesmen of Grasmere, under the sycamores and yews of a country churchyard, by the side of a beautiful stream, amid the mountains he loved."

Keep fresh the grass upon his grave
O Rotha, with thy living wave!
Sing him thy best, for few or none
Hear thy voice right now he is gone.

We leave his grave with these words of Matthew Arnold, one of the great successors of Nature's master singer, in our minds.

Nature's Own Poet

THE poet of the Lakes, where nearly all his years were spent, and from whose vast output of verse can be distilled some of the purest lines of English poetry, was nearing 70 before his countrymen recognised his worth. He had not to wait, as some poets have done, till his death for fame. When he was 73 he was offered the Laureateship, vacant through the death of his friend Southey, and honours flowed in on him till he passed away seven years afterwards.

It seems strange now that a writer in whose lines so often gleams

The light that never was on sea or land,

and whose thought embraced not merely the beauty of Nature and the pervading Presence,

Whose dwelling is the light of setting suns
And the round ocean, and the living air
And the blue sky, and in the mind of man,

but the glory and honour of the English people as well, should have found so little appreciation among them. Who can think now of the writer of the lines beginning

Milton! thou shouldst be living at this hour
England hath need of thee

as any but an Englishman of the strongest patriotic fibre? And who can read the sonnet on the Venetian Republic:

Once she did hold the gorgeous East in fee
And was the safeguard of the West,

without seeing in him a citizen of the world as well as a poet capable of finding a matchless image to express his thought?

The explanation of the indifference towards him (amounting to contempt) is twofold. The first was offered by Wordsworth himself, who observed that every great or original writer, in proportion as he is great or original, must himself create the taste by which he is to be appreciated; and Wordsworth believed himself to be a crusader who should lead taste away from the artificial literature and the sentimental diction of his time. He got no sympathy from the critics. The second reason lay in the circumstances of his early manhood.

He lost both his parents when he was young, his mother, a gentle and pious woman, when he was eight, and became the charge of two kindly uncles who sent him eventually to Cambridge. There he did none too well. The ancient quadrangles and gardens did not inspire him. His poetic gift seemed hardly born, and to be still awaiting the inspiration of his native hills and dales, the sounding cataract, the tall rock, the deep and gloomy wood.

He went on a walking tour in Switzerland and Italy, and, caught in the revolutionary mood which influenced Byron and Shelley, found a spiritual home in France. There he was almost involved in the terrors of the French Revolution, but got away before they descended on the noble and the innocent. It was the turning point in his life, and in his verse, which at that time had a revolutionary tinge. He returned to England, and to its sequestered countryside, to become a pastoral and a philosophic poet, from whose lines all traces of his inflammatory doctrines gradually disappeared.

We cannot think that ever he regretted his quiet contemplative life, or the loss of the earlier fevered life. Nor can we, the inheritors of his bequest of poetry, regret it when we call to mind such lines as those which among many others glorify his chosen surroundings:

I wandered lonely as a cloud
That floats on high o'er vales and hills,
When all at once I saw a crowd,
A host, of golden daffodils;
Beside the lake, beneath the trees,
Fluttering and dancing in the breeze.

Continuous as the stars that shine
And twinkle on the milky way,
They stretched in never-ending line
Along the margin of a bay:
Ten thousand saw I at a glance,
Tossing their heads in sprightly dance.

But the known and expressed sentiments of his youth for long told against him with critics and with the public, and the Lyrical Ballads he wrote in association with Coleridge, and his long poem The Prelude, his Sonnets, his Happy Warrior, all fared ill; and The Excursion, written when he was 44, no better.

He went on his way unperturbed. His sister Dorothy to the end of her days was his faithful and revered companion. He took up his lifelong abode at Grasmere; he married Mary Hutchinson, the school companion of his boyish days, and then settled down, entirely and completely indifferent to neglect or criticism, to his task of expressing the thoughts within him, and his love of all things bright and beautiful, in English verse. Its worth all now know. Coleridge and Walter Scott knew it then, and before he died the Early Victorians were won over to its beauty and purity.

Of him, and of his work and his place in literature, the lines he wrote when watching a river flow past, are a just appreciation:

Enough, if something from our hands have power
To live, and act, and serve the future hour;
And if, as toward the silent tomb we go,
Through love, through hope, and faith's transcendent dower,
We feel that we are greater than we know.

In Grasmere churchyard among immortal poets lies a heroic figure who should not be forgotten, Sir John Richardson, friend of Franklin.

Sir John Franklin's Heroic Friend

A man of Dumfriesshire, born in 1787, he saw Burns nightly at his father's house, received a copy of the Faerie Queene from him, and entered school with his eldest son. At Edinburgh University Richardson distinguished himself in science and the classics, and then, having qualified in medicine, joined the Navy at 20 as a surgeon.

He had his share of the sea-fighting that followed, and in 1819 accompanied Franklin, as doctor and naturalist, on the great three-years overland expedition in Arctic North America. After two severe winters the party was reduced practically to starvation in the Barren Grounds, and headed for Fort Enterprise, first having eaten their old boots and straps and living on lichen, collected as they went.

They reached the frigid Coppermine River without boats or rafts, so Richardson, a man of immense courage and endurance, tried to swim it, towing a line. He had nearly reached the opposite bank when his legs failed, and turning on his back and swimming till his arms froze, he sank and was pulled back to his starting-point.

The river at last crossed, five men died and five more broke down. It being impossible to carry them, Richardson stayed with them while Franklin tottered on in search of relief. Three more collapsed, and Michel, an Indian guide, promised to lead them back to Richardson. Left to himself, he murdered them one by one, practised cannibalism, and arrived at Richardson's camp, nourished, insolent, and masterful. Richardson had only two white companions left alive. They fathomed the Indian's terrible secret, and realised that they might be his next victims, but were too ill and feeble to resist, and were not surprised when, in the temporary absence of two of them from camp, Michel shot their helpless companion dead.

It was now a question whether the Indian would murder Richardson or whether Richardson, barely able to move, should dispose of the Indian, who had an arsenal of weapons. There was no alternative: he must kill Michel or be eaten. Chance gave him the opportunity; he had just strength to pull the trigger of his revolver, and so to end the most terrible chapter in Arctic annals. He reached safety with the other survivor, witness of his act, and later published the whole story.

Accompanying Franklin on his second voyage, Richardson helped by his skill and foresight to keep every man healthy and relatively well fed. Afterwards he was a brilliant physician to the Royal Hospital at Haslar, where among his pupils was Huxley, who attributed his success in life to the start given him by his learned and heroic principal.

When he was 60 Richardson led an expedition in search of Franklin, who had loved and honoured him. It was another epic voyage, with almost incredible escapes from sea-ice, and from the perils of a great overland journey after the boats had been abandoned; but Richardson brought all his men safely home. After nearly half a century of public service he settled here at Lancrigg, the adventurer turned gardener. He wrote magnificent works on the animals, birds, fishes, and insects of the Arctic, and his books are still among the classics of science and Arctic knowledge.

A Queer Old Lady Passes By

GREAT ASBY. Its delightful cottages face each other across a stream, and the ancient rectory keeps watch over a church made new. There are traces of British settlements close by, and jewels lost by a wealthy Roman citizen have been found near Castle Folds.

Near the almshouses of 1812 is St Helen's well, and not far off is Asby Hall, with its imposing gates. It belonged to the Musgraves of Eden Hall in the 17th century and has their arms and crest over the door. But the rectory is older still and has something of a 14th-century tower, thick walls, a very old fireplace, and a great wooden lock made in 1670. The lock has the initials of Lady Anne Clifford, Countess of Pembroke, and is treasured because it is thought to have been given for kindness shown to her when she sheltered here from a storm. She was the wonderful lady we come upon all over Westmorland, and her story belongs to Appleby.

Not far away from here is what is called Pate Hole, a much-visited cave with a stream running through it.

The Garlands of Midsummer Day

GREAT MUSGRAVE. It lies by the river Eden and is almost hidden among the Pennines, its 19th-century church resting on ancient foundations.

It has a beautiful brass over 400 years old with a portrait of old Thomas Ouds, the rector who met the rushbearers at the church door in Tudor days. Musgrave is one of the few villages where every midsummer day a procession of girls with garlands comes to the church with music. They sit through the service with their rushes and flowers, and the garlands are afterwards hung over the door. Rushbearing Day goes back to the time when the youths and maidens of a village would take flowers and rushes to strew on the old clay floor of the church.

Thomas Ouds's brass portrait is not all that is left of the old church. A beautiful tombstone, carved in the 13th century with a lovely cross and a sword, is now set in a wall. Two bells may be 15th century, and the font perhaps 17th.

Three Surprises

GREAT ORMSIDE. It has two Halls and an ancient church near the River Eden, in the beautiful valley going down to Appleby. Here are fine old houses, and with them a magnificent sycamore where the market cross stood till it was used as a pedestal for a sundial in the churchyard.

Ormside Hall keeps a little of its ancient grandeur. It has many quaint passages and a fine courtyard, its windows looking across to the church on a hill. Built for strength in the days when the Scots came over the border to burn and plunder, its grand 13th-century tower is a place of refuge as strong today as when its Norman builders left it. Though it has lost some of its dignity, it keeps two very old bells.

Much Norman work remains in the church, in the masonry of the north and west walls, and the arcade of two bays leading to the north aisle, with round arches and pillars and scalloped capitals. The bowl of the font is Norman. Older still is the blocked south doorway into which a new window is set, for it comes from the end of the 11th century.

The west tower with a gabled roof is about 1200, and only eleven feet square. The porch, made new with its old masonry, has many remains of carved coffin lids, and one used as a lintel of a window in the nave has a cross and a sword; others are in the outside walls. Three bells may be 15th century, and the fine oak chancel roof with king-posts is 400 years old.

Three surprises have been found in the churchyard. One was a hoard of brass and pewter vessels dug up in the 17th century, perhaps hidden in the Civil War; a Viking sword was found in 1899, a weapon used perhaps a thousand years ago, now in Carlisle; and in 1823 the famous Ormside Cup was found here. A glorious piece of gold and rich enamel, it was fashioned by a craftsman who may have lived in Alfred's day. It is one of the rarest of our Saxon treasures, a gem of beauty in its day, lost in the dark earth for centuries and now among the treasures of York Museum.

Robert Bruce Slips Past

HARTLEY. A company of limes by a stream, silver birches feathering in the breeze, a little bridge, a few houses below the grandeur of the Pennines, this is Hartley, a quiet spot under a hill with nine great stones centuries old.

A little way from the village is the romantic Podghill, with huge stones covered with bright mosses; and an uphill road with many sycamores brings us to the red ruins of Hartley Castle, once a stronghold keeping watch over the valley. A farmhouse stands on its foundations and many of its stones have gone to Eden Hall in Cumberland, but we can still see fragments of the castle walls, and of a tower with a vaulted room. In the 13th century the castle belonged to Sir Thomas Musgrave and in Tudor days to Sir Richard, but the Harclays were here long before the first Musgrave, among them Andrew, one of the chief men of his time. It has been said that he was the first Englishman to fight the Scots with soldiers on ponies. He distinguished himself in the wars of Edward the First, and Edward the Second made him Earl of Carlisle and immensely rich. But in 1322 he allowed Robert Bruce to slip past him and invade the north of England, and the king had him executed in his own town.

The Stricklands of Sizergh

HELSINGTON. It is as modest as a place can be, for it has neither street nor shop nor inn, and not a group of houses. Only the little 18th-century church and a school stand side by side on

Scout Scar high above the broad Lythe Valley. Like a stretch of green silk shot with buttercup gold the fields spread below them to Whitbarrow Scar across the valley.

Yet this modest hamlet has a home so grand that it must be called one of the noblest in all England. It is Sizergh Castle, as charming a fortified house as we have seen. For 700 years the Strickland family has lived in this place in unbroken occupation, a record rarely surpassed in any house in England. They fought at Hastings, they fought through the Wars of the Roses with the kings; they were at Agincourt with Henry the Fifth and with Charles Stuart at Edgehill. Stricklands everywhere have coveted the honour of having their pedigrees traced back to the Stricklands of Sizergh; and through more than 20 generations this great family has filled this house with treasure.

Everyone who loves an ancient building full of youthful vigour will delight in Sizergh as we see it outside, and everyone who loves beautiful things must delight in its possessions.

The ancient Hall, built round its more ancient pele tower and flanked by Elizabethan wings, is attractive in itself, its situation, and the treasures it has accumulated through the ages. It has fine Tudor panelling, exquisite Flemish tapestry of the 17th century, and lovely portraits. Panelling from the Inlaid Chamber has been sold to South Kensington, but the room still has its 16th-century plaster frieze, beautiful with leafy scrolls and flower sprays, leading up to the lavishly decorated ceiling.

There is a tradition that in a splendid bedroom hung with tapestry Catherine Parr once slept. She was born at Kendal a few miles away and may have visited her relations the Stricklands before she became Queen of England, Henry the Eighth's lucky widow. Treasured in the castle are a tablecloth and a counterpane of white satin embroidered with pictures of flowers and gorgeous birds and butterflies, said to have been worked by her. Here is kept the privy purse of Catherine of Braganza, the wife of Charles the Second.

One of the rarest possessions of this great house is in the chapel, a portable altar, remarkable for itself and interesting for its story. It is 500 years since a Pope granted Sir Thomas Strickland a licence for a portable shrine, and Sir Thomas was fortunate in being able to obtain an altar perhaps unique in this country. It is made of Italian leather and painted by a 15th-century craftsman with cherubs in bright colours, the background burnished in silver and gold.

A Discovery for the Last Day

HEVERSHAM. It is a village of old things and much charm, and proud particularly of a rare treasure it has from King Alfred's England.

Close to the estuary of the River Kent, it is only a mile or so from the famous Levens Hall, and has a Hall of its own, a 16th-century house with a fragment of a tower 200 years older, a fine courtyard, and massive walls. One of its rooms has a grand Tudor roof, and two of its notable possessions are an oak staircase and an oak table 13 feet long and four centuries old.

Keeping company with the Hall are the grammar school and the church. Built in Shakespeare's day, the school has memories of a scholar who made a name for himself in the 17th century, Ephraim Chambers, whose Dictionary of Art and Science went through six editions in 18 years, was translated into French, and was praised by Dr Johnson, who said he was partly indebted to the author for his style.

In a churchyard with a 17th-century sundial is a church begun soon after the Conquest but much damaged by fire at the end of Tudor days. From the close of Norman days comes the south arcade of the nave, the north being modern. The chancel, with a good 15th-century east window, has a 400-year-old arcade leading to the north chapel, the opposite bays and the chancel arch being new. The entrance to the porch and the doorway within are 14th century. A massive iron-bound chest nearly nine feet long is about 500 years old. The altar rails in a chapel, and most of the panelled screenwork of the opposite chapel, are early 17th century. There is some old heraldic glass, and old ironwork is on the south door. One of the monuments shows Lady Dorothie Bellingham with her child, a pathetic pair who have been here 300 years. The mother died in bringing the little one into the world, and it is sad to see them here between two grinning skulls of Death.

On a stone in the graveyard we are told of William Whalley, "whose character will be discovered at the last day"; and looking down on this irony is a gargoyle with a grin, near a sundial which has kept it company since they brought William Whalley here 200 years ago.

The oldest possession of the village is a stone in the porch, a fragment of a cross much worn and sadly battered, but carved with delightful vine foliage and what may be little foxes. It is a relic of Saxon England and may have been carved by a craftsman of King Alfred's day. Another fragment of the same shaft is in a wall.

They Live for Evermore

HUTTON ROOF. It once belonged to St Mary's Abbey, now in ruins at York, and it must have had a church in medieval times. It had a chapel built in the 18th century, and the present trim church was built in the 19th. It has little ancient history, but what history could surpass in human appeal its brave and tragic memory of a hero of our time?

We think of no one but Theodore Hardy as we walk here, where so many things appear to speak of him. Born in Devon, he had been a schoolmaster before he came to Hutton Roof in 1913, at 50. For five years he was vicar, but for much of the time was far away answering a stern call for one so gentle and humane. Going to France as a chaplain, he set himself the heroic task of saving and tending the wounded. Appalling it is to think that such a man should have had to spend himself following in the trail of war, yet so it was, and the honours showered on him can have seemed only a mockery to one striving to relieve the bitter suffering before his eyes.

In the autumn of 1917 he won the D.S.O. for helping to bring in the wounded and for comforting a dying man under fire; a month later came the M.C. for working with the stretcher-bearers during a bombardment; and in his last summer the V.C. was all they had left for "his most conspicuous bravery and devotion to duty."

Words seem to have failed those who were trying to reward him. His energy and endurance at 55 would have been wonderful in a man half his age. He followed an infantry patrol going out to attack the enemy, and, finding an officer dangerously wounded, stayed with him till help came. He set to work under fire to extricate men buried by an enemy shell, getting out one man who had been completely buried. He took out a party to fetch a wounded soldier left behind in a wood from which all the rest had gone.

So the tale goes on, and it seemed inevitable that he would throw away his life for others. He fell in action as the war was ending, leaving behind a memory of bravery and sacrifice never to be forgotten. King George wrote of it to his daughter, almost all the soldiers who had known him came to the memorial service, and a fellow-officer declared that he would be famous in history, adding that "his retiring nature made it almost a penance to wear those ribbons which most of us would give our right arm for."

Such a man would be loved and respected anywhere, and it is hardly surprising to find three memorials of him here. In a corner of his charming churchyard his name has pride of place on the peace memorial, inscribed to him and to three privates. In the chancel are two tablets to him, one by the officers and men of his battalion, the other by his diocese, as a tribute to his "heroic courage, sympathetic service, and spiritual labours." We may feel sure that in our time this place will never see his like again.

Wordsworth's Story of the Village Boy

INGS. Wordsworth loved this little place in the heavenly country round Windermere, and gave to one of its sons an earthly immortality in his poetry.

Here is High House, with a great round chimney and walls nine feet thick; and on Hugill Fell are fragments of a British village about 160 yards square. We can still see its wall and traces of hut circles, and a stone with curious cup markings.

One of the first men to investigate this ancient village was the botanist Peter Collinson, born at Hugill Hall in 1694, a great lover of these fells. A celebrated antiquarian, he was a great authority on insects and flowers. Among his friends were Sir Hans Sloane and Benjamin Franklin.

A few stones of the old church of Ings are in the new church, and an arch is hidden away in a farm, but the new church, like the almshouses with their lovely gardens, have a story of their own, for they were Robert Bateman's thankoffering to the village which gave him his opportunity of making a fortune. He built the church in 1743, and gave it a floor of lovely Italian marble. It is a memorial to the Dick Whittington of Ings whose portrait is in the nave, where his smiling eyes look out on this church he gave to his village but never saw, for it was destined so to be.

Here is set in enduring brass his story as Wordsworth told it:

There's Robert Bateman, thought she to herself,
He was a parish boy—at the church door
They made a gathering for him, shillings, pence,
And halfpennies, wherewith the neighbours bought
A basket which they filled with pedlar's wares;

And with this basket on his arm the lad
Went up to London, found a master there,
Who, out of many, chose the trusty boy
To go and overlook his merchandise
Beyond the seas; where he grew wondrous rich
And left estates and moneys to the poor,
And at his birthplace built a chapel floored
With marble which he sent from foreign lands.

It is a wonderful story of how a poor boy became rich, but we are sorry it all ends so unhappily, for less than a year after the first stones of his church were laid Robert was killed by an Italian captain as he was sailing home in one of his own ships. Far away in some strange grave he sleeps, or in the sea, but here are his good works, and we found the gardens of his almshouses gay with flowers.

The Home of Catherine Parr

KENDAL. It comes into Shakespeare and it gave England a queen. A grey old town in the lovely valley of the River Kent, it remembers the Young Pretender, has memories of one of our great artists, and has a ruined castle and a grand old church.

With glorious views of river and mountain scenery, it has all the charm of the Serpentine Woods, Abbot Hall, and many old houses in its streets. Near the road to Milnthorpe is Collin Field manor house of Tudor days, its remarkable oak door with a lock and key made when Lady Anne Clifford was here. In Stramongate is a house which has been here since 1546 and has still its wooden mantelpieces; and in Wildman Street is Castle Dairy, a curious place with round chimneys perhaps 600 years old. Among its treasures are carved oak beds, a fine chest, and fragments of 16th-century glass. Here also is one of the few snuff mills left in England; in 200 years it has made 5000 tons of snuff.

Shakespeare mentions three knaves dressed in Kendal green, and though Kendal green is no more the town has something older, a few quaint courts hidden from the streets, their narrow entrances reminding us of the days when houses were grouped in this way so that the people could defend themselves from the Scots who so often came over the border. On Castle How, with its ancient mound, is an obelisk in memory of the Revolution of 1688.

But Kendal goes back to Roman times and has traces of a Roman camp at Watercrook. Fragments of pottery, a broken statue, and an altar with festoons and grapes, have been found and can be seen in the museum; and the British Museum has the tombstone of an officer buried here. A Roman station stood on a hill above the town, where the ruins of Kendal's castle now stand proudly in their loneliness. With walls of astonishing thickness, there are fragments of domestic buildings, and, though the drawbridge has gone and the walls by the entrance have crumbled away, three towers keep watch.

The castle is famous as the birthplace of Catherine Parr, the lucky widow of Henry the Eighth. She was the daughter of Sir Thomas Parr, who rose to be controller of the king's household and died when Catherine was five. His widow, refusing all offers of marriage, devoted herself to teaching her daughter languages, and Catherine's education and character impressed themselves on Henry's children. She proved a model stepmother to them, and among the most interesting possessions of her native town today is one of the books from which she taught the children who were to grow up to be Edward the Sixth, Queen Mary, and Queen Elizabeth.

This little book was happily discovered at an antique dealer's in London, marked £500, and there was much risk of its being sold to America when a Kendal citizen realised its historic value and with the help of the Corporation formed a Committee to raise a fund for buying it. The book is now in the safe possession of the town, kept in the mayor's parlour. It is very small, only two-and-a-half inches by one-and-a-half, and is bound in silver. It was Catherine's book of prayer and meditations and we may picture her reading from it on quiet evenings to the king's children. She herself was 31 when she married the king, and she had been married twice before and was a stepmother, too, as Lady Latimer. No one knows what England does not owe to her and to this book which inspired her. The education of the little prince and princess was her special care, and the handwriting of Edward has a marked resemblance to hers. He admired it in his childish way, for in one of his letters he praises her pretty writing which made him so ashamed of his own.

That letter is dated 1544; and in the same year we find Princess Elizabeth, then eleven years old, sending to her for correction her English translation of a French poem, beautifully written on vellum. Mary, a woman only four years younger, softened to her influence, for there exists Catherine's letter to her urging her to publish a translation she had made of the Paraphrase of the Gospels by Erasmus.

Kendal has still the house in Strickland Gate where the Young Pretender slept. He is said to have proclaimed his father King at the market cross, but a few days afterwards retreated to Scotland.

The town hall is notable for its lofty tower, its corporation plate of the 17th century, its silver seal with a quaint picture of the town in Elizabeth's day, and its portraits by Romney who sleeps in his own town of Dalton. It was here that he fell in love with Mary Abbott, whom he married when he was 22. He left her for 40 years while living in London, meeting everybody, and making an imperishable name for himself, and then he came back to Kendal to die in her arms.

Among the men Kendal is proud to remember are two John Goughs, one who wrote a history of the Quakers, and one, sleeping in the churchyard, remembered as a blind naturalist with a wonderful knowledge of local plants and fossils. Another of Kendal's men was Anthony Askew, born here in 1722, a doctor best known as a collector of curious manuscripts. An odd story is told of his kindness to a Chinese, who showed his gratitude by making a model of him in clay, which can still be seen in London at the College of Physicians. Yet another famous son of this town was Daniel Gardner, an 18th-century painter notable for his small portraits in pastel and oils.

The church, which was here before the Conqueror's day, was made new about the time of Magna Carta. It is notable for its square tower 80 feet high, and its double aisles which make this spacious place impressive with many arches. The chancel has 13th-century arcades except for the modern pillars, and its hammerbeam roof (new like the rest of the roofs) is enriched with angels.

Over the medieval nave arcades are corbels supporting the shafts between the windows of the 15th-century clerestory, carved with grotesque heads, beasts, a Holy lamb, and a bust of a man. A 400-year-old arcade of nine bays leads to the outer north aisle and the Bellingham Chapel, and the nine bays of the outer south aisle and the Parr Chapel are perhaps a little younger.

Two treasures are a 13th-century coffin lid carved with a lovely cross, a shield and a sword; and a fragment of a cross-shaft, carved perhaps in the eighth century with vine scrolls and grapes. The black marble font is 15th century. Among old glass fragments are arms and the head of a king. An altar table is 300 years old; there is screenwork of about 1500, and two finely traceried poppyhead bench-ends of this time are in a modern desk.

A battered memorial recalls Sir Augustine Nichols, Chief Justice of England in the time of James the First. There is a cenotaph to Romney set up by his son; it was here that Romney died, and the tribute on the cenotaph tells us that "as long as genius and talent shall be respected his fame will live." A marble group by Flaxman shows the mourning widow and six children of Zacchary Hubbersty. Under a flat canopy on four pillars lies a boy in a shroud, his head on a pillow; he was Walter Strickland who died in 1656, son of Sir Thomas. A tomb with shields may be that of Sir Walter Strickland of 1528, and one in the Parr chapel is believed to be that of Sir William Parr, grandfather of Queen Catherine.

In the beautiful Bellingham Chapel, with original bosses in its roof, is a brass of Alan Bellingham of 1577 in armour. Here too is an altar tomb with a modern brass to Sir Roger Bellingham of 1533 and his wife. A helmet here has a curious story which has brought it into literature.

It had a thrilling adventure during the Civil War, when it was dramatically knocked off the head of Major Robert Philipson, who lived on Belle Isle in Lake Windermere, and thought himself so great a fellow that in searching for a Cromwellian officer with whom he had a quarrel he rode his horse into church while service was on. Somebody knocked the helmet off his head and it has been kept as a memorial of his insolence. Sir Walter Scott used the idea with fine effect in the last part of his poem Rokeby, where he describes how Bertram Risingham rode into the church at Rokeby, shot Oswald, and was himself killed in the nave.

There are those who will say that the most precious possession of Kendal is its distant views of the mountains. No other town has such a vast panorama as Kendal sees from many points, but best of all is the scene from Scout Scar two miles outside the town. Here the whole of the southern ranges are within view from Coniston Old Man and the Scafell massive round to the Fairfield Range. It is a noble sight to live with, though it stresses the fact that Kendal is not in the mountain zone.

The Extraordinary Story of Mr and Mrs Romney

IT was at Kendal that Romney fell in love and never was a stranger story in the world than his. Romney was one of the eleven children of a Lancashire cabinet-maker, a dunce at school, but proficient with his father's tools and making admirable fiddles, and apprenticed to an artist here at Kendal because he was so good at drawing.

His master made a Gretna Green marriage, and Romney, having been nursed through an illness by his landlady's daughter, a domestic servant, followed his master's example and married in haste when the master ordered him to join him at York. The bride returned to service, but eventually the bridegroom was released from his apprenticeship and was able to return to Kendal to paint portraits. Here they set up house; but his powers needed greater scope and at 28 he went to London, leaving the little home, his wife, and their two children with half his savings, and he did not return home again for 37 years.

He gave his life to art, and became famous. Although shy and ill-educated, he claimed the chief figures in royal, learned, and society circles for his sitters. His chief inspiration was Nelson's Lady Hamilton. For a while Romney lived to paint her, depicting her in no fewer than 30 characters, such a gallery of art as never honoured a woman before. All the time he was growing rich; but he did not send for his wife, though he paid her brief visits very occasionally, and liberally supported her as well as members of his own family.

He exhausted himself with labour. Scores of his pictures were left unfinished to decay on damp walls. His highest fee for a portrait was 120 guineas, but one of those portraits sold for 60,000 guineas. He began to suffer from fear, fits of morbid despondency, followed by mad elation.

Then, when he was 65, broken in health and in mind, the famous man, without a word of farewell to anyone, quietly returned to Kendal to the wife of his youth. She received him with loving greeting, as if he had just come home, and for his last three years was a tender and unwearying nurse to him.

Those last years live imperishably in Tennyson's poem on Romney's Remorse, in which the poet makes the artist, rambling in his illness, say this to his nurse, not knowing that she was his wife:

Nurse, were you hired? or came of your own wil.
To wait on one so broken, so forlorn?
Have I not met you somewhere long ago?
I am all but sure I have—In Kendal church—
O yes! I hired you for a season there,
And then we parted; but you look so kind

That you will not deny my sultry throat
One draught of icy water. There—you spill
The drops upon my forehead. Your hand shakes . . .
Your hand. How bright you keep your marriage ring!

She, devoted soul, uttered no reproach, but was as a good angel to him to the hour when, in 1802, he ceased to breathe. He was carried to a grave at Dalton-in-Furness, where he had lived as a boy, and his son, who wrote his life with such kindly understanding, set up the cenotaph here in Kendal, a memorial not only of a great painter, but of one of the strangest marriage stories we know.

Kendal has on her roll of fame hero, John Gough, whose story is perhaps unsurpassed in the heroic annals of the blind.

The Blind Man Who Loved Nature

HE was born here in 1757 into a Quaker household. Blinded by smallpox in early childhood, he was denied the solace of music by his father who forbade him to practise on the violin, so he cultivated his remarkable gifts by the study of plants and animals.

He proved an eager and successful pupil at the Quaker School, attaining an astonishing mastery of natural history, of mathematics, and of classical poetry, which lingered fresh in his mind throughout his life. For his mathematical problems he invented an elaborate plan of his own by which he made himself master of algebraic symbols and of geometrical figures.

Not only could he learn: he taught. Botanists applied to him for data as to the character and classification of plants; parents sent their sons to him for instruction in mathematics. Among his pupils was the immortal John Dalton. Gough wrote as well as he taught, and on a great variety of topics—on geology, on sound, motion, on seed-germination and on gases, on the migration of birds, on the nutrition and hibernation of plants, and on other such varied themes as ventriloquism and the atmosphere.

His high gifts and unquenchable courage attracted the wondering attention of many of his illustrious contemporaries, among others of Coleridge, who venerated him as mathematician, botanist, and zoologist; and of Wordsworth, who made him the hero of a stirring passage in The Excursion, picturing him, "blind and alone, advancing straight towards some precipice's airy brink":

No floweret blooms
Throughout the lofty range of these rough hills,

Nor in the woods, that could from him conceal
Its birthplace: none whose figure did not live
Upon his touch. The bowels of the earth
Enriched with knowledge his industrious mind:
The ocean paid him tribute from the stores
Lodged in her bosom; and, by Science led,
His genius mounted to the plains of heaven.

A happy husband and the father of nine children, Gough died in 1825, unique in his era as a blind man who had taught, led, and inspired those who had eyes to see.

The Lonely Depths of the Valley

KENTMERE. It is lost to most of us in the lonely depths of the Kentmere Valley. The upper part of the valley, in which Kentmere is the only village, has nobly impressive scenery. The valley runs up into the hills for miles beyond the village, narrowing gradually until it is circled by steep heights. Between parallel ranges on a height of nearly 1000 feet lies Kentmere Reservoir with the gaunt cliffs of Ill Bell towering 1500 feet above it. Down the vale the precipitous Rainsbarrow Crag, descending from Yoke, acts like a gateway to this topmost part of the dale. Only the rough roads from the Reservoir leave this grim recess; the one other way out is by climbing the steep foot track.

Not one traveller in ten thousand who see the smooth and graceful peak of Ill Bell on its western side from Windermere sees or suspects that rugged drop on its eastern side into Kent Dale. Kent river, the one Westmorland river reaching the sea entirely through the county so placidly at Arnside, has its highest springs in the midst of the most lonely grandeur.

We may think of the village as living in a continual Great Silence. About a hundred years ago its great lake was run dry to make good pasture land, and now its ancient church stands at the head of a marsh. It has a yew which has kept sentinel in this lonely place for about 500 years. To this spot they brought St Cuthbert in his coffin on his way to Durham; here the Saxon saint lay in the church all night. But there is nothing now of those days. The church is 16th century, the painted reredos in red and blue is modern, two brightly painted angels stand guard at the altar. The tower is 19th century.

Near the foot of the rugged Garburn Pass from Kentmere into Troutbeck Vale stands the old hall, with its 14th-century tower crumbling away. It has a vaulted cellar and a stairway to the battlements. Here lived 12 generations of a marvellous family. Little is left of their home, but their names are woven in our Island story. They grew up in this remote valley to be preachers, artists, writers, and doctors, men of rare capacity, one of them at least among the choicest spirits of his day, Bernard Gilpin, the Apostle of the North, who died at Houghton in Durham, where he sleeps.

The Place John Ruskin Loved

KIRKBY LONSDALE. John Ruskin said of this small town that it had moorland, sweet river, and English forest at their best. It has long been famous for its church and its bridge. It has Stone Age graves on the hills, a Roman camp close by, a Tudor grammar school rebuilt, and a cross 600 years old. It has old squares, charming streets, and Georgian houses little changed since the Young Pretender came this way in 1745. By the river is the lovely Underley Hall; and not far off is Biggins, a 19th-century house with a drive in two counties. Beyond the limes in the churchyard is a glorious view of the Howgill and Casterton Fell, which Turner painted.

The church, with its venerable stones and quiet dignity, has been much changed through the centuries, but the lower part of the tower and its boldly carved doorway are Norman. Part of the nave arcades is also Norman, the capitals remarkable for grotesques among strange carvings, and some of the pillars having diamond ornament rather like those of Durham Cathedral. There are two other reconstructed Norman doors and a Norman window in the south aisle.

In the belfry hangs a set of quaint orders for ringers to ring well with hand and ear, keep stroke and time and go not out. From the 17th century comes two chests and a chair, and the charming six-sided pulpit with its richly carved panels. A cupboard has still older work. There are fragments of a handsome screen 500 years old, and a pretty piscina niche in a pillar of the south arcade is 700 years old.

A battered figure over 400 years old, perhaps a man with his head on a helmet, lies on an altar tomb with shields in the Middleton Chapel, founded a year or two before Columbus set sail for America. Here too is an old stone coffin, found last century with a medieval carving of the Madonna among angels.

A black marble monument is to the mother of the Earl of Bective, and a quaint inscription to William Sturgeon, a boy of the neighbourhood who became a notable electrical experimenter. He has been sleeping at Prestwich since 1850, but some of his experiments were carried out in Kirkby Lonsdale, where he studied electric storms.

Of all the outdoor possessions of this village none is more valued than the old bridge over the Lune. We do not know exactly how old it is, but it was old enough to need repairing about 600 years ago. It has three beautifully ribbed arches, one 40 feet above the river, and all a triumph of simplicity and grace. Since 1673 it has had an inscription which calls on all who cross to Fear God, Honour the King, and for centuries it has been used by knights and pedlars, monks and soldiers. Its work is done and its burden is carried by a new bridge close by, but we shall all feel that it is a very gracious thing for the town to keep this honourable servant now that its useful days are over.

Out from this village went forth a Lakeland lad whose fine character and great gifts of learning made him Lord Langdale, Master of the Rolls.

The Strange Story of the Missing Heir

ALL the Langdales are in Westmorland, the village, the fell, the beck, the noble Pikes, and when Henry Bickersteth of Kirkby Lonsdale, a local apothecary's younger son who had made his way to London, became Master of the Rolls, he remembered his native county and took Langdale for the title of his barony.

Unflagging industry allied to outstanding genius and conscientiousness carried him towards his goal at the Bar, and at 52, feeling that the future was safe, he married Lady Jane Hardy, daughter of the Earl of Oxford. She was 37, and he had loved her from a child.

The misdoings of the old Chancery Court were as real as Dickens paints them in Bleak House, and at last the Government was shamed into the determination to reform the whole system. Bickersteth was the predestined hero of the great reform. While he was still very poor, and was driven to change his chambers, such was his integrity that he pasted across the chimney piece a notice of warning for any possible tenant: "The chimney of this fireplace smokes incurably, and every experiment has been tried to remedy the evil, and no expense spared."

He demanded for the administration of the law the same high standard of care and deliberation which marked his own life, and most romantically he was justified in one famous case. A sum of money was in Court waiting distribution in proof of the death of a man who had been missing for thirty years. Langdale was not satisfied, on the evidence before him, that the death of the missing man was established. Eventually new evidence was forthcoming and Lord Langdale at last made an order for the distribution of the estate to three parties. The order was taken to the law office to be entered, and the clerk into whose hands it was given was—*the missing heir!*

He had got into disgrace long years before, had fled the country, and after a long absence, things having been forgotten, had returned to England and obtained a situation in the office to which came this extraordinary revelation of his unknown fortune. Let us hasten slowly, the good Lord Langdale would ever afterwards say as he told this strange story.

Bound For a Thousand Years

KIRKBY STEPHEN. It has kept a prisoner bound hand and foot for a thousand years, a Saxon captive in its ancient church. A town with narrow passages and spacious squares, it looks up to some of the grandest scenery in England. Like ageless giants are Wild Boar Fell and Hugh's Seat, both over 2300 feet high; and beyond is the great waste of Stainmore where Yorkshire and Westmorland meet on the lonely Pennines. A romantic spot is Stenkrith Bridge, where the River Eden roars into Coopkarnal Hole among huge rocks; Lammerside Castle is a lonely ruined fortress with a background of splendid hills.

Curfew rings here every night as it has rung for 700 ye rs. Here are crooked little 17th-century houses, a quaint market hall, a vicarage with a fine view of the fells, and an inn in the market square with a curiously carved stone which may have been in the Saxon church. The church of today has traces of Norman and Saxon work, and a 16th-century tower, one of the most graceful in Westmorland.

Like a small cathedral this church is, a noble building which is one of the largest in the county, with a stately nave notable for its length and its magnificent 13th-century arcades under a modern clerestory. The crossing between the transepts has a 13th-century arch and two modern ones. The chancel and its chapels were made new last century, but the fine 13th-century sedilia and piscina still remain in the chancel. A bracket as old is in a chapel, where there is a 14th-century coffin lid carved with a cross, a sword, and a shield.

There is a 16th-century roof, a 17th-century cupboard, and fragments of an old screen. Four carved offertory boxes used in Cromwell's day are being used still. A pathetic inscription is in memory of a young doctor of last century who gave up his life fighting an outbreak of fever in France.

In the church are some remarkable stones, one, a fragment of a Norman capital, has two grotesque animals which seem to be squeezing a little man to death. Among fragments of Saxon crosses from the old churchyard is one showing a queer horned figure with a beard, his arms and legs bound, perhaps meant for Satan. Carved when the Confessor ruled in England, it is of great interest to antiquarians, and one of the quaintest stones we have seen. A hogback stone has a gabled top resembling tiles.

In the Musgrave Chapel, with its old piscina and its fine oak roof with six carved bosses, lies a stone figure, thought to be Sir Richard Musgrave, on his early 15th-century altar tomb, wearing armour with hip belt, his feet on a lion. Another Sir Richard Musgrave has been sleeping here with his wife and son since 1464, their plain tomb under a lovely arch. A monument of red stone has a cross in memory of Sir Thomas Musgrave, perhaps the founder of the chapel, who died about 1376.

In the Wharton Chapel lie the rather battered stone figures of Thomas, first Lord Wharton, and his two wives. He is a knight in armour, his feet on a beast; his wives wear French caps and gowns with tight bodices and full skirts. Two sons and two daughters kneel on the sides of their handsome tomb. Another monument to him is at Heelaugh in Yorkshire, where he has been sleeping since 1568.

Sir Thomas made his name with the sword, and was the ancestor of Philip Wharton who made his name with the Bible. Their old home was at Wharton Hall, now a farm but once a stately place with an embattled gatehouse and a banqueting hall where James the First came to dinner. Among the ruins are buildings of the 14th and 15th centuries and a chapel which still has its old benches. The ancient glass, magnificent ceilings, and beautiful panelling have gone, but the Whartons will be remembered when the ruins themselves have disappeared.

They were here in the days of Edward the First and rose to importance in Tudor days. When the English Bible came it was a Wharton who left money here for the distribution of Bibles in four English counties. It was a Philip Wharton who helped to bring

William of Orange to England, and his splendid portrait by Van Dyck is well-known. The last of the family, who died in a monastery in Spain while still a young man, was a staunch supporter of the Old Pretender.

Three Precious Old Things

KIRKBY THORE. Here met two Roman roads; here they had a camp on a green mound a bowshot from where the church now stands. Their altars, coins, and ornaments have been found round about, and one of their milestones is still erect by the mountain road to Hadrian's Wall.

Not far off is a ruined manor house built by the Whartons soon after the Battle of Bosworth Field. Their home for 13 generations, it was once a noble house with stones from a ruined castle. Little of its glory is now left. Of the 14th-century hall only broken walls remain, with a lofty window still beautiful.

In the loveliest corner of this village below the Pennines stands a group of white cottages with bright gardens, near a small hill called the Cross. Here is the sturdy church begun by the Normans, with stones from the Roman camp. With Norman work in its walls, it has a medieval nave and chancel much restored by the Whartons, whose shields have been on the battlements of the tower since the 15th century. The splendid altar rails and a font with three greyhounds on it were the gifts of Thomas Machell, a rector of Charles the Second's day. The nave arcade is 13th century, and the porch is a little younger.

A fine pulpit, an ancient bell, and fragments of old glass are among the best possessions of the church. The glass is thought to have been here before Queen Elizabeth, and its bright colours still enrich two windows. Strikingly beautiful is the oak pulpit with flowers, foliage, and figures carved by a craftsman of Charles Stuart's day. The bell is older still; one of the biggest in Westmorland, it is said to have rung in the tower of Shap Abbey long before the monks were turned out by Henry the Eighth.

Wordsworth Sees a Great Splendour

LANGDALE. There are two Langdales, visited from Ambleside or Grasmere, draining into Lake Elterwater and then into Windermere, and overlooked from the north by the impressive Langdale Pikes, 2300 feet high, mountains which have a resemblance to lions crouching, side by side.

There are 40 higher Lakeland mountains than the Langdale Pikes, but not so many making such an individual impression. Apart from the Pikes, the two dales (Great and Little Langdale) make the most convenient approach to the sterner mountain features of Westmorland, Cumberland, and Lancashire.

Little Langdale descends from the Wrynose Pass eastward to the head of Windermere, with the Brathay as its accompanying stream, and the top of the pass is a meeting-place for those three counties. The Brathay is here the boundary for Lancashire and Westmorland down Little Langdale, and it is a pleasant region of the lower hills, with little lakes, waterfalls, and woodlands—Loughrigg Tarn and Skelwith Force below Elterwater, and Colwith Force and Little Langdale Tarn above Elterwater, with not much sense of the higher mountains.

But Great Langdale is different. The boundary between Westmorland and Cumberland, from the Three Shire Stone on Wrynose Pass, follows north the topmost rocky ridges of some of the spurs of the highest mass of the Cumbrian mountains, and beyond Elterwater the Great Langdale valley runs into their very midst. From a green strath by the beck we look south to where the boundary line runs, at an elevation of nearly 3000 feet, over crags seamed with steep gullies, to the noble peak of Bow Fell westward, while the Langdale Pikes rise precipitously overhead to the north. The whole vale is walled around with mountains. Here villages are nothing; the mountains and the impression they make are everything.

The best entrance to the upper part of Great Langdale is up Little Langdale by the road between Lingmoor and Pike of Bliscoe and past Blea Tarn, "the little lowly vale and yet uplifted high," where the Solitary of Wordsworth's Excursion lived, and where we have the best view of Langdale Pikes, Wordsworth's lusty twins, "echoing back, in the grim and breathless hour of noon, the thunder's greeting." It was up here that a single step out of the mist brought the poet to a splendour without end:

Glory beyond all glory ever seen
By waking sense or by the dreaming soul!
Fabric it seemed of diamond and of gold,
With alabaster domes, and silver spires,
And blazing terrace upon terrace, high
Uplifted; here serene pavilions bright,

In avenues disposed; there towers begirt
With battlements that on their restless fronts
Bore stars—illumination of all gems!
O, twas an unimaginable sight!

But the place is not now as it was when Wordsworth described it, for it is no longer treeless.

In Great Langdale the one thing seen by all is the well-hidden little waterfall of Dungeon Gill:

Into a chasm a mighty block
Has fallen and made a bridge of rock;
The gulf is deep below
And in a basin black and small
Receives a lofty waterfall.

The fall is about 90 feet. The amount of water varies so greatly that it eludes description. It may be a shower-bath or a small torrent, but Nature's artistry is very choice. Great Langdale is stern and repellent at first sight, but it is the lowland that is nearest to the finest mountain scenery of England, conveniently within a six-mile walk to the topmost point of the land.

The Hall in the Enchanting Garden

LEVENS. For centuries it has been, and for centuries it surely must be, a place of pilgrimage. A tiny village with one of the most beautiful houses and perhaps the loveliest garden in Westmorland, it lies on the banks of the river Kent, and in the green plain below the hills it has a 19th-century church, an old mill, and its second ancient house, Low Levens Hall, with round chimneys and walls that have braved about six centuries.

The great house, one of the wonders of Lakeland, is Levens Hall near Levens Bridge, set in a delightful park of 100 acres with the river winding among its venerable oaks and beeches. Here are broad avenues and shady paths and a glorious sanctuary for squirrels and birds.

Like most of Westmorland's old houses, Levens Hall began as a peel tower in the 14th century, a place of refuge against the Scots, as all these peel towers were. From this stronghold the Redmaynes went to fight on the border. Richard was Speaker of Parliament in the year of Flodden Field; another Richard rebelled, was pardoned, and became Bishop of Ely. Most of the old peel tower is gone, but the great house has been built about it, an Elizabethan manor built round a Plantagenet fortress. It is a wonderful structure, built in the days when money could be spent like water and artists were available to make even rain pipes and chimney stacks beautiful. Here the rain pipes are adorned with cherub heads, and the great house is made attractive by every architectural device of gables and wings and charming windows. Inside and out it is as rare a treasure house as England has to show, with all the graciousness the Elizabethan builders could give it, a wealth of exquisite oak panelling, wonderful plastered ceilings, magnificent chimney-pieces, panelled rooms, and deep friezes, the whole house filled with 17th- and 18th-century furniture and set in an evergreen garden of almost incredible loveliness.

Three of the rare treasures of the decoration of Levens Hall are the fireplaces in the small drawing-room, the great drawing-room, and the smoking-room. They are all of oak. In the small drawing-room the features of the chimney-piece are its carved figures. In two panels are groups of the Four Seasons and the Four Elements, and the side figures at the base are Samson with the jawbone of an ass and Hercules in a lion's skin, armed with a club. The five other separate figures representing the five senses, Touch, Smell, and Taste, standing by the two group panels, and Hearing and Seeing reclining at the top of the pediment. In the great drawing-room is a three-decker chimney-piece with magnificent heraldic panels, the whole rising on Doric, Ionic, and Corinthian columns. In the windows of this room are six heraldic oval panels of stained glass. The smoking-room mantelpiece has five oak figures in it, three representing Wisdom, Justice, and Truth. It was Sir James Bellingham who ordered all this beauty to be made. He lived to enjoy it until 1641 and his dream house has lived on to be a wonder of today. It has long been famous for its pictures, and for a quaint guide to good conduct written in 1682, perhaps the work of one of the Levens stewards. It tells the guests of Levens Hall that they must be up in good time in the morning, and says

None to the kitchen shall repair
To wash their hands or comb the hair.

Among the treasures understood to be in the house when we called were the despatch box used by Pitt, and a bowl said to have been bowled by Drake when playing his historic game on Plymouth Hoe; there was time to bowl it, he said, and to beat the Spaniards too.

The gardens are enchanting. They were planted by the gardener who remodelled the grounds of Hampton Court for James the Second, and he laid them out that they might be impressive all the year round, with marvellous battlemented hedges, with beech and box cut into every conceivable shape, with archways and arbours, the Beech Walk and the Beech Circle, the group of yews that stand for Queen Elizabeth and her maids of honour, and, in short, a collection of formal shrubs and trees that could hardly be surpassed. The marvellous square masses of beech in the Beech Walk are probably unequalled for a hundred miles around; it is a wonderful sight, and everywhere the beeches keep brown all through the hard northern winter, a memorable sight to see clothed in their white mantles, and glowing with warmth when the winter days are fine.

This wonderful garden, a paradise of colour when the carpet beds are all aglow, is immediately round the house, and we have seen no home more beautiful or more nobly set. In spite of their formality the gardens have all the charm of something irregular and haphazard, for these yews and hollies and the pretty little box are clipped into fantastic shapes, living cones or squares or pyramids, evergreens bewitched into strange birds or beasts, giant chessmen, peacocks that have not moved for a hundred years, a judge's wig, a green lion: it may seem to a pilgrim as queer as the garden Alice found so bewildering in Wonderland, and yet in spite of all that is fantastic it is a thing of beauty that we should like to feel will be a joy for ever.

A Gem of Tudor England

LITTLE STRICKLAND. It has grand views across miles of wooded hills. Its 19th-century church, not far from Lowther Castle, has fine oak seats from the older church, and an inscription to Thomas Fletcher of 1695, recorder of Appleby and founder of a village charity.

But the best of its sights is the Hall on a little hill above the green, which has charming windows with carved bosses at the ends of the drip-stones, and is reputed for its splendid Tudor woodwork and fine plaster ceilings. One of the rooms has a ceiling ornamented with roses, and a small bedroom is a gem of Tudor England, with exquisite plasterwork above the panelling, and a Jacobean mantelpiece richly carved in oak with the figure of a woman. The ceiling of this tiny chamber is lavishly ornamented with birds and flowers.

The Old Doorways

LONG MARTON. Its small church has fragments from Norman England. Its tower has been here 300 years. One of its possessions is a medieval chest, a massive thing with great oak planks and much strong ironwork, the lid too heavy for one man. There is a piscina over 500 years old and stone seats in which the priests sat long before the Reformation. One bell is about 1400, and another is a hundred years younger.

But we come to see the stones over two doorways, with their bold carvings by Norman sculptors. Over the south doorway are worn carvings of two monsters, a shield with a cross and a sword. Over the west doorway is carving of lattice ornament, and two queer creatures, one with its tail tied in a knot, the other with wings. It is thought the carvings on these doorways have something to do with the legend of St Margaret of Antioch, to whom 200 churches are dedicated.

Robert Elsmere's Country

LONG SLEDDALE. We found the valley golden with kingcups and the lane a winding way through mists of bluebells. Above the village is Goat Scar, and on Harter Fell are the beginnings of the little River Sprint, which goes down to meet the Kent near Kendal. Very fine are the mountains here, with Shap Fell at one side and Ill Bell and Rainsborrow Crag at the other, though the most beautiful part of the valley is near Sad Ghyll.

The small 19th-century church looks across to white farms on the hillsides. It has an 18th-century oak locker and an Elizabethan chalice.

Here came Mrs Humphry Ward, her mind full of a book she wanted to write, and in this valley she found the setting for her novel Robert Elsmere. She calls it Long Whindale, and what she wrote of it in 1888 is still true. She found the narrow road between the crags lined with blossom, a line of white through the green sloping pastures.

The House With 3000 Acres

LOWTHER. Its great house is the pride of Westmorland and the church stands in its park, a spreading place of 3000 acres. The Newtown has dignified houses with clipped shrubs, and the Village has delightful cottages with trim gardens, and wide views of the hills going up to Shap Abbey.

The trees of its glorious park, near the river Lowther, make a green wall behind the village; high above the river is a green bank 1000 yards long, and the stately terrace in front of the castle is 500 feet long and 90 feet wide with a strong rampart, two watch-towers, and an imposing lodge. The house has been made new several times and only part of the tower is left from the 13th century. Among its treasures are some early Hogarths and two fine 8th-century cross-shafts. In the grounds are many carved stones from Shap Abbey and round about, as well as part of a 9th-century cross-shaft. The gardens, especially the Italian garden and the scented garden, have an unforgettable beauty.

Its south front has a room 60 feet long, the central tower is 90 feet high inside, and the grand staircase is adorned with statues and stained windows. One of the windows was given by the last German Kaiser, who stayed here in his friendly days. From the tower the peaks of Skiddaw and Helvellyn can be seen. Wordsworth thought it all like a cathedral with its parapets and towers, spires and pinnacles:

Lowther! in thy majestic pile are seen
Cathedral pomp and grace in apt accord
With the baronial castle's sterner mien.

To an older house here, now gone, came Mary Queen of Scots, and she was always grateful for the kindness she received from Sir Richard Lowther. Sir Richard joined a rebellion to put her on the throne, but was careful of his safety and lived to a good old age. He has been sleeping in the church since 1607, and his alabaster figure shows him with a fine ruff and doublet.

Among the trees and behind fine gates, stands the church, with a dome and lantern crowning its central tower. An old mounting stone and a medieval cross keep it company together with three Saxon stones known as hogbacks, little low gravestones made as little houses of the dead in imitation of the low long cottages common in the North until the 18th century, and their curved tops are generally carved to represent tiles. The sculptor would often carve on them a pair of muzzled bears hugging the ends of the roof. Only a few hogbacks have survived, and they are generally dug up in graveyards or found built into churches, usually over the doorway. Many were made before the Danish invasion, and they did not die out until the Norman Conquest. On one of Lowther's hogbacks we see a figure between a group of armed men, and other armed men in a ship; another has heads of beasts, a bird, and foliage. Part of a tombstone with interlacing work, and fragments perhaps of a cross-shaft with interlacing and key pattern, are also in the churchyard, both stones perhaps 11th century.

The church has been much changed in several centuries, but there still remains the Norman north arcade, its capitals carved with foliage, monsters, and grotesque beasts. The other arcade is a little younger, and over them is the 17th-century clerestory. The chancel is also of this time. There is a 13th-century arch in each transept. Two chairs, the altar table with a modern top, the rails, and a chest are 17th century.

In the mausoleum outside sleep generations of Lowthers. On his plain tomb lies Sir Richard Lowther of 1607, Lord Warden of the Marches, in armour and ruff. A marble wall monument has draped busts of Sir John Lowther and his son of Stuart days. John, Viscount Lonsdale and Lord Lowther of 1700, reclines in his wig and peer's robe, with his sword and holding his coronet, his tomb adorned with drapery and cherub's heads. He struck a blow for William of Orange by leading a troop of men to capture a ship loaded with arms landing at Workington. He rebuilt the castle, brought in Italian artists to paint the ceilings, laid out its spacious gardens, planted the park, and restored the church.

In a white marble tomb lies Sir William of the 19th century, who made the house as we see it. He was a patron of art and literature, and Wordsworth dedicated his Excursion to him, saying:

Oft through thy domain, illustrious Peer,
In youth I roamed on youthful pleasures bent.

There is a fine statue of his son, second Earl of Lonsdale. He had immense wealth and befriended the roadmaker John Macadam.

The first Earl of Lonsdale used his silver to acquire an evil reputation.

The Rich Bad Earl

THREE lines of the family dying during his lifetime, James Lowther, born in 1736 and created Earl of Lonsdale, found himself possessed of great riches, in money, land, and minerals. Very ill he employed them. He used his wealth to buy political influence.

Certain constituencies he owned, others he bought, so that he had a group of nine members in the House of Commons, his people, as he called them, elected by his favour and there to do his bidding. He spent great sums in bribing electors to return him and his creatures to Parliament; and they did return him and them.

In politics he veered from side to side, from the Whigs to the Tories, whose leader Bute became his father-in-law; from the Tories back to the Whigs. His political life and his means of entering and continuing it were a scandal, yet it was he who, as owner of Appleby, in 1781 brought Pitt into the House of Commons.

He had a passion for electioneering, and, not content with Parliament, carried his methods into municipal and rural politics, and endeavoured to override the electors of Carlisle by wholesale creation of freemen. He died in 1802 with seven thousand guineas at hand in readiness for a forthcoming election; but he left a host of poor creditors he had refused to pay, including Wordsworth's father, his own lawyer.

He was known throughout the North as the rich bad earl, and it was said of him that he was the most detested man alive. Yet there was method in his madness, and he had a shrewd eye for industrial development where his estates lay, boasting that all the land, fire, and water of Whitehaven belonged to him, and helping the town by the introduction of the steam engine and textile industries.

If ever the men who fought so long and wearily for the Reform Bill had needed a text they had it in the bad Earl of Lonsdale.

Pendragon's Castle

MALLERSTANG. It is among the highest of all these mountains, a lonely little place in the valley of the River Eden between Wild Boar Fell and High Seat, both over 2300 feet. Here are ancient graves on the hills and a few houses in the valley. On the Yorkshire border is a stone pillar with an inscription to Sir Hugh Morville, the gift of Lady Anne Clifford, who restored the ancient church and rebuilt the castle, one of the most romantic ruins in Westmorland.

Once a home of the Cliffords, it is a massive pile with a name that brings to our minds legends a thousand years old. They had fine names in those days for hills and valleys and castles. The great hill opposite High Seat was Wild Boar Fell, the valley between them was Mallerstang, and the castle from which the Cliffords bore rule had the romantic name Pendragon. It was all there as early as 1314. It is all there now as a fine piece of scenery, except that the castle is a ruin. The Cliffords, too, have gone. How came they by the ghostly name Pendragon?

There is no doubt that when the Norman castle was built the legends of King Arthur were circulating through the dales of Westmorland 700 years after the days of the Table Round, if ever there were such days. It was rumoured that King Arthur's legendary father Uther Pendragon had had a castle on the hill in the valley, and that he had tried to lead the river to encircle it like a moat. He had failed, and the memory of it was kept alive by the rhyme.

Let Uther Pendragon do what he can,
Eden shall run as Eden ran.

So some romantic Clifford boldly claimed the name of Pendragon for his new stronghold, across the waste of 700 silent years.

It has persisted very well as a name through rough vicissitudes. The Scots came and burnt it in 1341, but the doughty Cliffords built it up again. The Scots burnt it a couple of centuries later and in the 17th century the remarkable Lady Anne, Countess of Pembroke and last of her race, found it ruinous and left it "a neat little place." She built it anew in defiance of parliament and kings, but her successor saw no reason why he should waste wealth on such a useless structure and so he kept it for Time to put its seal on the aged thing, and there it stands, a legendary ghost.

Pendragon is a fine-sounding name to appropriate for an eerie region of the Pennine wilds, and it may give some comfort to those who hold that King Arthur was really a hero of the Cumbrian and Strathclyde Britons, and not of Cornwall, Wessex, or Wales.

A Village Under Sentence of Death

MARDALE. Mardale will soon be no more; it is waiting to be drowned. Below Kidsty Pike, it is a tiny place in a lovely valley hidden in the mountains. Far above is a green lane which was once a Roman road, perhaps the highest in England. Near the parsonage is Castle Crag with traces of a British fortress. Harter Fell 2300 feet high and what are known as the Giant's Graves are not far off. The old village has known the Holme family, called Kings of Mardale, for over 600 years, and one of them built a little church here in the 14th century.

Very delightful is Mardale Hall, thought to have been the summerhouse of Lord William Howard, the Belted Will of Scott's Last Minstrel. Not far off is the beautiful Thornthwaite Hall, a lonely Elizabethan house described by Anthony Trollope.

From Mardale we can go by a company of firs to the open fell above Riggindale and then to the cairns on Harter Fell, where there is a splendid view of the valley with Hawes Water like a mirror for the trees at the edge. Another track from the village takes us along the mountain path to Shap, the way the people of Mardale took their dead till two centuries ago.

It is Hawes Water that is to drown Mardale when the valley becomes a reservoir for Manchester. The old inn will go, and the ancient yews by the church are like the little church itself, only a memory. There was little to preserve, for the black watch beetle had crept into its rough-hewn beams, the fine spandrels of the roofs, and the handsome screen. The graves in the churchyard had been opened and the bodies removed to Shap. The stone bridges, the quaint houses, and the noble pines will go, but when the waters close over all this beauty a little island with a few trees will show where the lost village lies.

A Traveller Home at Last

MARTINDALE. Above the wooded shores of Ullswater lies Martindale, with wild mountains about. Guarded by Beda Fell and Gowk Hill, it has streams running down to Howgrane, and a forest home for wild red deer. High on Bampton Common is the astonishing Roman road over Weather Hill, and among the solitude of moors a thousand feet above the sea is a 15th-century church.

The old church at Howgrane was here soon after the Conqueror's day, but was made new in 1633 and again in 200 years more. One of the loneliest churches in Westmorland, deserted and unused when we found it, it still has its 17th-century woodwork—the pulpit with good carving, 12 beautiful pews, panelling on the walls, and massive beams in the roof. A bell and a stoup are perhaps medieval. Close by is a yew which may have been a sapling here soon after the Normans left. About 20 feet round its trunk, it is magnificent with far-spreading branches.

Not far off sleeps a traveller who knew the wonders of four continents, but loved this romantic bit of Lakeland best of all. He was Andrew Wilson, who has been sleeping here since 1881. The son of a famous missionary, he wrote vivid accounts of his journeyings. He mastered 15 languages, edited papers in India and China, and became an authority on all Eastern questions. He wrote a remarkable history of Gordon's Chinese campaigns, visited the United States, and had an adventurous journey over the Himalayas into Tibet. He made an excursion into one of the wildest States of India and wrote a popular account of 20 years of African travel, and after all his excitements came to spend his last years among the glory of the Lakes.

MIDDLETON. Close to the Yorkshire border and only a few miles from Sedbergh, it is between Middleton Fell and the River Lune. The Romans must have loved it, and one of their milestones still encourages us on our way as we pass the vicarage. From the small church of 300 years ago, made new last century, is a delightful peep of the river through the trees.

There are old fragments of Beckside Hall in the modern farmhouse which has taken its place. The home of Sir John Otway in the 17th century, it has oak which has been admired since Shakespeare's day.

But it is Middleton Hall the traveller remembers here, a fine 15th-century house by the river. It has a massive outer wall and wide doorways into its spacious courtyard. Its great hall has fine windows and an arched fireplace 400 years old; and another room has much old woodwork over the mantelpiece. Perhaps its chief treasure is a medieval oak door beautifully panelled and studded with iron.

Richard Atkinson's Lost Days

MILBURN. It may have hoped for the best but it certainly prepared for the worst. Always in danger of being destroyed by the Scots, its houses were built facing the spacious green to make a protection for cattle; the church was hidden in a hollow enshrined in trees, and its castle was built for strength.

Now a farmhouse, Howgill Castle has still something of its 14th-century grandeur. It stands finely above a deep ravine and has 17th-century buildings between huge towers with walls ten feet thick and vaulted basements for the keeping of cattle when the Scots were raiding Westmorland. It has fragments of its battlemented parapet, a handsome pillared entrance, a 17th-century staircase with massive balustrades, and a great chamber with an elaborate mantelpiece and a splendid oak table that must have been made there, for it would be impossible to get it out.

Not far from the village, with an old maypole set in the base of an ancient cross, is the church with a modern bellcot, keeping a Norman doorway which has been rebuilt, Norman masonry in the north wall, and two Norman carved stones in the west wall. The nave arcade and a piscina are over 600 years old. A chest is 17th century, and on the chancel wall are several scratch dials.

There is a 13th-century gravestone with a cross and shears; and from the churchyard has come indoors for shelter a medieval stone figure. A window with white horses in the angry waves is in memory of a young doctor who was drowned at sea. Perhaps we can hardly help being amused at old Richard Atkinson, who died in 1760, and of whom we are told that he lived 71 years and 350 days, though the reform of the calendar robbed him of ten of his days.

Built into a wall of Underwood House, within a mile of the church, is a Roman inscribed stone relating to the work of the 20th Legion.

He Sleeps Under the Tree He Planted

MORLAND. Easily missed is this lovely village of the beautiful valley near the River Lyvennet.

One of the most delightful houses for miles round is its Newby Hall, with a little flagged garden, an old fireplace nine feet wide, and a kitchen with a bakehouse, once a feature of Westmorland houses. Morland house has been the companion of the church since Stuart times, and has a charming old garden glorious with lawns, yews, flowers, and a wonderful box hedge as high as the roof.

In a churchyard sweet with lavender and roses, watched over by a magnificent Spanish chestnut, stands the venerable and dignified church of Norman and medieval times, two storeys of its sturdy tower thought to have been here before the Conqueror came. Its top storey is 16th century, and inside are heavy oak ladders which some folks think have been here as long as the tower. There are fragments of Norman work in the 13th-century nave arcades, and in the sides of the 600-year-old chancel arch; and some stones carved with zigzag are in a window.

A beautiful coffin lid, with leaves growing from the stem of its cross, looks little older than the day it was carved nearly 700 years ago. The font has a 17th-century bowl and a carved pyramid cover as old as itself, but its stem and base are medieval, as is some ironwork on the north door. Some old timbers are in the roofs, and from the 17th century come the altar rails, some panelling in the aisles, a chest (which may be older still) and a poor-box.

The splendid carved oak in the chancel is the work of a man who lived before America was known in Europe, a man with a rare sense of humour, for his 22 heads are as quaint as anything we have seen in Westmorland, kings, queens, bishops, monks, angels, patriarchs, and a demon in their midst.

A palimpsest brass which may have come from Shap Abbey has a figure of a young man in armour on one side, and on the other an inscription to John Blythe, who was vicar here for 35 years of Tudor reigns.

Here sleeps Frederick Markham, grandson of Archbishop William Markham, a soldier and a sportsman who made a remarkable journey into the interior of Kashmir and Tibet, bringing home rare specimens of deer. He was at the storming of Sebastopol, and died soon afterwards. Only a month or two before he left for the Crimea he had planted a tree in the churchyard, and we found it healthy and strong, throwing its shadow over his grave.

At Newby Head not far off is a Quaker cemetery where Thomas Lawson has been sleeping 200 years. He gave up his curacy to join the Friends, and George Fox mentions him in his Journal.

The Fighting Archbishop

MURTON. Brown streams, glorious fells, winding lanes sweet with wild roses, glimpses of red earth reminding us of Cornwall—this is Murton, the tiny village below the mighty Pennine range.

Its church is modern, with a modern three-decker pulpit, and round about are gracious old houses, among them Murton Hall with fragments of Elizabethan work in its mullioned windows, a charming porch, and a quaint chimney-stack, finished with a 14th-century gabled lantern. The east part of the main block, perhaps also 14th century, is now a cow-house, and the traceried head of a 14th-century window is built into a garden wall.

Not far off is Roman Fell, nearly 2000 feet high, and below is Hilton, a hamlet which gave England a fighting archbishop. He was Christopher Bainbridge, born in this lovely corner of Westmorland in 1464. A quick-tempered man, he was faithful to Henry the Seventh who made him Archbishop of York, and to Henry the Eighth who sent him as an ambassador to the Pope. He became a cardinal and was given command of the Pope's Army to march against France. He made peace soon afterwards but was poisoned at the height of his power in 1514; it is said the deed was done by his Italian steward, in acknowledgment of a blow he had received from the cardinal, but there are other stories.

Natland Has No Treacle Mines

NATLAND. With two things that were here 1700 years ago, and a church built a year or two before the war, it is known to every child in Westmorland as the place with treacle mines. When they ask too many questions their mothers and fathers say teasingly, "I haven't time for any more questions now; I'm going to Natland treacle mines," a quaint saying baffling not only children but older folk, not one of whom knows how it began.

It has no treacle mines, but Natland has joyous trim gardens, and little houses facing a green, and a modern church with a spacious nave, graceful arches, and massive pillars in the tower. Its story goes back to the days when the Romans had two camps close by. One was a sort of look-out post built on the ruins of a British fortress on Helme Hill, where there is a glorious view; the other was a bigger station 500 feet long and 400 wide, protected on three sides by a loop of the River Kent known as the Watercrook. Of this stronghold, a great Roman post in Agricola's day, a few green mounds remain, and hereabouts have been found many treasures, among them an inscribed gravestone and an altar now in the British Museum. The gravestone has a quaint inscription to a soldier of the 20th Legion, and ends with the odd threat that anyone putting another body in his grave will be fined!

Among the old houses not far from the church is Natland Hall with its original fixed table, panelled screen, and 17th-century staircase; Natland Abbey, built perhaps in the middle of the 16th century, like a letter H, with 17th-century doors and staircase, and some original roofs; and High House with 17th-century panelling, doors, and staircase and chimney-stacks with oval shafts. Watercrook, nearly a mile away is L-shaped; one wing may be 16th century, and another a century younger; there are two 300-year-old staircases.

Two Watchmen on the Housetop

NEWBIGGIN. A little place below a high moor where a Roman road runs over British earthworks. It had a priory 600 years ago, and has still, near St Helen's Well, the foundations of an ancient chapel.

In a lovely group of cottages stands the church made almost new but keeping something of the Norman church rebuilt 600 years ago. The chancel has several 14th-century windows, there is a coffin lid of the same age, and in the 16th-century chapel is a 14th-century doorway.

Among old glass fragments, medieval and 17th century, are heads of a bearded king and a saint. Some 17th-century panelling is in the chancel, which has a 600-year-old piscina, but the treasure here is a pillar piscina from the end of Norman days, its group of eight shafts crowned with a simple foliated capital.

There is a medieval sundial on a buttress, and remains of an old cross in the churchyard.

The village has two brave knights in armour above the village roofs. With their arms akimbo, they stand on the battlements of the Hall, remarkable men in stone, where they have been keeping watch since Christopher Crackenthorpe made new this part of the house 400 years ago. The house has fragments of an older one, great stones of a 14th-century tower belonging to the home of the Crackenthorpes 600 years ago. With its battlements, turrets, and spouts like little guns above the walls, the old place proudly guards the border. It was from this house that the Crackenthorpes went to fight for our first King Edward. In the Wars of the Roses they were ardent Lancastrians, and two of them died at Towton, all for a red rose.

OLD HUTTON. It was a noble house built in the last years of Queen Elizabeth. Much of the grandeur of Bleaze Hall has gone, but it has an imposing front, beautiful plaster ceilings, and rich woodwork; one of its spacious rooms has oak panelling with elaborate figures and foliage, and a mantelpiece of Stuart times.

The church, refashioned more than once, has a 14th-century window in the organ chamber, and two chairs and a poor-box over 200 years old. Its one possession, which will long be treasured, is a chalice of exquisite beauty, the work of a medieval silversmith. On the base is engraved a Crucifix with foliage, and round the stem is an enriched boss, with an unusual and lovely pattern.

The Indomitable George Whitehead

ORTON. It lies below Shap Fells and Orton Scar, where a beacon flamed when the Scots came over the border and the people drove their cattle into a walled enclosure. There are magnificent views from the moors above, where ancient Britons have been sleeping two thousand years.

It has an Elizabethan Hall, with a great iron door richly ornamented. The small church has a chancel made new, and a 15th-century bell in its fine tower built over 400 years ago. A 17th-century porch and a door almost as old leads us inside, where an arcade built late in the 15th century leads to the north aisle; the south arcade having one 700-year-old bay and two 300 years younger.

The roofs of the nave and aisles are over 400 years old. A bracket carved with nail-head, a piscina in the south aisle, and two coffin lids in the porch are 13th century. The stone coffin of a child is in the tower. The font and the altar rails in an aisle are 17th century, and the simple pulpit was made from an old three-decker. A medieval dug-out chest six feet long, with a coved lid, was hewn out of a single tree which was once one of the glories of Lowther Park. A great stone in the churchyard, at which the village folk would gather to hear the news in the days before newspapers, may be an old altar.

In the churchyard sleeps William Farrar, an 18th-century doctor well known in the hills, where the people believed he practised black magic.

With this sham wise man are remembered three men truly wise. One was Richard Burn, remembered for his legal writings and a valuable book of local history; he was vicar of Orton for half of the 18th century. One who would hear him preach was Thomas Barlow, famous for his knowledge of logic and philosophy, Bishop of Lincoln. But the greatest of Orton's three wise men was George Whitehead, a Quaker who suffered much persecution, one of the founders of the Society of Friends.

He Called on Kings to Set the Quakers Free

GEORGE WHITEHEAD was born here in 1636, educated at Blencow free school, fell under the irresistible magic of George Fox, and, to the distress of his family, turned Quaker while still a youth. The times were perilous for Quakers; prisons were full of them. They were hated by Anglicans, Presbyterians, and Baptists, and it was sport to bait and bludgeon them.

In these conditions Whitehead set forth on a crusade that occupied him for 65 years. He preached, he conducted disputations with parsons and professors, he wrote pamphlets, visited imprisoned Quakers, and then began to join them himself as a captive. Beginning at Norwich, where he was in gaol for 18 months, he was placed in the stocks at Saffron Walden and whipped.

He preached his way home again, and there held services on the wild hillsides till he suffered fresh imprisonment at Ipswich, Peterborough, and Norwich, where gaol fever nearly killed him. With the Restoration he appeared at the House of Commons as a proud suppliant for justice to Quakers, but for the next five years he was hardly ever out of prison.

Nothing shook or deterred him; he went quietly on, until by his unruffled complacence he found a way into the presence of Charles. In his gay indifference the king was not in the least hostile to Quakers and at Whitehead's request freed every captive Quaker, including Bunyan. But the wheel turned full circle again, and a measure aimed at the Papists threw 1500 Quakers into gaol and pitilessly robbed them of their estates.

With the accession of James the Second the resolute Quaker secured immunity from a king who desired to free all creeds so that Roman Catholicism might again be legalised. Not until after the Revolution, however, were the old lion's efforts finally crowned. Then an Act of Parliament recognised Quakers as citizens.

Fox was the creator of the Society of Friends; indomitable, clear-headed, legal-minded, George Whitehead was the law-giver, the Moses of his creed. He stood before seven sovereigns unabashed, and obtained concessions that were fused in the Quaker's Magna Carta of 1696. He personally congratulated William, Anne, and George the First on their accession, and finally visited the future George the Second to urge him to grant liberty of conscience when the time came. He died in 1723, aged 86, and was buried in Bunhill Fields.

The Way Up Helvellyn

PATTERDALE. One of Westmorland's most romantic dales, it looks up to Kidsty Pike (with a Roman road over the mountains) and down to the majesty of Ullswater. Nestling among trees near the lake, the village is loved by all travellers for its natural charm, and its wonderful walks and climbs.

From Patterdale we can climb by Kidsty Pike and across the Roman road to a track which goes down to Mardale, or can take the road to Ambleside, with fine views of Windermere and Troutbeck. A ramble up Deepdale to St Sunday Crag brings us to glorious heights. High on Tarn Crag, a few yards before Grisedale Tarn comes into sight, is a rock with an inscription recalling that here Wordsworth came on his last walk with his brother John, not long before John, who was commander of the "Earl of Abergavenny," went down with his ship. Beyond Red Tarn is a track to Striding Edge, where we seem to be on the roof of the world. It was up here, on what De Quincey called the awful curtain rock, that Charles Gough was killed in Trafalgar year, his faithful dog watching by his body for three months. The story has been told by Scott and Wordsworth, one writing of it in the immortal lines:

How long didst thou think that his silence was slumber?
When the wind waved his garment, how oft didst thou start?

and the other, wondering about the source of this dog's strength:

He knows, Who gave that love sublime,
And gave that strength of feeling—great
Above all human estimate.

One of the best ways up Helvellyn is from Patterdale, up a pony track and by Kepple Cove Tarn and Swirrel Edge, where there are still traces of the effect of seven million cubic feet of water rushing down the fell some years ago. From the top of Helvellyn we can see 20 mountains, seven lakes and tarns, the hills of Scotland, and a glimpse of the Irish Sea. Just below the summit is a cairn with an inscription to Hinkler and Leeming, who landed here, the first airmen to land on an English mountain.

At Hartsop, a hamlet near Patterdale, is a fine 15th-century house with beautiful windows, a noble oak staircase with handsome balustrades, splendidly ornamented beams, and a vaulted cellar. A queer little hollow in the wall of an outbuilding is thought to have been a hiding place for priests. Patterdale Hall, long the home of the Mounseys, known as Kings of Patterdale, has magnificent views; some of the Mounseys sleep in the churchyard, a quiet place below the fells.

A stone's throw from St Patrick's Well is the quaint church made new last century, near the site of a Tudor chapel. It has a curious looking tower. Among its possessions is a Bible of 1611 (rebound in two volumes), altar plate of Helvellyn silver, a font with a medieval stem and base and a much later bowl, and a cracked bell in the vestry perhaps 500 years old. One of the windows is in memory of John Thompson, rector for nearly 60 years of last century.

In the churchyard is a noble company of firs and yews from many parts of the world, young giants of great promise. With them is an old giant whose greatness was destroyed by the gale which brought down the Tay Bridge. A yew which must have been here 600 years ago, it has a broken trunk 23 feet round. It was one of the glories of Patterdale when Adam Walker was a boy here. He was one of the first men to make astronomy popular and to invent machines.

A Hero of Scholarship

WORDSWORTH celebrates less heroic figures than Adam Walker, who was born here about 1731. His father was a woollen manufacturer, too poor for the boy's schooling, so Adam faced life without even having mastered reading. Put to work while still a child, he used his leisure in constructing, at a brook near the cottage, models of the corn mills, paper mills, filling mills, and other works in the neighbourhood.

Having borrowed a few books, he built himself a hut in a thicket, and studied to such purpose that his scholarship became noised abroad and he was appointed, at 15, usher in a school at Ledsham, Yorkshire. While teaching he learned, became a good mathematician, and as such was made a master at the free school at Macclesfield while still only 18.

Here came a crisis. He traded, lost his little all, went bankrupt, and decided on a hermit's life on one of the islands of Lake Windermere. Laughed out of this folly, he ventured on a lecture at Manchester, won immediate success, opened a school, and prospered; but he was a wandering scholar, and, embarking on a lecture tour, taught natural philosophy all over England. Then he met the famous Joseph Priestley, who persuaded him to open a great London theatre for the continuance of his discourses.

Adam acted on the advice with such success that he was able to take a good house off Hanover Square and hold a regular series of meetings throughout successive winters, and to accept invitations from the headmasters of Eton, Winchester, Westminster, and elsewhere to lecture at their schools.

The boy-modeller was father of the man. Walker invented and installed revolving lamps to light the deadly rocks of the Scilly Isles. He would have won the undying admiration of Tristram Shandy's Uncle Toby by his invention of vehicles to go by wind and steam. He invented engines to raise and distribute water, improved mills and ploughs, made a novel harpsichord, and evolved a system for both warming and ventilating houses that was ingenious if prohibitive in cost.

Born poor and denied any education except what was self-acquired, he was a gifted teacher, instructing from knowledge acquired with difficulty, but tested and proved by his own efforts, contacts, and experiments. He died at Richmond in Surrey.

All the Glory of the Pennines

RAVENSTONEDALE. It is within hail of Yorkshire and sees all the glory of the Pennines. It is hidden among mountains and has Gallows Hill in Lord's Park, a curious cattle refuge cut in the rocks below Ash Fell, and traces of our Ancient Britons.

The old home of the Fothergills a mile away, Tarn House, has still its medieval windows and its Jacobean doorway. Perhaps the oldest natural monument the village has is a noble beech with a trunk 15 feet round, and the oldest man-made monument is the foundation of a tower on the site of a monastery, where there are two gravestones with finely carved crosses.

A few fragments of the old church have been built into the church made new in the 18th century. Some of the stones of the chancel arch, and its capitals, are 13th century, and the entrance archway of the porch is as old. There is a 15th-century bell, and the font has a medieval stem and a later bowl.

A 17th-century door opens to the vestry, and panelling of this time is in the seats. Two old panels are painted with the Commandments, the Creed, and the Lord's Prayer, and figures of Moses and Aaron, Peter and John.

But its chief possession is a remarkable pulpit of the three-decker type. It is in panelled oak and came from Lowther Park, and it has a distinction we do not remember elsewhere—a little seat high up for the parson's wife. It is behind the top tier from which the sermon was preached.

A stone corbel in the tower, with beakhead ornament, is a Norman relic. Older still may be the shaft and base of a cross in the churchyard, for it is perhaps Saxon. Here too are three medieval coffin lids with crosses, one having a chalice.

There is a brass in the chancel paying tribute to Robert Mounsey, who was vicar here for over half of the 18th century; he must have got used to the idea of seeing his congregation facing each other instead of looking east as in most churches. In the churchyard is the grave of Sir Lazarus Fletcher, who was in our own day the Director of the Natural History Museum at South Kensington. Here also is a window in memory of a brave woman from this village, Elizabeth Gaunt, burnt at Tyburn in 1685 for sheltering a fugitive rebel.

The Pitiful Fate of Elizabeth Gaunt

IT is in a tallow-chandler's shop in Whitechapel that the story begins of the last woman to suffer death in England for a political offence.

Elizabeth Gaunt was a kindly God-fearing Baptist, who ran her humble shop in quiet prosperity, and devoted her small gains to the relief of the sick and suffering, especially those imprisoned in the reeking, infamous gaols of Stuart England. Although convinced that the only way to heaven lay through the chapels of her own denomination, she brought solace and material comfort to all who needed it, irrespective of their religious tenets.

It was in keeping with her selfless generosity that she gave shelter to James Burton, a minor figure in the Rye House Plot in 1683. She pitied him, not as a conspirator, but because a price was set on his head, and because he was friendless. Admitting him into her home, she hid him until she could hire a boat to take him to Gravesend, whence he might escape to Holland. At his departure she gave him money for his sustenance that was a small fortune to so poor a woman. Burton escaped, returned in 1685 with Monmouth, and after the Battle of Sedgemoor fled to London. There he denounced his benefactress to the Government and himself appeared as the chief witness against her.

Tried at the Old Bailey in October 1685, Elizabeth Gaunt was found guilty and sentenced to be burnt at Tyburn. On the night before her execution she wrote a declaration setting forth the insolence of her judges and the brutality of her gaoler. As for her fault, it was one which, she said, a prince might well have forgiven. "I did but relieve a poor family, and lo! I must die for it." She forgave all who had persecuted her, not excepting the King, for whose pleasure she and so many other victims had been sacrificed.

Among those who attended the execution was William Penn, who left a moving picture of the poor woman arranging the straw about her so that she might burn the sooner, a sight at which all burst into tears. Her martyrdom sent a thrill of horror through the country.

The Home of Nature's Poet

RYDAL. It is a lake (the smallest of them all), a village, and a park; they occupy the course of the River Rothay between Grasmere and Ambleside. The lake is steeply constricted between the rocky hill Nab Scar on the north and the expansive plateau of Loughrigg Fell on the south. It is a beautiful situation, traversed by the central highway of the Lake District for more than half a mile along the northern shore of the lake, which is shallow and in places encumbered with reeds, but for its situation and its sweet placidity much admired. Dora's Field here, also known as the Rashfield because of the rushes that once grew in it, was planted by Wordsworth and given to his daughter Dora. In spring it is golden with wild daffodils. Before his death at Rydal in 1935 Mr Gordon Wordsworth, the poet's grandson, gave the field to the nation.

Before the advent of the Lake Poets the notable people of Rydal were the Flemings, who had held the Rydal Hall estate for four centuries. Sir Daniel, a stout Royalist, became after the Restoration an equally active repressor of such people as Quakers and Dissenters, and was knighted. He had antiquarian tastes, and traced the evidences of Norwegian influence in the Lake District. His son Sir George became Bishop of Carlisle. Rydal Park, with fine timber, is a pleasing variation in the scenery. In the grounds of the Hall are two pleasing waterfalls on the Rydal Beck, which may be visited.

Not far off is Wordsworth's Seat, a little rock where he loved to look across the lake, and at Fox How is the house built by Dr Arnold of Rugby, where Wordsworth would often look in for a chat. It was Arnold who gave nicknames to the three roads from Rydal Water to Grasmere. One was Old Corruption, another Bit-by-Bit Reform, the other Radical Reform. We love Old Corruption for its view of Rydal Water, and Radical Reform for its sudden prospect of Grasmere.

Not far from the Hall, a little east of Rydal Water, a road strikes off northward past the modern church and rises steeply. This road is Rydal Mount, for 37 years the home of Wordsworth; here he wrote nearly half the poems he published in his day. Here he built up his fame and gathered his friends about him. Here De Quincey came, and here came into Wordsworth's life the tragic Hartley Coleridge.

On the highroad, midway along Rydal Water, is a cottage with

1732 over the door. Behind it towers Nab Scar, and the cottage is called Nab Cottage. In the cottage lived old Farmer Simpson, and De Quincey lived at Dove Cottage a mile away. He fell in love with the farmer's daughter, and when he was 31 she married him, though he was then a confirmed opium-eater. Notwithstanding his wandering habits, she was a most devoted wife till her death 20 years afterwards, De Quincey surviving her 22 years.

It was on one of his walks hereabouts that Wordsworth explained one of his most magical and intriguing passages, the famous lines in the Ode to Immortality:

Not for these I raise
The song of thanks and praise;
But for those obstinate questionings
Of sense and outward things,
Fallings from us, vanishings;
Blank misgivings of a Creature
Moving about in worlds not realized,
High instincts before which our mortal Nature
Did tremble like a guilty Thing surprised.

Walking with the poet near the sycamores under Nab Scar one day, a friend asked Wordsworth if he could explain what he meant by these lines. He drew himself erect, crossed the road to a five-barred gate, grasped it firmly, and in these memorable words explained his mysterious lines:

There was a time in my life when I was often forced to grasp, like this, something that resisted to be sure that there was anything outside of me. This gate, this bar, this road, these trees fell away from me and vanished into thoughts. I was sure of the existence of mind—I had no sense of the existence of matter.

In Nab Cottage for the last 11 years of his life lived poor Hartley Coleridge, ending one of the most pathetic and tragic lives a genius ever lived. His birth and youth were celebrated in poems by his father and by Wordsworth, his lifelong friend. His father wrote—and where has it been excelled?

But thou, my babe, shall wander like a breeze
By lakes and sandy shores, beneath the crags
Of ancient mountains. So shalt thou see and hear
The lovely shapes and sounds intelligible
Of that eternal language which thy God
Utters.

But when the boy was six years old Wordsworth had fears for him, and wrote those famous lines which have such infinite pathos now:

O blessed vision! happy child!
Thou art so exquisitely wild,
I think of thee with many fears
For what may be thy lot in future years.

It was Wordsworth's fear that proved true. The child grew up a poet, but utterly unable to withstand the shocks of life. Weak of will, a slave to wayward fancy, he died in Nab Cottage, helped in vain by everybody, a persistent failure, a victim of Drink, yet by everyone beloved. Wordsworth, then in his eightieth year, chose the ground for his grave in Grasmere churchyard. "Let him lie by us," he said; "he would have wished it," and so near by the Wordsworths he lies.

This is what the young poet wrote of Rydal:

Nigh to the mansion of a titled dame,
A village lies, and Rydal is its name.
Its natives know not what is meant by fame;
They little know how man in future time
Will venerate the spot. . . .

Hartley Coleridge was right about the failure of the natives to understand Wordsworth. They all agreed that Poet Hartley was a better poet than Poet Wordsworth.

It is Rydal Mount itself that is the precious spot in this small place, not for what Wordsworth wrote there but because he died there. He lived at the Mount while his fame increased and honours showered upon him. From this hillside house he set out to tramp across the mountains, to come up to London Town, to make a tour of the Continent; and here it was that in the end his strength began to fail. The death of Southey gave him the Laureateship but robbed him of a friend. His sister died soon after, and then came the tragic blow of Hartley Coleridge. But nothing could disturb the serenity of his spirit, and the evening of his life at Rydal Mount was as calm and radiant as the sunsets he had loved. He was at the church in the spring of 1850, and as he walked home for the last time he felt the fresh glory of the spring and saw the little celandine making a new wonder in the woods. A few more days and he saw a greater wonder still, for though they laid him in a corner of Grasmere churchyard his spirit was dwelling in the light of setting suns, freed on April 23, the day also of Shakespeare's passing.

Mingled with Rydal's proud memories of an immortal are her sorrowful recollections of one who might have been immortal.

The Tragedy of Hartley Coleridge

THE poet Coleridge, spending perhaps the happiest days of his life with the Wordsworths in Somerset, announced Hartley's birth to Charles Lamb in a sonnet, and celebrated it in a prophetic poem.

Wordsworth loved the frail little lad (a gem that glitters while it lives, he called him), and Hartley grew up in an atmosphere of poetry, more interested in fancy than in fact. In Southey's household at Keswick, where he was brought up, Hartley had none of the discipline which might have helped him to develop his undoubted poetic genius. His friends and he himself had great hopes that he would win a deathless name, but he went to Oxford University ill-prepared for life and fell astray. He went from bad to worse, and he said of himself at this time that "with few habits but those of negligence and self-indulgence, with principles honest and charitable but little applied to particulars, with much vanity and diffidence, with wavering hopes and uncertain spirits, I was sent among men."

Although he did fairly well in his examinations and won much admiration for his fine flow of language, his failure to win the Newdigate Prize for verse depressed him excessively. "I have lost the race I never ran," he wrote in one of his sonnets, and he counted himself a failure almost before he had begun. Pitiful it was to see one in whom Wordsworth had reposed such affection, and such high hopes, falling to ruin in his youth. He stayed in London for two years, doing casual literary work, and then retired to the Lakes, where he did little for the rest of his life but "wander like a breeze by lakes and sandy shores." Making his headquarters at Nab Cottage, he became well known to the country people, more beloved by them than any of the more successful poets who have lived there.

Wordsworth, who had hoped so much from the dreamy child, remained a close friend of the dreamy man. When Hartley died at 52 Wordsworth asked the sexton at Grasmere to keep the next grave for him. Within a year the old poet was sleeping by the side of the young one, whose life had been saddened by his consciousness of failure and his sheer demoralisation, for even in his youth he was a moral wreck; and he wrote of himself:

Though my ship was fraught
With rare and precious fancies, jewels brought
From fairyland, no course I cared to keep.
Nor changeful wind nor tide I heeded aught.

Perhaps he brought more of his precious cargo to shore than he realised, for he mastered the sonnet and left many gems in this form.

The Only Abbey in Westmorland

SHAP. High up is this bare village, with little that is beautiful except its grand view of the hills, and its ruin of the only abbey in Westmorland. It has plain 17th-century houses, grey and rather forbidding; an old market hall with curious windows and sturdy arches, and many inns with memories of the bustle of coaching days.

Close by is Hardendale, where John Mill the Greek scholar was born. He gave most of his life to making a remarkable New Testament from manuscripts, and died in 1707, a fortnight after finishing the work which had taken him thirty years. Here also is a farm where the Young Pretender spent a night, and by the road from Kendal to Carlisle is a drinking fountain on which is a lovely girl's face; she was the little daughter of James Shepherd-Rae and died far away in the West Indies, being remembered by this memorial in the village her father loved.

Almost lost in trees is St Michael's church made partly new last century, its one Norman relic being a stone corbel in the south aisle, carved with the head of a beast. A 13th-century arcade leads to the aisle which has some of the old masonry, and a medieval coffin lid and fragments of others are built into the walls. A chest, a table in the vestry, and the altar rails are over 200 years old. It has three fonts, and has lost a fourth which was the oldest, a veteran of 600 years now in a garden at Sleagill.

Round about Shap are many traces of the Stone Age, among them a group of stones known as Carl Lofts, and a stone circle at Brackenber; but travellers come here to see the ruins of Shap Abbey in a sheltered valley. They make a fine picture with the background of the distant Mardale Hills and a beautiful river. The Abbey was founded 800 years ago by Thomas Gospatric, and disappeared soon after Henry the Eighth. Not even its gateway is standing. But fragments remain of its 12th-century church, with stones of the 13th century and a noble tower built about 1600.

Like a lonely sentinel it keeps watch over the desolation round about, its great arch a frame for the hills beyond. There are a few fragments left of the presbytery, among them a tomb of the 14th century. The nave, nearly 90 feet long, has two doorways to the cloisters. In the ruins of the chapter house is a stone coffin, and not far off are one or two gravestones with crosses. There are also parts of the transepts and an altar, pathetic memorials of departed glory.

Across the fields at Keld is a 15th-century chapel, with some original windows and a doorway, which was probably served from the Abbey. After the Reformation it was used as a house, but it is now cared for by the National Trust.

It has been a pathetic experience for this village to receive in the last few years over a hundred people of Mardale who had rested in the churchyard that is waiting to be drowned. The bodies were removed when Mardale Church was demolished to make way for the Hawes Water Reservoir which is to give Manchester its drinking water, and they were laid here in a cemetery prepared for them.

Like a Village of the Fairy Tales

SKELSMERGH. Almost surrounded by streams (the Sprint, the Kent, and the Mint) it has an ancient hall, old grey houses in the shadow of towering firs, and dark woods round about. It is like a village of the fairy tales.

One of its quaint old houses is Dodding Green, with many secret cupboards where priests are said to have hidden. It has had a chapel since the 18th century, and in the library are many precious books, some printed less than forty years after Caxton's day.

Down the lane from Dodding Green the 19th-century church stands by the old farmhouse called Skelsmergh Hall, with walls 300 and 400 years old and a 14th-century tower. Here when we called was still an oak staircase, much handsome panelling, a chest in which the lord of the manor kept his armour, and a cradle in which the babies were rocked in Queen Anne's day.

Westmorland Meets Yorkshire

STAINMORE. We wonder if even the spacious solitudes of Dartmoor have a deeper silence than the great moors and fells dividing Westmorland from Yorkshire. Between 1400 and 1600 feet high, wild and impressive, splendid in their desolation, they have a glory of their own, and perhaps there is truth in the old saying that no one passes this way only once. To travel the road from Barnard Castle to Brough, to see the commanding beauty of Stainmore, is to feel that we must come back.

Among the grandeur of these lonely hills is the village of Stainmore with a small 19th-century church and a quaint bridge built by Sir Cuthbert Buckle, Lord Mayor of London in 1593. Not far off is Maiden Castle, a grassy mound said to be the site of a Roman camp and near the ancient road where Britons, Romans, Vikings, and Normans have travelled.

Rere Cross rises like a silent watcher of the centuries. A grey stone pillar, it was once protected by entrenchments and must have been of much importance. It is perhaps a thousand years old, and though it is now the boundary stone between two counties, it is said to have marked the old borders of two countries. There is a tradition that it marks a battle between three Irish chieftains who settled in Lakeland, and the story may be true, for Rere Cross is older than anyone knows, and, like the moors about, it keeps its secret.

Master and Scholar

STAVELEY. It has a school as old as Queen Elizabeth, a church with a Burne-Jones window, and the story of a man who outwitted a king.

The Burne-Jones window is the great possession of the long and handsome chancel in the 19th-century church. It shows the Crucifixion and the Ascension with angels grouped on a starry background. Only the noble tower of the 15th-century church remains, a magnificent monument to its builders, its west window set between lovely niches. The weathervane may be 300 years old. Other relics are a medieval font, a 17th-century chest, and old glass fragments of heraldry and the half figure of a man.

It was in the shadow of this tower that a company of men met one winter's day 300 years ago. Summoned by James Smith, they came together to protest against the king's decision to take from them certain lands. The men were brought before the Star Chamber, and their case was so strong that for once the court decided in favour of the people, and this brave group of Staveley men were confirmed in their possessions.

Staveley had not a fine little school for nothing in those days. One of the school's distinguished scholars was Sir John Wilson, an

18th-century judge, and one of its distinguished headmasters was Joseph Martindale, who sleeps in the churchyard. They laid him here in the year the war began, schoolmaster and friend of the village for nearly half a century, and a musician, geologist, antiquarian, and botanist who gave far more to the world than he took out of it.

The Village Drowned

SWINDALE. It was a pathetic place to reach in our tour of the Lakes, for here had just been held the last service in the little church on the lonely moors. The church was doomed by Manchester's water scheme, and in a few years more must be submerged.

At the last service the vicar said it was the second church to be sacrificed in a short time to the needs of a great city, but they parted with their beautiful little home in the knowledge that pure water from their mountainside was being sent to city people. He was preaching to the largest congregation ever seen in one of England's smallest churches. One man in the congregation came to say farewell to the church in which he was christened 61 years before, and among those who followed the prayers by the light of stable lamps and oil lamps were exiles from their native dale, some of whom had come 50 miles. The parish clerk of Shap was the only one in the congregation who remembered the last resident vicar 75 years ago. He was Mr Roddick, who had tolled the bell for half a century, and now tolled it for the last time.

From this valley came the brave parson John Hodgson, who was born here in 1780. The son of a mason, he helped Sir Humphry Davy with his invention of the safety lamp and was the first to use it in a coal mine. He is best known as a historian of Northumberland, and has been sleeping in Hartburn church since 1845, but it should be remembered for ever that he dared to go down a mine with the first safety lamp, risking his life for his faith in Sir Humphry Davy.

Forts and Castles of Long Ago

TEBAY. The tower of its church, below Langdale Fell, on the road from Appleby to Kendal is seen far off. Its stalls, pulpit, and reading desk are made from American walnut, and its handsome font is carved out of a single block of granite, richly ornamented.

The story of Tebay goes back to Roman times. We can trace a Roman road through Tebay Gorge, and at Low Boroughbridge are remains of a Roman camp with four gateways. At Castle How and

Greenholm Castle are the remains of ancient fortresses, and one of the quaint old things here is the Brandreth Stone in Galloper Field, which may have marked an ancient boundary or may have been used by farmers for branding sheep.

Queen of Westmorland

TEMPLE SOWERBY. It loves to be called the Queen of Westmorland villages. Certainly it is a very old queen, for it was the home of Stone Age men long before the Romans came this way. The village is charmingly grouped round its 18th-century red stone church. It goes back 20 centuries and there is a Roman milestone on the way from Appleby to Penrith.

With all the loveliness of the Eden valley round about, it has two greens, old cottages, a tall maypole, and the delightful Crowdundle Beck. Here is a beautiful bridge of four arches, its fine balustrades and turrets over 200 years old; but the mill by the stream is three times older. Though it has seen many changes, it makes an enchanting picture with its background of grand old oaks.

Once owned by the Knights Templars, the village is proud of its ancient manor house, Acorn Bank. It is a charming place, much rebuilt in the 18th century, with fragments of a 14th-century stronghold. Its courtyard has fine buildings round three sides, and the house has a magnificent oak staircase of Cromwell's day. It has an ancient sundial with a curious inscription giving a conversation between the Passenger and the Dial, but it has something new better than all it has old, for it has roses, roses everywhere.

Three Artists and a Window

TROUTBECK. It has some of the noblest views in Lakeland, and much loved is the village, with houses built 400 years ago, many with quaint gables and round chimneys showing finely among sycamores and apple-trees. One of the oldest is Townend, still owned by the family which built it in Tudor days, with splendid oak carving.

With streams in its old streets, the village has many water troughs in cool recesses, relics of the coaching days when horses had to be watered before beginning the hard climb over Kirkstone Pass to Patterdale. Rather lonely is the simple church, twice rebuilt in 200 years, though it still keeps a fine roof with massive oak beams. In its noble little 18th-century tower is a bell which was ringing before the Civil War, and its plain oak altar table is 300 years old. Its chief treasure is the beautiful east window, one of the first designed by Sir Edward Burne-Jones. It is said that William Morris and Ford Madox Brown happened to be fishing here when Burne-Jones was at work in the church, and that they helped him with the window; it shows the Crucifixion, and makes Our Lord a clean-shaven, young-looking man. We may wonder how many churches have a window to which such a famous group of artists have contributed.

Two Brothers and Far Away

WARCOP. Time seems to have passed it by, so old and gracious is this village of the Eden valley, sheltered by great fells going up to the Yorkshire border. On the hills are stones, cairns, entrenchments, and circles older than the Roman road close by. Under Warcop Fell are ruins of what is said to have been a Druid temple, and behind Warcop Hall are traces of a prehistoric camp.

Very charming is the Hall above the village, its windows looking on to a beautiful garden with splendid examples of topiary work, and up to the hills beyond the river. Warcop tower was a fortress; and there was once a castle near Kirksteads, though nothing of it is left. Here is an old smithy, an ancient cross, and a striking bridge with massive piers said to be older than any other bridge in Westmorland.

It is a delightful picture the church gives us in the village street, its warm red walls and its grey porch among the ancient yews. By it stands a Tudor arch leading to the rectory, a rambling farmhouse long ago and before that a sort of fortress, of which some of the entrenchments can still be seen.

Like nearly everything else in Warcop the church is very old, for it was first built by the Normans whose masonry is in the lower part of the north wall of the nave. The walls of the transepts are 13th century, the south aisle is 200 years younger, and the chancel is new except for its 13th-century arch. Other arches of this time lead to the transepts, and two of the 15th century divide the nave and the aisle. There are two piscinas and a stone seat, all medieval. The 17th-century altar table has a new top, and the old door has an oak lock.

Two of three coffin lids in the church are over a doorway, and there are six others in the churchyard, all about 1300; most of them have crosses, some have shears or swords. The worn stone figure of a woman in the churchyard, wearing veiled headdress, may be 14th century. Here too are remains of the old cross.

Two windows are memorials to brothers who died far from the village they loved. They were Henry Preston who fell at Sebastopol, and Moyes Preston who lost his life at Lucknow. But the man of whom Warcop is most proud is James Wilkinson Breeks, a village boy who became a civil servant in India and spent much of his time collecting ornaments, dresses, tools, and implements of the natives of Madras. He visited many villages, opened cairns, collected dialects, and prepared a most valuable account of the primitive tribes of South India. His work was cut short by his death when only 42, but his book was finished by his wife who had helped him in all his labours.

Warcop is one of the few villages where the rush-bearing ceremony is kept up. It has a merry day once every summer when girls wearing flowers in their hair walk to the church, as in the days when the floors of churches were made of clay and rushes were spread to last a year. Now after service the floral crowns are hung above the door, where they are treasured till Rushbearing Day comes round again.

The Magic Lake

WINDERMERE. Who does not love the very name; and who that has seen it does not love its memory all his life? It is the biggest lake in England, set in some of the loveliest scenery in Westmorland. It has grown up to bring into itself the lovely little port of Bowness, which has enchanting views of Windermere. Here is all the charm of blue water, mountain peaks, fells, and islands. The lake, over ten miles long, is best seen from Orrest Head, where it is like a blue mirror for all the beauty and grandeur about it. After a fall of snow it is a view to hold us spellbound, yet what can surpass it on a summer's evening, with lake and hills in a golden mist? From Orrest Head we see the Langdales, bold and stern, the gentle Grasmere mountains, the great peak of Ill Bell, and the fine curves of the Coniston Fells.

It is for what Nature gave it that Windermere is justly famed throughout the world. What man has given it (except for a clock tower in memory of John Baddeley, the guide-book man) are two companions, the rectory and the church. The rectory is one of the oldest houses in Westmorland, built soon after Agincourt, and it has still some of its original beams. Its gracious porch and its delightful chimneys keep watch above the lake.

The church is the pride of Windermere, St Martin's, and the pride of St Martin's is in two great possessions—a magnificent east window, and an old wood carving of the patron saint. Finely the church stands by the lake, with stately yews about it that have seen the centuries come and go.

It is the east window that catches the eye, glowing with crimson and blue. Most of it has been here only two generations, but some of it was in the old church, some was new when the church was made new in the 15th century, and some was brought from Cartmel Priory. It is crowded with figures and full of colour.

Its central picture is the Crucifixion, with angels, the Madonna, and St John set in a blue background. In one of the other scenes a fine St George is slaying the dragon, and by him is St Barbara with her symbol of the tower and three windows. On the other side is St Catherine with the Wheel, wearing a martyr's crown, and above these saints are angels playing musical instruments. There are splendid pictures of knights in armour, many kneeling figures of monks, and, of remarkable interest, the arms of a 15th-century John Washington, one of George Washington's ancestors. Here in this window the stars and stripes are older than the flag of the United States.

There are many small fragments in the upper part of the window, on one of which a Madonna of the 14th century is fading away. The glass has been repaired, but in the main it stands as a splendid piece of 14th and 15th-century craftsmanship.

The font has an early bowl adorned with four heads, but it rests on a modern stem; it has two small crosses cut in the stone, one perhaps as old as itself, the other probably carved at the rebuilding in the 15th century. The marks of the fire which destroyed the church in those days are still on the font.

The figure of St Martin is one of the rare carvings of a saint in wood, it is believed to be the work of a local craftsman and to be over 300 years old. It shows the saint sitting on a horse, wearing a queer hat and dividing his cloak and sharing it with a beggar standing by with a stick. The sculpture is about six feet high and is interesting because it is one of a very small group of equestrian statues in our English churches. There is, of course, the famous equestrian statue on Wellington's tomb in St Paul's and there are two kings on horseback in the wonderful chantry of Henry the Fifth in the Abbey; but in our parish churches we have come upon only four in England, two in bronze, one in marble, and this at Windermere in wood. It was lost sight of for nearly half a century, though it was known to have been in the church before its restoration in 1870. In 1915 the saint on horseback turned up again and was presented to the church by one of its friends.

The spirit of St Martin is finely shown in the story of the Bowness Carrier, set in the window known as the Carrier's Arms. It is said that at the 15th-century rebuilding half the people wanted the old site and half the new, and the matter was settled by the generous offer of a carrier, who said he would carry the lead for the roof on his packhorses if they used the old site. They used it and the carrier's arms are here in 15th-century glass, a rope, a wanty hook, and five skewers.

Next to the Carrier's Arms window is a fine Te Deum window set up by Sir William Forwood as a thankoffering for 40 happy summers on the shores of Windermere. It was Sir William Forwood who gave the church its handsome chapel to the memory of the 71 men of Windermere who did not come back.

In an aisle off the chancel is a monument by Flaxman in memory of a bishop of Llandaff who was a chemist as well as a bishop, and is said to have saved the Government £100,000 a year by his experiments with gunpowder.

The church has some old Bibles and chained books, painted texts on its great beams, and frescoes of the Wise Men and the Entombment, on the chancel walls. An odd inscription in Latin under the crown of one of the arches reminds us of a day of great rejoicing in the history of our Motherland. This is what it means:

This is a day more famed as each year brings it round. Rejoice, ye who are good! The mischief conspired in Stygian darkness has been made an empty tale by the hand of Providence. England, which was to be conspicuous for the greatness of its ruin, may now sing hymns, since she has remained free by the aid of Heaven.

The Deliverance for which all this gives thanks was the discovery of the Gunpowder Plot, and the inscription was put here by "Christopher Philipson, Junior, Gentleman," in 1629. It was a kinsman of this Christopher who rode on horseback into Kendal Church and was known as the Daredevil.

Two pathetic links with history the churchyard has. One is the grave of Poor Tom—Thomas Ullock who left this peaceful scene to fight our battles far away; we read on his stone that

Poor Tom came here to lie
From Battles of Dettigen and Fontenoy.

Not far away sleeps a poor Abyssinian slave; he was Rasselas Belfield, who must have worked on the Belfield Estate in Windermere. Glad we are to know that he "found his freedom on Britannia's Strand" and that the touch of our Blest Isle unbound for him the chains of slavery. It all happened just after Waterloo.

The 19th-century church of St John has a richly carved oak screen made by the people who worship there, and by the vicar, who himself carved the Cross.

A little outside Bowness, on the banks of the lake, Storrs Hall stands among the trees. It is open today for all who will come, but 200 years ago it was the great house of Sir John Legard, who smuggled rum and slaves into the country, using a secret passage from the shore to the cellars of the Hall.

Under the roof of this great house have come a little host of people whose names the world will not forget. Wordsworth and Scott and Southey were ever welcome here, and Shelley would drive over from Keswick. Perhaps the most brilliant day in the history of the Hall was when a procession of fifty barges came to pick up Sir Walter Scott and George Canning—soon to be Prime Minister—who sat facing each other in their barge of honour, both wearing white hats.

He Walked Here With Wordsworth

WINSTER. We wondered if anything had changed here since Wordsworth saw it. A winding lane among grand old chestnuts and beeches brings us to a spot too easily missed by travellers in the Motor Age. On the Lancashire border, it is just a group of quaint houses with a white inn, a tiny school, and a small church among the trees. In springtime it is lost in a glory of apple and damson blossoms; in summer it is a rare corner of wild flowers.

Its 19th-century church has a few curious texts on wooden tablets from the old church walls, and the old post-office has a charming porch. At Wood Farm is an ancient ford and bridge. Brime House, where Jonas Barber made grandfather clocks, is much the same as when he knew it 300 years ago. Here lived William Pearson, a poet and naturalist who was never happier than when he was showing Wordsworth the loveliness of this lonely valley.

Three Village Boys

WINTON. We found it golden with gorse in spring, this hamlet of neat cottages by a green, with memories of a tragic group of rebels against Charles the Second and of three village boys at school here who became learned men. The rebels rose against Charles the Second and were hanged at Appleby; the three boys were Richard Burn and the two brothers Langthorne.

Richard Burn was a legal writer and topographer who helped Dr Nicholson with a history of the Lake Country and has been sleeping at Orton since 1785. William and John Langhorne were born about 200 years ago, both poets and translators. John was the more notable, though no one reads his poetry now. He is best remembered for his translation of Plutarch's Lives, a fine piece of work for which he received much help from his brother.

Peter the King's Physician

WITHERSLACK. It has known three men it does not forget, two brothers greatly loved in their day and an outlaw who sleeps in a wood close by.

Between Grange-over-Sands and Lake Windermere, it is a small place with an imposing Hall among beautiful trees below Whitbarrow; and Halecote, in 100 acres of loveliness with splendid views of Morecambe Bay and Cartmel Fells.

A lane through the orchards brings us to a church keeping company with gnarled old yews. It has a fine canopied pulpit, once a three-decker; and a charming marble figure of a baby which has been sleeping here since last century. Like the small school, the church was the gift of John Barwick, a Royalist who became Dean of St Paul's. His shield is in one of the windows and has the red-and-gold rose given him by Charles the Second for his loyalty; his marble monument has his arms.

His brother Peter was the King's physician, and a friend of William Harvey. He was one of the few doctors who did not run away from the Plague in 1665. Every day he attended old St Paul's to minister to miserable sufferers, and when the Great Fire destroyed his home he lived very simply at Westminster. He was blind for his last 11 years, but even then he advised poor people free, and few men of his day were more beloved.

The outlaw sleeping somewhere among the wooded hills was Sir Thomas Broughton, who joined Lambert Simnel's rebellion against Henry the Seventh and had to flee for his life. It is said that for months he was hiding in a cave hereabouts, and that his tenants took him food. He died in hiding, and was buried in the forest.

Witherslack has a proud record in its vicar's list, for John Dawson, who died in 1843, was its vicar for 65 years.

The county has given us few finer characters than John Barwick, Dean of Durham and London, who was born here.

Parson Hero

BELIEVING devoutly in the righteousness of his cause, John Barwick, without firing a shot or drawing a sword, played a part of unexcelled heroism on the Royalist side during the Civil War. Born in 1612, he was one of two brothers whom a splendid village family here chose to be educated as scholars, while the remainder of the family toiled on their little farm to support them. Both attained a modest immortality, John the Dean, Peter the noble doctor.

John reached Cambridge University by way of Sedbergh, proved a brilliant scholar, and at 26 was M.A., D.D., and a Fellow of his college. When the war broke out it was he who made the famous journey from Cambridge to Nottingham, conveying money to Charles, brilliantly eluding Cromwell and a troop that lay awaiting him. That, followed by two Royalist tracts that he wrote, cost him his Fellowship and cast him penniless adrift upon the world.

After various wanderings he secreted himself with his ciphers in the London house of the Bishop of Durham, and there won over waverers to the King's cause, maintaining a voluminous correspondence with Charles at Oxford, keeping him informed of everything that was happening in the capital.

His brother Peter shared his perils by himself going to the post office to collect letters so that John should remain hidden. The execution of Charles shattered John for a time, but he recovered, to transfer his fidelity to Charles the Second, with the result that a vigilant official at length discovered him, and John, a mere skeleton, was committed to the Tower for treason, and expected to expire out of hand.

But, absence of worry restored him to the picture of health, and his goodness and charm so won over his opponents that he was allowed to leave the Tower, not acquitted, but ignored.

Then he set to work again as hard as ever on his perilous work for Charles! He was the cleverest secret correspondent in Europe. Having burnt his old ciphers, braved the threat of torture, and refused reward rather than betray his trust, he carried on his task until the Restoration.

Then, lest it should be thought he had acted for gain, he refused bishoprics and reluctantly accepted the deanery first of Durham and then of St Paul's, where he toiled unremittingly till he died in 1664, to be buried in the cathedral, two years before its destruction by the Great Fire.

Peter, his brother, was a noble character, a godly man who consented to act as physician to Charles the Second. His real mission lay among the poor, whom he attended without fee. He gave them medicine, food, and comforts at his own cost, and, when others fled, stood by them in the Plague, a ministering angel.

He wrote a beautiful Life of his brother John, and, pious soul, actually laboured to put it all into Latin simply in order that he might include in it the Latin thesis with which his beloved hero had gained his doctorate of divinity. He died in 1705. Rarely has a village given England two such brothers.

TOWNS AND VILLAGES OF THE LAKE COUNTIES

In this key to our map are all the towns and villages treated in this book. If (as may rarely happen) a place is not on the map its square is given here, so that the way to it is easily found, each square being five miles. One or two hamlets are in the book with their neighbouring villages; for these see Index.

CUMBERLAND

Place	Square
Abbey Town	C7
Aikton	E6
Ainstable	H7
Allhallows	D8
Allonby	B8
Alston	K7
Arlecdon	B11
Armathwaite	H7
Aspatria	C8
Bassenthwaite	D10
Beaumont	F6
Beckermet	B13
Bewcastle	H4
Birdoswald	J5
Blencow	G9
Bolton Gate	D8
Bootle	C15
Borrowdale	E11
Bowness	D5
Brampton	H5
Bridekirk	C9
Brigham	B9
Bromfield	D7
Broughton	B9
Burgh-by-Sands	E6
Buttermere	D11
Caldbeck	E8
Calderbridge	B12
Camerton	B9
Carlisle	F6
Castle Carrock	H6
Castle Sowerby	F9
Cleator	B12
Clifton	B10
Cockermouth	C9
Corney	C14
Croglin	J7
Crosby-on-Eden	G6
Crosscanonby	B8
Cumrew	H7
Cumwhitton	H7
Dacre	G10
Dalston	F7
Dean	B10
Dearham	B9
Distington	B10
Drigg	B13
Eaglesfield	C10
Edenhall	H9
Egremont	B12
Ennerdale	B11
Eskdale	D13
Frizington	B11
Garrigill	L8
Gilcrux	C8
Gilsland	J5
Glassonby	J8
Gosforth	B13
Great Corby	G6
Great Orton	E6
Great Salkeld	H9
Greystoke	G9
Haile	B12
Hallthwaites	D15
Harrington	A10
Hayton	C8
Hensingham	A11
Hesket-in-the-Forest	G7
Holme St Cuthbert	C7
Hutton-in-the-Forest	G9
Ireby	D9
Irthington	H5
Irton	C13
Isel	C9
Ivegill	G8
Keswick	E10
Kirkandrews-on-Esk	F4
Kirkbampton	E6
Kirkbride	D6
Kirkcambeck	H4
Kirkland	B11
Kirklinton	G5
Kirkoswald	H8
Lamplugh	B11
Lanercost	H5
Langwathby	J9
Lazonby	H8
Little Salkeld	J9
Longtown	F5
Lorton	C10
Loweswater	C11
Maryport	B9
Matterdale	F10
Melmerby	J8
Millom	D16
Moresby	A11
Mosedale	F9
Muncaster	C14
Mungrisdale	F9
Naworth	H5
Nenthead	L8
Netherby	F4
Newlands	F8
Newton Arlosh	D6
Newton Reigny	G9
Nichol Forest	G3
Ousby	J9
Over Denton	J5
Penrith	H9
Plumbland	C8
Plumpton Wall	H8
Ponsonby	B13
Raughton Head	F7
Ravenglass	C14
Renwick	J8
Rockcliffe	F5
St Bees	A12
St John's-in-the-Vale	E10
Scaleby	G5
Scotby	G6
Seascale	B13
Sebergham	F8
Setmurthy	D9
Silloth	C6
Skelton	G9
Skirwith	J9
Stanwix	F6
Stapleton	H4

TOWNS AND VILLAGES OF THE LAKE COUNTIES

Place	Map ref.
Threlkeld	E10
Thursby	E7
Torpenhow	D8
Ulpha	D14
Waberthwaite	C14
Walton	H5
Warwick	G6
Wasdale	C13
Watermillock	G10
Westward	E8
Wetheral	G6
Whicham	C15
Whitbeck	C15
Whitehaven	A11
Wigton	E7
Workington	A10
Wreay	G7
Wythburn	E12
Wythop	D10

WESTMORLAND

Place	Map ref.
Ambleside	G13
Appleby	K11
Arnside	G15
Askham	H10
Bampton	H11
Barbon	J15
Barton	H10
Beetham	H15
Bolton	J10
Brough	L11
Brougham	H10
Burneside	H13
Burton	H16
Casterton	J15
Cliburn	J10
Clifton	H10
Crackenthorpe	K10
Crosby Garrett	K12
Crosby Ravensworth	J11
Crosthwaite	G14
Eamont Bridge	H10
Firbank	J14
Grasmere	F12
Great Asby	K11
Great Musgrave	L11
Great Ormside	K11
Hartley	L12
Helsington	H14
Heversham	H15
Hutton Roof	H16
Ings	G13
Kendal	H14
Kentmere	G13
Kirkby Lonsdale	J15
Kirkby Stephen	L12
Kirkby Thore	J10
Langdale	F12
Levens	G15
Little Strickland	J11
Long Marton	K10
Long Sleddale	H13
Lowther	H10
Mallerstang	L13
Mardale	H12
Martindale	G11
Middleton	J15
Milburn	J9
Morland	J10
Murton	K10
Natland	H14
Newbiggin	J10
Old Hutton	J14
Orton	J12
Patterdale	G11
Ravenstonedale	K12
Rydal	F12
Shap	H11
Skelsmergh	H14
Stainmore	L11
Staveley	G13
Swindale	H11
Tebay	J12
Temple Sowerby	J10
Troutbeck	G13
Warcop	L11
Windermere	G13
Winster	G14
Winton	L12
Witherslack	F15

INDEX

This index includes all notable subjects and people likely to be sought for, and a special index of pictures appears at the beginning of the volume.

INDEX

INDEX

INDEX

INDEX

INDEX

INDEX

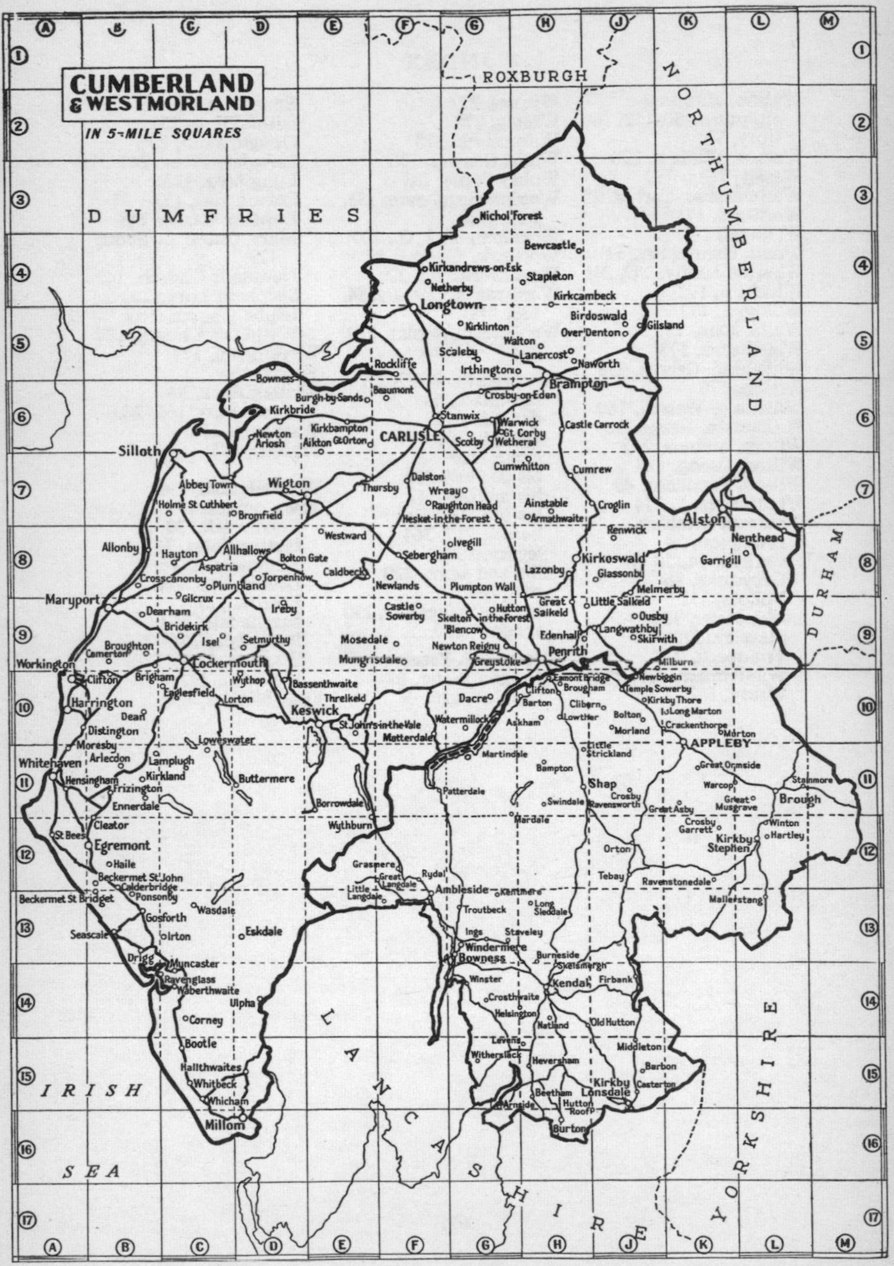

CUMBERLAND & WESTMORLAND
IN 5-MILE SQUARES
DUMFRIES
ROXBURGH
NORTHUMBERLAND
DURHAM
YORKSHIRE
LANCASHIRE
IRISH SEA
Nichol Forest
Bewcastle
Kirkandrews-on-Esk
Stapleton
Netherby
Longtown
Kirkcambeck
Birdoswald
Gilsland
Over Denton
Kirklinton
Walton
Lanercost
Naworth
Scaleby
Irthington
Rockliffe
Brampton
Bowness
Beaumont
Burgh-by-Sands
Crosby-on-Eden
Kirkbride
Stanwix
Warwick
Gt. Corby
Wetheral
Castle Carrock
Newton Arlosh
Kirkbampton
Aikton
Gt. Orton
CARLISLE
Scotby
Silloth
Cumwhitton
Cumrew
Abbey Town
Wigton
Thursby
Dalston
Wreay
Raughton Head
Holme St Cuthbert
Bromfield
Hesket-in-the-Forest
Ainstable
Armathwaite
Croglin
Alston
Westward
Ivegill
Renwick
Nenthead
Allonby
Hayton
Allhallows
Bolton Gate
Sebergham
Kirkoswald
Garrigill
Aspatria
Caldbeck
Lazonby
Glassonby
Crosscanonby
Torpenhow
Plumbland
Newlands
Plumpton Wall
Melmerby
Maryport
Gilcrux
Ireby
Castle Sowerby
Hutton in the Forest
Great Salkeld
Little Salkeld
Dearham
Skelton
Ousby
Bridekirk
Blencow
Edenhall
Langwathby
Isel
Setmurthy
Mosedale
Newton Reigny
Skirwith
Broughton
Camerton
Penrith
Mungrisdale
Greystoke
Workington
Cockermouth
Milburn
Clifton
Brigham
Wythop
Bassenthwaite
Eamont Bridge
Newbiggin
Eaglesfield
Threlkeld
Dacre
Brougham
Temple Sowerby
Harrington
Lorton
Barton
Kirkby Thore
Keswick
Cliburn
Bolton
Long Marton
Dean
St John's in the Vale
Watermillock
Askham
Lowther
Crackenthorpe
Distington
Matterdale
Morland
Murton
Moresby
Loweswater
APPLEBY
Whitehaven
Arlecdon
Lamplugh
Martindale
Little Strickland
Hensingham
Kirkland
Bampton
Great Ormside
Frizington
Buttermere
Shap
Stainmore
Patterdale
Warcop
Ennerdale
Borrowdale
Swindale
Crosby Ravensworth
Great Musgrave
Brough
Great Asby
Cleator
Mardale
Crosby Garrett
Winton
St Bees
Wythburn
Hartley
Kirkby Stephen
Egremont
Orton
Haile
Grasmere
Rydal
Great Langdale
Tebay
Ravenstonedale
Beckermet St John
Calderbridge
Little Langdale
Ambleside
Kentmere
Ponsonby
Long Sleddale
Mallerstang
Beckermet St Bridget
Troutbeck
Wasdale
Gosforth
Seascale
Irton
Eskdale
Ings
Staveley
Windermere
Drigg
Muncaster
Bowness
Burneside
Skelsmergh
Ravenglass
Winster
Kendal
Firbank
Waberthwaite
Ulpha
Crosthwaite
Helsington
Corney
Natland
Old Hutton
Bootle
Levens
Middleton
Witherslack
Heversham
Hallthwaites
Barbon
Whitbeck
Kirkby Lonsdale
Beetham
Casterton
Whicham
Arnside
Hutton Roof
Millom
Burton